Communicate to Connect

Interpersonal Communication for
Today's Relationships

FIRST EDITION

EDITED BY Elizabeth Dorrance Hall, Ph.D.

Michigan State University

cognella®
SAN DIEGO

Bassim Hamadeh, CEO and Publisher
Jennifer Codner, Senior Field Acquisitions Editor
Michelle Piehl, Senior Project Editor
Casey Hands, Production Editor
David Rajec, Editorial Assistant
Emely Villavicencio, Senior Graphic Designer
Greg Isales, Licensing Associate
Natalie Piccotti, Director of Marketing
Kassie Graves, Vice President of Editorial
Jamie Giganti, Director of Academic Publishing

Cover image: Copyright © 2019 iStockphoto LP/Prostock-Studio.

Printed in the United States of America.

cognella® | ACADEMIC PUBLISHING

3970 Sorrento Valley Blvd., Ste. 500, San Diego, CA 92121

CONTENTS

PREFACE

Welcome to *Communicate to Connect: Interpersonal Communication for Today's Relationships*. The readings that appear in this textbook were handpicked with you in mind! As I have taught interpersonal communication to over a thousand students in the past ten years, I have taken note of the topics students want to know more about that tend to be missing from traditional interpersonal communication textbooks. Those include online dating, maintaining relationships at a distance, how to communicate with people who are different from you, how to communicate with difficult people at work, why we hurt the ones we are closest to, and understanding *why* we communicate and make sense of the world in the ways that we do. You will find all of those topics and more covered here.

INTRODUCTION

T he purpose of this book is to introduce you to the rich and exciting world of interpersonal communication. Researchers have been working hard for decades to understand how humans share meaning with one another and why miscommunication is so common in the process of sharing meaning. After reading this book you will understand more about your own style of communicating and have tools for improving your ability to communicate clearly and effectively with others to build, maintain, and dissolve relationships and to achieve your goals in life.

The book begins with the basics of interpersonal communication: defining communication and learning about the meaning and importance of words. Next, we move on to nonverbal communication and listening. After that, we dive into the social psychology behind the words we say and how we make sense of the things that other people say. You will also learn about persuasion and how to use communication strategically to achieve your goals. In the following couple of chapters we dive into romantic relationships, including how long-distance dating relationships are maintained, how (and why) people in close relationships hurt and sometimes forgive one another, and how to give and receive support online. The book concludes with a few chapters on other types of relationships including relationships in organizations/work settings, in families, and across cultures.

At the beginning of each chapter, you will find an introduction that previews the content to come. The introduction will alert you to the most important sections of the reading, and as you read, you should keep the topics mentioned in the introduction in mind.

At the end of each chapter, you will find a "Real-World Lab" (RWL) activity. I designed these activities to get you out of the classroom and into the "real world," practicing what you have just read. These RWL activities sometimes ask you to interview others about their experiences when you have not had an experience yourself. Other times you will be asked to go and observe or interact with people in your community. These activities will enrich your learning experience if you take them seriously, so please do! All the activities are accompanied by reflection questions to help you connect your "real-world" experience with what you have been learning. Blank spaces are provided so you can do your reflecting right in this book.

Enjoy the journey you are about to take in examining your own communication abilities and taking notice of the communication happening all around you, every day! If you put in the effort, you will become a better communicator who is more aware of how communication creates meaning and how it can bring people together or tear relationships apart.

CHAPTER 1

Defining Communication

Introduction to the Chapter

What exactly do people mean when they talk about "communication"? Why is communicating with others so challenging at times? These are important questions that will be answered throughout this book. In this introductory chapter, you will learn the basics of communication, including the definition of communication, messages, and social interaction. You will also read about two schools of thought on what communication is: communication as message exchange and communication as meaning making. Later in the text you will read more about communication as both message exchange and as meaning making.

Introduction

What Is Communication?

By John Fiske

....

Communication is one of those human activities that everyone recognizes but few can define satisfactorily. Communication is talking to one another, it is television, it is spreading information, it is our hair style, it is literary criticism: the list is endless. This is one of the problems facing academics: can we properly apply the term "a subject of study" to something as diverse and multi-faceted as human communication actually is? Is there any hope of linking the study of, say, facial expression with literary criticism? Is it even an exercise worth attempting?

The doubts that lie behind questions like these may give rise to the view that communication is not a subject, in the normal academic sense of the word, but is a multi-disciplinary area of study. This view would propose that what the psychologists and sociologists have to tell us about human communicative behaviour has very little to do with what the literary critic has.

This lack of agreement about the nature of communication studies is necessarily reflected in this book. What I have tried to do is to give some coherence to the confusion by basing the book upon the following assumptions.

> I assume that communication is amenable to study, but that we need a number of disciplinary approaches to be able to study it comprehensively.

> I assume that all communication involves signs and codes. Signs are artefacts or acts that refer to something other than themselves; that is, they are signifying constructs. Codes are the systems into which signs are organized and which determine how signs may be related to each other.

I assume, too, that these signs and codes are transmitted or made available to others: and that transmitting or receiving signs/codes/communication is the practice of social relationships.

I assume that communication is central to the life of our culture: without it culture of any kind must die. Consequently the study of communication involves the study of the culture with which it is integrated.

Underlying these assumptions is a general definition of communication as "social interaction through messages".

[...] [T]here are two main schools in the study of communication. The first sees communication as the *transmission of messages*. It is concerned with how senders and receivers encode and decode, with how transmitters use the channels and media of communication. It is concerned with matters like efficiency and accuracy. It sees communication as a process by which one person affects the behaviour or state of mind of another. If the effect is different from or smaller than that which was intended, this school tends to talk in terms of communication failure, and to look to the stages in the process to find out where the failure occurred. For the sake of convenience I shall refer to this as the "process" school.

The second school sees communication as the *production and exchange of meanings.* It is concerned with how messages, or texts, interact with people in order to produce meanings; that is, it is concerned with the role of texts in our culture. It uses terms like signification, and does not consider misunderstandings to be necessarily evidence of communication failure—they may result from cultural differences between sender and receiver. For this school, the study of communication is the study of text and culture. The main method of study is semiotics (the science of signs and meanings), and that is the label I shall use to identify this approach.

The process school tends to draw upon the social sciences, psychology and sociology in particular, and tends to address itself to *acts* of communication. The semiotic school tends to draw upon linguistics and the arts subjects, and tends to address itself to *works* of communication.

Each school interprets our definition of communication as social interaction through messages in its own way. The first defines social interaction as the process by which one person relates to others, or affects the behaviour, state of mind or emotional response of another, and, of course, vice versa. This is close to the common-sense, everyday use of the phrase. Semiotics, however, defines social interaction as that which constitutes the individual as a member of a particular culture or society. I know I am a member of western, industrial society because, to give one of many sources of identification, I respond to Shakespeare or *Coronation Street* in broadly the same ways as do the fellow members of my culture. I also become aware of cultural differences if, for instance, I hear a Soviet critic reading *King Lear* as a devastating attack upon the western ideal of the family as the basis of society, or arguing that *Coronation Street* shows how the west keeps the workers in their place. Both these readings are possible, but my point is, they are not mine, as a typical member of my culture. In responding to *Coronation Street* in the more normal way, I am expressing my commonality with other members of my culture. So, too, teenagers appreciating one particular style of rock music are expressing their identity as members of a subculture and are, albeit in an indirect way, interacting with other members of their society.

The two schools also differ in their understanding of what constitutes a message. The process school sees a message as that which is transmitted by the communication process. Many of its followers believe that intention is a crucial factor in deciding what constitutes a message. Thus pulling my earlobe would not be a message unless I deliberately did it as a pre-arranged signal to an auctioneer. The sender's intention may be stated or unstated, conscious or unconscious, but must be retrievable by analysis. The message is what the sender puts into it by whatever means.

For semiotics, on the other hand, the message is a construction of signs which, through interacting with the receivers, produce meanings. The sender, defined as transmitter of the message, declines in importance. The emphasis shifts to the text and how it is "read". And reading is the process of discovering meanings that occurs when the reader interacts or negotiates with the text. This negotiation takes place as the reader brings aspects of his or her cultural experience to bear upon the codes and signs which make up the text. It also involves some shared understanding of what the text is about. We have only to see how different papers report the same event differently to realize how important is this understanding, this view of the world, which each paper shares with its readers. So readers with different social experiences or from different cultures may find different meanings in the same text. This is not, as we have said, necessarily evidence of communication failure.

The message, then, is not something sent from A to B, but an element in a structured relationship whose other elements include external reality and the

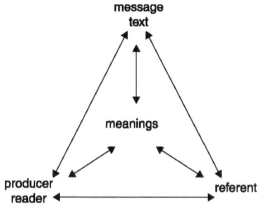

Figure 1.1 Messages and meanings.

producer/reader. Producing and reading the text are seen as parallel, if not identical, processes in that they occupy the same place in this structured relationship. We might model this structure as a triangle in which the arrows represent constant interaction; the structure is not static but a dynamic practice (see figure 1.1).

Introduction to Communication
Real-World Lab

Competent communicators understand how to produce effective messages and can also do so in practice. The know-how is referred to as process competence. The ability to actually send and interpret messages successfully is called performative competence.

Name: _____

Date: _____

Name of place observed: _____

1. Go to a public place for 45 minutes and observe. Good options include libraries, cafeterias, coffee shops, or stores. You can also choose to observe an activity like soccer club practice, a staff meeting, a student organization event, or another event you are curious about.

2. Write down what you notice. For this lab, you will turn in your observation notes along with the worksheet. Try to be as curious as possible about the act of communication during your observation time.

3. What happened at the activity or place where you were observing? Include sights, sounds, and what people spoke about.

_____

_____

_____

_____

_____

_____

_____

_____

_____

_____

4. Write down and explain any clear nonverbal signs you understood (for example, a customer shaking their head to indicate "no" to a server). How do you know what the nonverbal signs meant?

_____

_____

_____

_____

_____

5. How did people respond to you at the activity/place? Did they take notice of you? Did anyone interact with you? If yes, describe the interaction. If no, explain why you think people did not interact with you.

_____

_____

_____

_____

_____

_____

6. What did you learn about the people you observed?

_____

_____

_____

_____

_____

_____

CHAPTER 2

Verbal Communication

Introduction to the Chapter

The way humans come to understand the world is through communication and language. In fact, the language you speak shapes the way you see the world. And in return, the world humans inhabit has shaped language over time. The process of humans forming or writing words and then attaching shared meaning to those words is pretty amazing. That process is what you will learn about in this chapter. You will learn about signs to understand "communication as meaning" and how meaning is made through conversation with others. You will read about denotative and connotative meanings of words and the relationships words have with one another that help humans understand each other.

Selection from "Communication, Meaning, and Signs"

By John Fiske

....

We now turn our attention to a radically different approach to the study of communication. Here the emphasis is not so much on communication as a process, but on communication as the generation of meaning. When I communicate with you, you understand, more or less accurately, what my message means. For communication to take place I have to create a message out of signs. This message stimulates you to create a meaning for yourself that relates in some way to the meaning that I generated in my message in the first place. The more we share the same codes, the more we use the same sign systems, the closer our two "meanings" of the message will approximate to each other.

This places a different emphasis on the study of communication, and we will have to familiarize ourselves with a new set of terms. These are terms like sign, signification, icons, index, denote, connote—all terms which refer to various ways of creating meaning. So these models will differ from the ones just discussed in that they are not linear: they do not contain arrows indicating the flow of the message. They are *structural* models, and any arrows indicate *relationships* between elements in this creation of meaning. These models do not assume a series of steps or stages through which a message passes: rather they concentrate on analysing a structured set of relationships which enable a message to signify something; in other words, they concentrate on what it is that makes marks on paper or sounds in the air into a *message*.

Semiotics

At the centre of this concern is the sign. The study of signs and the way they work is called semiotics or semiology, and this will provide the alternative focus in this book. Semiotics, as we will call it, has three main areas of study:

1. The sign itself. This consists of the study of different varieties of signs, of the different ways they have of conveying meaning, and of the way they relate to the people who use them. For signs are human constructs and can only be understood in terms of the uses people put them to.

2. The codes or systems into which signs are organized. This study covers the ways that a variety of codes have developed in order to meet the needs of a society or culture, or to exploit the channels of communication available for their transmission.

3. The culture within which these codes and signs operate. This in turn is dependent upon the use of these codes and signs for its own existence and form.

Semiotics, then, focuses its attention primarily on the text. The linear, process models give the text no more attention than any other stage in the process: indeed, some of them pass it over almost without comment. This is one major difference between the two approaches. The other is the status of the receiver. In semiotics, the receiver, or reader, is seen as playing a more active role than in most of the process models (Gerbner's is an exception). Semiotics prefers the term "reader" (even of a photograph of a painting) to "receiver" because it implies both a greater degree of activity and also that reading is something we learn to do; it is thus determined by the cultural experience of the reader. The reader helps to create the meaning of the text by bringing to it his or her experience, attitudes, and emotions.

In this chapter I wish to start by looking at some of the main approaches to this complex question of meaning. I shall then go on to consider the role played by signs in generating this meaning, and to categorize signs into different types according to their different ways of performing this function.

Signs and Meaning

Basic Concepts

All the models of meaning share a broadly similar form. Each is concerned with three elements which must be involved in some way or other in any study of meaning. These are: (1) the sign, (2) that to which it refers, and (3) the users of the sign.

A sign is something physical, perceivable by our senses; it refers to something other than itself; and it depends upon a recognition by its users that it *is* a sign. Take our earlier example: pulling my earlobe as a sign to an auctioneer. In this case the sign refers to my bid, and this is recognized as such by both the auctioneer and myself. Meaning is conveyed from me to the auctioneer: communication has taken place.

In this chapter we shall study the two most influential models of meaning. The first is that of the philosopher and logician C. S. Peirce (we will also look at the variant of Ogden and Richards), and the second is that of the linguist Ferdinand de Saussure.

Peirce (and Ogden and Richards) see the sign, that to which it refers, and its users as the three points of a triangle. Each is closely related to the other two, and can be understood only in terms of the others. Saussure takes a slightly different line. He says that the sign consists of its physical form plus an associated mental concept, and that this concept is in its turn an apprehension of external reality. The sign relates to reality only through the concepts of the people who use it.

Thus the word CAR (marks on paper or sounds in air) has a mental concept attached to it. Mine will be broadly the same as yours, though there may be some individual differences. This shared concept then relates to a class of objects in reality. This is so straightforward as to seem obvious, but there can be problems. My wife and I, for example, frequently argue over whether something is blue or green. We share the same language, we are looking at the same piece of external reality: the difference lies in the concepts of blueness or greenness that link our words to that reality.

Further Implications

C. S. Peirce

Peirce (1931–58) and Ogden and Richards (1923) arrived at very similar models of how signs signify. Both identified a triangular relationship between the sign, the user, and external reality as a necessary model for studying meaning. Peirce, who is commonly regarded as the founder of the American tradition of semiotics, explained his model simply:

> A sign is something which stands to somebody for something in some respect or capacity. It addresses somebody, that is, creates in the mind of that person an equivalent sign, or perhaps a more developed sign. The sign which it creates I call the *interpretant* of the first sign. The sign stands for something, *its object*. (In Zeman, 1977)

Peirce's three terms can be modelled as in figure 2.1. The double-ended arrows emphasize that each term can be understood only in relation to the others. A *sign* refers to something other than itself—the *object*, and is understood by somebody:

that is, it has an effect in the mind of the user—the *interpretant*. We must realize that the interpretant is not the user of the sign, but what Peirce calls elsewhere "the proper significate effect": that is, it is a mental concept produced both by the sign and by the

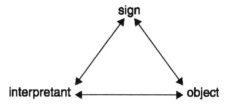

Figure 2.1 Peirce's elements of meaning.

user's experience of the object. The interpretant of the word (sign) SCHOOL in any one context will be the result of the user's experience of that word (s/he would not apply it to a technical college), and of his or her experience of institutions called "schools", the object. Thus it is not fixed, defined by a dictionary, but may vary within limits according to the experience of the user. The limits are set by social convention (in this case the conventions of the English language); the variation within them allows for the social and psychological differences between the users.

One additional difference between the semiotic and the process models is relevant here. This is that the semiotic models make no distinction between encoder and decoder. The interpretant is the mental concept of the user of the sign, whether this user be speaker or listener, writer or reader, painter or viewer. Decoding is as active and creative as encoding.

Ogden and Richards (1923)

Ogden and Richards were British workers in this area who corresponded regularly with Peirce. They derived a very similar triangular model of meaning. Their referent corresponds closely to Peirce's object, their reference to his interpretant, and their symbol to his sign.

In their model, referent and reference are directly connected; so too are symbol and reference. But the connection between symbol and referent is indirect or imputed. This shift away from the equilateral relationship of Peirce's model brings Ogden and Richards closer to Saussure (see below). He, too, relegated the relationship of the sign with external reality to one of minimal importance.

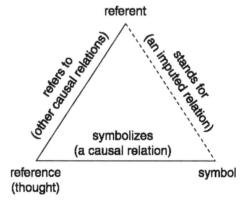

Figure 2.2 Ogden and Richards's elements of meaning.

Like Saussure, Ogden and Richards put the symbol in the key position: our symbols direct and organize our thoughts or references; and our references organize our perception of reality. Symbol and reference in Ogden and Richards are similar to the signifier and signified in Saussure.

Saussure

If the American logician and philosopher C. S. Peirce was one of the founders of semiotics, the other was undoubtedly the Swiss linguist Ferdinand de Saussure. Peirce's concern as a philosopher was with our understanding of our experience and of the world around us. It was only gradually that he came to realize the importance of *semiotics*, the act of signifying, in this. His interest was in meaning, which he found in the structural relationship of signs, people, and objects.

Saussure, as a linguist, was primarily interested in language. He was more concerned with the way signs (or, in his case, words) related to other signs than he was with the way they related to Peirce's "object". So Saussure's basic model differs in emphasis from Peirce's. He focuses his attention much more directly on the sign itself. The sign, for Saussure, was a physical object with a meaning; or, to use his terms, a sign consisted of a *signifier* and a *signified*. The signifier is the sign's image as we perceive it—the marks on the paper or the sounds in the air; the signified is the mental concept to which it refers. This mental concept is broadly common to all members of the same culture who share the same language.

We can see immediately similarities between Saussure's signifier and Peirce's sign, and Saussure's signified and Peirce's interpretant. Saussure, however, is less concerned than Peirce with the relationship of those two elements with Peirce's "object" or external meaning. When Saussure does turn to this he calls it *signification* but spends comparatively little time on it. So Saussure's model may be visualized as in figure 2.3.

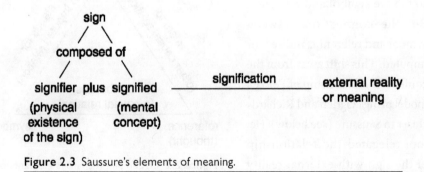

Figure 2.3 Saussure's elements of meaning.

For illustration, I might make two marks on the paper, thus:

O X

These might be the first two moves in a game of noughts and crosses (or tick-tack-toe), in which case they remain as mere marks on the paper. Or they might be read as a word, in which case they become a sign composed of the signifier (their appearance) and the mental concept (oxness) which we have of this particular type of animal. The relationship between my concept of oxness and the physical reality of oxen is "signification": it is my way of giving meaning to the world, of understanding it.

I stress this, because it is important to remember that the signifieds are as much a product of a particular culture as are the signifiers. It is obvious that words, the signifiers, change from language to language. But it is easy to fall into the fallacy of believing that the signifieds are universal and that translation is therefore a simple matter of substituting a French word, say, for an English one—the "meaning" is the same. This is not so. My mental concept of oxness must be very different from that of an Indian farmer, and teaching me the sound of the Hindu word (signifier) for ox does not get me any nearer to sharing his concept of "oxness". The signification of an ox is as culture-specific as is the linguistic form of the signifier in each language.

Sign and System

The deceptively simple question is "What is an ox?", or, to put it more linguistically or semiotically, "What do we mean by the sign *ox*?" For Saussure the question can be answered only in the light of what we do *not* mean by that sign.

This is a new approach to the question of how signs signify. The similarity between Saussure and Peirce here is that they both seek meaning in structural relationships, but Saussure considers a new relationship—that between the sign and other signs in the same system: that is, the relationship between a sign and other signs that it could conceivably be, but is not. Thus the meaning of the sign *man* is determined by how it is differentiated from other signs. So *man* can mean *not animal* or *not human* or *not boy* or *not master*.

When Chanel chose the French star Catherine Deneuve to give their perfume an image of a particular kind of sophisticated traditional French chic, she became a sign in a system. And the meaning of Catherine-Deneuve-as-sign was determined by other beautiful stars-as-signs that she was not. She was not Susan Hampshire (too English); she was not Twiggy (too young, trendy, *changeably* fashionable); she was not Brigitte Bardot (too unsophisticatedly sexy); and so on.

According to this model of meaning, the signifieds are the mental concepts we use to divide reality up and categorize it so that we can understand it. The boundaries between one category and another are artificial, not natural, for nature is all of a piece. There is no line between man and boy until we draw one, and scientists are constantly trying to define more accurately the boundary between humans and other animals. So signifieds are made by people, determined by the culture or subculture to which they belong. They are part of the linguistic or semiotic system that members of that culture use to communicate with each other.

So, then, the area of reality or experience to which any one signified refers, that is the signification of the sign, is determined not by the nature of that reality/experience, but by the boundaries of the related signifieds in the system. Meaning is therefore better defined by the relationships of one sign to another than by the relationship of that sign to an external reality. This relationship of the sign to others in its system is what Saussure calls *value*. And for Saussure *value* is what primarily determines meaning.

Semiotics and Meaning

Semiotics sees communication as the generation of meaning in messages—whether by the encoder or the decoder. Meaning is not an absolute, static concept to be found neatly parcelled up in the message. Meaning is an active process: semioticians use verbs like create, generate, or negotiate to refer to this process. Negotiation is perhaps the most useful in that it implies the to-and-fro, the give-and-take between person and message. Meaning is the result of the dynamic interaction between sign, interpretant, and object: it is historically located and may well change with time. It may even be useful to drop the term "meaning" and use Peirce's far more active term "semiosis"—the act of signifying.

Categories of Signs

Basic Concepts

Peirce and Saussure both tried to explain the different ways in which signs convey meaning. Peirce produced three categories of sign, each of which showed a different relationship between the sign and its object, or that to which it refers.

In an *icon* the sign resembles its object in some way: it looks or sounds like it. In an *index* there is a direct link between a sign and its object: the two are actually connected. In a *symbol* there is no connection or resemblance between sign and object: a symbol communicates only because people agree that it shall stand for what it does. A photograph is an icon, smoke is an index of fire, and a word is a symbol.

Saussure was not concerned with indexes. Indeed, as a linguist, he was really concerned only with symbols, for words are symbols. But his followers have recognized that the physical form of the sign (which Saussure called the signifier) and its associated mental concept (the signified) can be related in an *iconic* or an *arbitrary* way. In an iconic relationship, the signifier looks or sounds like the signified; in an arbitrary relationship, the two are related only by agreement among the users. What Saussure terms *iconic* and *arbitrary relations* between signifier and signified correspond precisely to Peirce's *icons* and *symbols*.

Further Implications

Though Saussure and Peirce were working in the different academic traditions of linguistics and philosophy respectively, they none the less agreed on the centrality of the sign to any understanding of semiotics. They also agreed that the first task was to categorize the variety of signs in terms of the way that, for Saussure, the signifier related to the signified, or, for Peirce, the way that the sign related to the object.

Peirce and the Sign

Peirce divided signs into three types—icon, index, and symbol. Once again, these can be modelled on a triangle (figure 2.4). Peirce felt that this was the most useful and fundamental model of the nature of signs. He writes:

> every sign is determined by its object, either first, by partaking in the character of the object, when I call the sign an *Icon*; secondly, by being really and in its individual existence connected with the individual object, when I call the sign an *Index*; thirdly, by more or less approximate certainty that it will be interpreted as denoting the object in consequence of a habit ... when I call the sign a *Symbol*. (In Zeman, 1977)

An *icon* bears a resemblance to its object. This is often most apparent in visual signs: a photograph of my aunt is an icon; a map is an icon; the common visual signs denoting ladies' and gentlemen's lavatories are icons. But it may be verbal: onomatopoeia is an attempt to make language iconic. Tennyson's line

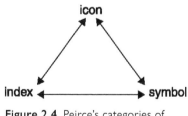

Figure 2.4 Peirce's categories of sign-types.

Figure 2.5 Icon-index-symbol.

"The hum of bees in immemorial elms" makes the sound of the words resemble the sound of the bees. It is iconic. Beethoven's "Pastoral" Symphony contains musical icons of natural sounds. We might think that some perfumes are artificial icons of animal smells indicating sexual arousal. Peirce's model of sign-object-interpretant is an icon in that it attempts to reproduce in concrete form the abstract structure of the relationship between its elements.

An *index* is equally simple to explain. It is a sign with a direct existential connection with its object. Smoke is an index of fire; a sneeze is an index of a head cold. If I arrange to meet you and tell you that you will recognize me because I am bearded and will wear a yellow rose in my buttonhole, then my beard and yellow rose are indexes of me.

A *symbol* is a sign whose connection with its object is a matter of convention, agreement, or rule. Words are, in general, symbols. The red cross is a symbol. Numbers are symbols—there is no reason why the shape 2 should refer to a pair of objects: it is only by convention or rule in our culture that it does. The Roman number II is, of course, iconic.

These categories are not separate and distinct. One sign may be composed of various types. Take the road sign in figure 2.5, for example. The red triangle is a symbol—by the rule of the Highway Code it means "warning". The cross in the middle is a mixture of icon and symbol: it is iconic in that its form is determined partly by the shape of its object, but it is symbolic in that we need to know the rules in order to understand it as "crossroads" and not as "church" or "hospital". And the sign is, in real life, an index in that it indicates that we are about to reach a crossroads. When printed in the Highway Code, or in this book, it is not indexical in that it is not physically or spatially connected with its object.

Convention

Convention, or habit in Pierce's terms, plays an important variety of roles in communication and signification. At its most formal level it can describe the rules by which arbitrary signs work. There is a formal convention that the sign CAT refers to a four-legged feline animal and not an article of clothing. There is a formal convention that fixes the meaning of three signs in this order with this grammatical form: CATS HUNT RATS: we agree that the first word chases the third. It is also conventional that a final -s means plurality.

But there are also less formal, less explicitly expressed, conventions. We have learnt by experience that slow motion on television "means" one of two things: either analysis of skill or error (particularly in sports programmes), or appreciation of beauty. Sometimes, [...] it means both. Our experience of similar signs, that is our experience of the convention, enables us to respond appropriately—we know that it does not mean that people have suddenly started running slow laps; and our experience of the content tells us whether we are meant to appreciate the beauty or evaluate the skill of the movement.

Sometimes it is difficult to determine the relative parts played by convention and iconicity in a sign—that is, how highly motivated or constrained a sign actually is. A television camera zooming into close-up on someone's face conventionally means that that person is experiencing a strong emotion of some sort. We know, by convention, that it does not mean that we have suddenly pushed our face to within inches of his or hers. But that zoom also has an iconic element in that it represents, or reproduces, the focusing of our interest upon a person at such a moment.

Convention is necessary to the understanding of any sign, however iconic or indexical it is. We need to learn how to understand a photograph or even a life-size waxwork. Convention is the social dimension of signs (see also p. 73): it is the agreement amongst the users about the appropriate uses of and responses to a sign. Signs with no conventional dimension are purely private and thus do not communicate. So it may be of more help to consider the distinction between arbitrary and iconic signs or between symbols and icons/indexes as a scale, not as separate categories. At one end of the scale we have the purely arbitrary sign, the symbol. At the other end we have the notional pure icon, which cannot, of course, exist in practice. We can visualize the scale as in figure 2.6.

At the left-hand end of the scale are the signs that are 100 per cent arbitrary, conventional, unmotivated, unconstrained. In the middle are mixed signs, placed according to their degree of motivation. Thus the cross indicating a crossroads on a road sign would be further to the left than a map of a particular crossroads.

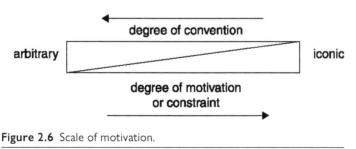

Figure 2.6 Scale of motivation.

The former we might estimate as 60 per cent arbitrary, 40 per cent iconic, whereas the latter may be 30/70 per cent. And we ought to chop off the last half-an-inch on the right, unless the development of holograms makes the purely iconic sign a possibility.

The Organization of Signs

Basic Concepts

Saussure defined two ways in which signs are organized into codes. The first is by *paradigms*. A paradigm is a set of signs from which the one to be used is chosen. The set of shapes for road signs—square, round, or triangular—forms a paradigm; so does the set of symbols that can go within them. Saussure's second way is the *syntagmatic*. A syntagm is the message into which the chosen signs are combined. A road sign is a syntagm, a combination of the chosen shape with the chosen symbol. In language, we can say that the vocabulary is the paradigm, and a sentence is a syntagm. So all messages involve *selection* (from a paradigm) and *combination* (into a syntagm).

Further Implications

We must remember that Saussure insisted that a sign's meaning was determined mainly by its relationship to other signs. It is here that his linguistic interest shows most strongly, and it is in this that he differs most radically from Peirce. The two main types of relationship which a sign can form with others are described by the terms *paradigm* and *syntagm*.

Paradigms

Let us take paradigms first. A paradigm is a set from which a choice is made and only one unit from that set may be chosen. A simple example is the letters of the alphabet. These form the paradigm for written language and illustrate the two basic characteristics of a paradigm:

i.   All the units in a paradigm must have something in common: they must share characteristics that determine their membership of that paradigm. We must know that M is a letter and thus a member of the alphabetic paradigm, and we must recognize equally that 5 is not, and neither is ÷.

ii. Each unit must be clearly distinguished from all the others in the paradigm. We must be able to tell the difference between signs in a paradigm in terms of both their signifiers and their signifieds. The means by which we distinguish one signifier from another are called the *distinctive features* of a sign: this is a concept of considerable analytical importance to which we will return later. In our current example we need to say only that bad handwriting is handwriting that blurs the distinctive features of the letters.

Every time we communicate we must select from a paradigm. Words are a paradigm—the vocabulary of English is a paradigm. Words are also categorized into other, more specific paradigms: grammatical paradigms, such as nouns or verbs; paradigms of use—baby language, legal language, lovers' talk, masculine swearing; or paradigms of sound—words that rhyme, day, may, say, etc. At a more detailed level still, the three Saussurian terms for analysing the sign form a paradigm and are frequently written Sn, Sr, Sd. Here the S indicates by convention the paradigm and the -n, -r, -d, are the distinctive features that identify the units within it.

Other examples of paradigms are: way of changing shot in television—cut, fade, dissolve, wipe, etc.; headgear—trilby, cap, beret, stetson, etc.; the style of chairs with which we furnish our living room; the type of car we drive; the colour we paint our front door. All these involve paradigmatic choices, and the meaning of the unit we choose is determined largely by the meanings of the units we did not. We can sum up by saying "where there is choice there is meaning, and the meaning of what was chosen is determined by the meaning of what was not."

Syntagms

Once a unit has been chosen from a paradigm it is normally combined with other units. This combination is called a *syntagm*. Thus a written word is a visual syntagm composed of a sequence of paradigmatic choices from the letters of the alphabet. A sentence is a syntagm of words. Our clothes are a syntagm of choices from the paradigms of hats, ties, shirts, jackets, trousers, socks, etc. The way we furnish a room is a syntagm of choices from the paradigms of chairs, tables, settees, carpets, wallpapers, etc. An architect designing a house makes a syntagm of the styles of doors, windows, etc., and their positions. A menu is a good example of a complete *system*. The choices for each course (the paradigms) are given in full: each diner combines them into a meal: the order given to the waiter is a syntagm.

The important aspect of syntagms is the rules or conventions by which the combination of units is made. In language we call this grammar or syntax; in music we call it melody (harmony is a matter of paradigmatic choice); in clothes we call it good taste, or fashion sense, though there are more formal rules as well. For instance, a black bow-tie with a black jacket and white collar means a dinner guest, but the same bow-tie with a tailed coat and a white wing collar would mean a waiter. In a syntagm, then, the chosen sign can be affected by its relationship with others; its meaning is determined partly by its relationship with others in the syntagm.

For Saussure, and the structural linguists who followed him, the key to understanding signs was to understand their structural relationship with others. There are two types of structural relationship—paradigmatic, that of choice; or syntagmatic, that of combination.

Traffic Lights

Traffic lights are a simple communication system that we can use to illustrate many of the analytical concepts introduced in this chapter. Figure 2.7 shows how Edmund Leach (1974) models the structural relationships of traffic lights. If we analyse the signifying in full we start by identifying the paradigm—that is, of traffic lights. A red light here means STOP and not BROTHEL or RECORDING IN PROGRESS. It is arbitrary, or a symbol, but not entirely so. Red is so widespread a sign for danger that we are justified in looking for some iconic element in it. It may be because it is the colour of blood, or because in moments of extreme rage or fear, the dilation of the blood vessels in the eye literally makes us "see red". So red is a crisis colour. If red, by a mixture of convention and motivation, means "stop", the rest follows logically. Green is the opposite of red on the colour spectrum, as GO is the opposite of STOP. Colour is the distinctive feature, and green is as distinctive from red as is possible. If we need a third unit in the system, we ought to go for yellow or blue, as these colours are midway between red and green in the spectrum. Blue is reserved for emergency services, so the choice is naturally yellow, or amber to give it a stronger form. Then we introduce a simple syntax: amber combined with red is a syntagm meaning that the change is in the direction of GO; amber on its own means that the change is in the direction of STOP. Other rules are that red can never be combined with green, and that red and green can never follow each other directly.

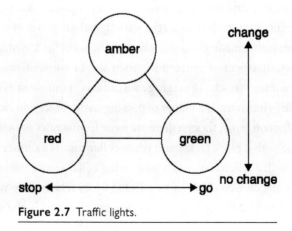

Figure 2.7 Traffic lights.

So there is a lot of redundancy built into the system. A red light is all that is strictly needed: "on" for STOP, "off" for GO. But even temporary traffic lights add redundancy by including a green. This prevents the possible error of decoding "off" as "the lights have broken down". The full system, of course, has high redundancy because it is vital to minimize errors of decoding and there may be a lot of "noise" (the sun in the eyes, other traffic to concentrate on).

References

Leach, E. (1974) *Lévi-Strauss*, London: Fontana.

Ogden, C. and Richards, I. (1923; 2nd edn. 1949) *The Meaning of Meaning*, London: Routledge & Kegan Paul.

Peirce, C. S. (1931–58) *Collected Papers*, Cambridge, Mass.: Harvard University Press.

de Saussure, F. (1974) (1st edn. 1915) *Course in General Linguistics*, London: Fontana.

Zeman, J. (1977) "Peirce's theory of signs" in Sebeok, T. (ed.) (1977).

Bibliography

Further Reading

In addition to the other titles in this series, the following books are recommended for those who wish to read further into the issues raised in this volume.

Barthes, R. (1973) *Mythologies*, London: Paladin. An original, lively, sometimes difficult collection of essays on contemporary, very varied "texts". Read the first half of "Myth today" at least—the second half is heavy going but worth the effort for serious students.

Barthes, R. (1977) *Image—Music—Text*, London: Fontana. Another collection of essays— "The photographic message" and "The rhetoric of the image" are not to be missed.

Cherry, C. (1957) (2nd edn. 1966) *On Human Communication*, Cambridge, Mass.: MIT Press. Early, comprehensive, though the mathematical angle has not proved as fruitful as was hoped—needs selective reading.

Cohen, S. and Young, J. (eds.) (1973) *The Manufacture of News*, London: Constable. A good selection of essays—specific, applied, theoretical, relevant, and sometimes funny: what more could you ask?

Corner, J. and Hawthorn, J. (eds.) (1980) *Communication Studies*, London: Arnold. A reader that makes a real attempt to cover the field; sections on: communication, definitions and approaches; perception, behaviour, interaction; language, thought, culture; meaning and interpretation; mass communication. Most of the major authorities are represented—a good support for this book.

Culler, J. (1976) *Saussure*, London: Fontana. A well-written account of the theories and significance of the great linguist.

Fiske, J. and Hartley, J. (1978) *Reading Television*, London: Methuen. Useful for its outline of semiotic theory and content analysis with examples. Applied, obviously, to television, but more widely applicable.

Guiraud, P. (1975) *Semiology*, London: Routledge & Kegan Paul. A short, useful little book that explains the main terms but is short on applied analysis. Rare in that it is an example of non-left-wing semiotics!

Hall, S., Hobson, D., Lowe, A., and Willis, P. (eds.) *Culture, Media, Language*, London: Hutchinson. A collection of some of the main work of the Birmingham Centre for Contemporary Cultural Studies. Some advanced work here, but important reading for the serious student. See especially the section on media studies.

Hawkes, T. (1977) *Structuralism and Semiotics*, London: Methuen. Literary in emphasis and examples, but gives a good account of the development and theory of semiotics.

McQuail, D. (1975) *Communication*, London: Longman. Comprehensive, sociological, not always easy reading but worth the effort for the theoretical framework it gives to the whole field.

Morley, D. (1980) *The Nationwide Audience*, London: British Film Institute. A highly recommended work, admirable in its combination of semiotic/cultural theory with empirical study.

Smith, A. G. (1966) *Communication and Culture*, New York: Holt, Rinehart & Winston. A large collection of essays—particularly useful for the number of models included. Essays by Weaver, Cherry, Newcomb, Westley and MacLean, Bernstein, Goffman, to name but a few. Not in paperback.

Webster, F. (1980) *The New Photography*, London: John Calder. This book is not specifically referred to in suggestions for further work, but it covers the reading of news photographs and advertisements. It is readable and thorough and can be recommended.

Books Recommended for Additional Reading

Readers

Hinde, R. (ed.) (1972) *Non-Verbal Communication*, Cambridge: Cambridge University Press. Excellent collection of essays, mainly on communication, codes, and cultural background. See especially those by MacKay, Lyons, Argyle, Leach, Miller, and Gombrich.

Sereno, K. and Mortenson, C. D. (eds.) (1970) *Foundations of Communication Theory*, New York: Harper & Row. Another impressive collection of essays which illustrates the variety of approaches to the study of communication theory. Some are advanced, but most are easily readable. Sections include: perspectives, systems, decoding–encoding, interaction, and social context.

Curran, J., Gurevitch, M., and Woollacott, J. (eds.) (1977) *Mass Communication and Society*, London: Arnold. Excellent reader covering all the burning issues of media studies. The list of contributors reads like a *Who's Who* of media studies. Some very advanced reading, little at introductory level, but a goldmine for those prepared to dig.

McQuail, D. (ed.) (1972) *Sociology of Mass Communications*, Harmondsworth: Penguin. Good reader, more at the introductory level than Curran *et al.* (1977). A wide range of topics by a prestigious series of authors.

Buscombe, E. (ed.) (1975) *Football on Television*, London: British Film Institute. Cheap, readable little book—excellent for the way it exemplifies various methods of analysis. Should spark off numerous ideas for group and individual work. Recommended.

(*Note*: all the BFI Television Monographs are well worth reading and are excellent value for money.)

Textbooks

Lin, N. (1973) *The Study of Human Communication*, New York: Bobbs Merrill. Good textbook, especially strong on the linguistic, psychological, and social-psychological approaches. Scientific in style.

Mortenson, G. (1972) *Communication: The Study of Human Interaction*, New York: McGraw-Hill. Another good textbook in the "transmission" school. Well illustrated, readable, more comprehensive than Lin (1973). Good introduction.

Semiotics

Monaco, J. (1977) *How to Read a Film*, New York: Oxford University Press. A thorough, well-illustrated review of semiotic theory and concepts, supported by ideas drawn from perception theory and applied to film. Good analysis of specifically filmic codes. Good alternative to Fiske, J. and Hartley, J. (1978).

Woollacott, J. (1977) *Messages and Meanings*, Milton Keynes: The Open University Press (DE 353, Unit 6). A succinct account of the main theory and methods of semiotics; readable applied Marxism—can't be bad!

Mass Media

Golding, P. (1974) *The Mass Media*, London: Longman. British version of Wright (1959) but shorter, more up-to-date, though lacking in any content study; but good.

Williams, R. (1962) (3rd edn. 1976) *Communications*, Harmondsworth: Penguin. Recommended brief book. Good history and very good chapter on content of the press that is crying out for comparisons with today's press.

Williams, R. (1974) *Television: Technology and Cultural Form*, London: Fontana. Good social/technological history followed by excellent chapters on the form and content of television; some American examples.

Wright, C. (1959) (2nd edn. 1975) *Mass Communication: A Sociological Approach*, New York: Random House. Good, readable introductory text, covering the functions, institutions, contents, and effects of the media, together with chapters on the communicators and the audience. Feels somewhat dated and locked into its sociological problem-free approach, but still a good point from which to start studies of the media.

Non-verbal Communication

Argyle, M. (1972) (3rd edn. 1978) *The Psychology of Interpersonal Behaviour*, Harmondsworth: Penguin.

—— (1975) *Bodily Communication*, London: Methuen. Two key works by the leading British authority on the social psychological approach to the study of non-verbal communication. Both are readable, though the 1972 one is probably the easier way in. That of 1975 is broader and takes more account of the social/cultural context.

Hall, E. (1973) *The Silent Language*, New York: Anchor Books. A useful balance to Argyle: as an anthropologist Hall gives greater emphasis to the part played by culture in non-verbal communication.

Sapir–Whorf Hypothesis: Verbal Communication Real-World Lab

Name: _____

Date: _____

The Sapir–Whorf hypothesis says that language determines how people interpret the world, and, because of this, speakers of different languages view the world differently. There are two main parts to the Sapir–Whorf hypothesis:

1. Linguistic determinism, which says that language determines how we interpret the world.

2. Linguistic relativity, which says that because language exerts a strong influence on perception; speakers of different languages view the world differently. For example, Inuit people have *many* more words for snow than English speakers in the United States do.

For this real-world lab, you will interview someone who speaks more than one language. This could be a relative, friend, roommate, or stranger. Ask them about their experience learning a second language.

1. How many languages do they speak and what are they?

   _____

   _____

   _____

   _____

2. Did they learn their second language at a young age or when they were older?

   _____

   _____

   _____

   _____

   _____

   _____

3. Ask them to reflect on words or phrases that *exist in one language but not the other*. Give them time to think about this and make sure to write down several examples they come up with. Have them think about words that exist in English but not in their other language and vice versa.

   ○ For example, *waldeinsamkeit* is a German word that means "the feeling of being alone in the woods." We do not have a single word for this feeling in English.

   _____

   _____

   _____

   _____

4. Once you have several examples written down, discuss together why these words exist in one language but not the other. Write your ideas. For the German example, the word might exist in German because much of Germany is wooded and this feeling is encountered more frequently than in English-speaking countries.

   _____

   _____

   _____

   _____

5. If you also speak a second language, reflect on these questions yourself and provide your own answers.

   _____

   _____

   _____

   _____

6. Who did you find to interview for this lab? Describe their relationship to you.

   _____

   _____

   _____

CHAPTER 3

Nonverbal Communication

Introduction to the Chapter

Today's world is a global one, and the chances you will work with people from other cultures are high. In order to benefit the most from these relationships, some knowledge about cultural differences in nonverbal communication will serve you well. This chapter dives into what you need to know about body language and nonverbal communication in cross-cultural conversations, especially ones you might have at work. The chapter breaks down nonverbal behaviors into three categories: body language, physical environment, and personal attributes. You will learn about the functions of nonverbal communication such as expressing emotion and managing the flow of conversations.

READING 3

Nonverbal Messages

Communication Beyond Boundaries

By Payal Mehra

··

> *Fie, fie upon her! There's language in her eye, her cheek, her*
> *lip, Nay, her foot speaks; her wanton spirits look out at every*
> *joint and motive of her body.*
> —Ulysses in William Shakespeare's Troilus and
> Cressida, IV.5.54-57

Introduction

From the time Charles Darwin published his epoch study—*Expressions of the Emotions in Man and Animals* in 1872, researchers from diverse disciplines such as anthropology, sociology, and, now, management, have been interested in exploring body language and its interpretation in various cultures. Nonverbal communication is an outward reflection of a person's emotional condition. More than verbal communication, it is the nonverbal communication that reveals the true attitudes and emotions of people, often without their conscious awareness. People both consciously and subconsciously tend to reveal their likes and dislikes through their body language.

Nonverbal communication is a product of culture and tends to be interpreted in a culture-specific way. People from native cultures speak their own language and follow particular cultural norms. In a multicultural workplace, negative micromessages may be sent to members of minority or ethnic groups (people who are perceived to be different from the majority), even if their verbal messages are polite and courteous. Negative micromessages can include a sneer, a cynical smile, raised eyebrows, a casual shrug, a smug facial expression, and the like. This subtle form of communication complicates relationships and provides a subconscious source of misunderstandings across cultures. It also has the potential to affect performance and output.

Randhir Garg, an Indian, working as a guest worker in Great Britain, is regarded by fellow British employees as nonassertive and lazy. Though they do not say anything to him verbally, they send him micromessages conveying a negative stereotype. Garg feels like an outsider, thus affecting his performance in the team.

Nonverbal communication includes all forms of communication excluding the language used to speak or write. Three types of nonverbal communication will be discussed in this text: body language (facial expressions, gestures, posture, and body movements); physical environment (using physical space, distance and proximity norms, and territorial control); and personal attributes (such as appearance, voice, and touch). Technically, the study of body language is termed as kinesics, oculesics, proxemics, haptics, vocalics, chronemics, and environment.

Nonverbal communication is very important in international business, partly because verbal communication can be (more often than not) misleading or unreliable. This is especially true in international business negotiations, cross-country presentations, international product launches, as well as all communication related to mergers and acquisitions. International marketing often relies on the nonverbal communication of target population participants in focus group discussions for brand decisions.

Types of Nonverbal Communication

Nonverbal communication can be classified into two categories: conscious messages and subliminal messages. Senders of conscious messages are aware that they are sending out a particular message and that the message has a definite implication. For example, a thumbs-up signal by an American is positive, denoting good job or go ahead. Receivers of the conscious nonverbal message know that the message is a positive one and a sign of motivation. In contrast, subliminal messages appeal to the subconscious mind of the receiver. A receiver is not consciously aware of the nonverbal message. Organizations that require its employees to wear uniforms subliminally communicate position, authority, and a desire for belongingness among those wearing them. The advertising media also uses subliminal messages. For example, in a movie, an actor is seen drinking cola of a reputed company. The use of these products in the movie would not be classified strictly as advertisements. However, the mere association of the movie with the brand and the product transmits subliminal messages that influence the viewers.

Nonverbal messages can be involuntary as well as voluntary. People unintentionally convey many messages through their facial expressions, hand movements, and eye contact. It is often said that liars can be caught merely by telltale signals: shifty eyes, gestures of touching nose and ear, and even by the way they smile. Because involuntary communication is unplanned, it represents a better assessment of people's true intentions than verbal messages. Nonverbal communication can also be voluntary. People knowledgeable about body language can control their nonverbal responses. They take special care to avoid the telltale signs that may reveal their true intent.

Functions of Nonverbal Communication

Mindful nonverbal communication has the following distinct functions:

Enhancing, Asserting, and Reflecting Identities

Nonverbal cues serve as identity badges. We tend to respond to others on the basis of stereotypes rather than personal content characteristics. The face, hair, eyes, clothes, and accessories are interpreted by others through the medium of stereotypes. Accent, posture, and gesture also reveal group membership (Asian? American? Japanese?). Categorical slotting takes place as a result of speech patterns, physical cues (such as hair and skin color), and clothing. Vocalics such as speech, accent, pitch intensity, volume, and articulation also characterize cultural origins. We tend to like people who sound like us in contrast to those who sound very different.

Expressing Emotions

Feelings and attitudes are inferred from kinesics and vocalics. The human face is said to be capable of producing 250,000 facial expressions. Culture shapes emotional expressions. Subconsciously, through the cultural reinforcement process, people internalize the nonverbal rules of their culture. They react spontaneously to situations through learned behavior. It is thus that human beings acquire nonverbal display rules. They learn when to suppress emotions and how and when to convey emotions. Thus, collectivists will learn to suppress display (to maintain relationships and preserve harmony), while the individualists will learn to express display of emotions, feelings, and behavior.

Though members of various cultures universally acknowledge happiness and surprise, feelings of disgust, anger, unhappiness, or hurt are more obviously demonstrated by the expressive cultures better than the reserved cultures. Additionally, the smile can be interpreted in different ways. While in the United States the smile is an expression of joy, in Japan, it may imply a myriad of emotions (including embarrassment, displeasure, or anger). Russians, for example, rarely smile at the beginning of a negotiation, but as it progresses in a favorable manner, they start to smile. In terms of vocalics, the Arabs, Italians, and Greeks tend to raise their voices and argue passionately; while they are not angry, to an American they might appear to be so. From an Arab's point of view, the American tone may sound cold, distant, and aloof, but to an Asian it may sound too aggressive and harsh. Thus, cultural relativism can impact how people perceive each other.

Meaning of a smile in various cultures

United States:	Friendliness
Asia:	Friendliness, covering for emotional pain, embarrassment, anger
Russia:	Agreement, satisfaction

Managing Conversations

People use kinesics and oculesics (eye contact) to manage their conversations with each other. Kinesics includes emblems, illustrators, regulators, and adaptors, and each of these has a specific communication objective. They are not, however, mutually exclusive. An emblem is an intentional hand gestures that has a specific meaning attributed to it. Consider the *ok* sign, for example. The use of this signal means good in the United States, money in Japan, a sexual insult in Greece, zero in French, and vulgar in Russia. The thumbs-up gesture means good or great in the United States and Great Britain, but is offensive to Arabs. The use of gestures may lead to misunderstandings, as a polite greeting in one culture may be considered rude in another culture.

Meaning of hand gestures in various cultures

Italy	In counting, thumb means one and index finger means two
Australia	Index finger is one and middle finger is two
United States	*V* is for victory with outward palm
Great Britain	*V* is for victory when the palm faces the receiver; it is an insult when palm faces the speaker (same for Australia, New Zealand)

Japan, Korea, Taiwan	*V* with outward palm (facing the receiver), especially when photographed
Philippines	*V* is for peace
Vietnam	*V* is for hello
Indonesia	Index finger is used to stop public transport
United States	People are beckoned with palm up
Korea	People are beckoned by snapping fingers
Europe	Thumbs-up gesture means one
Greece	Thumbs-up means "one up to you"
United States	Handshake to greet
Japan	Bow to greet (depth of the bow indicates respect for seniority and position)

Illustrators are hand gestures that complement the spoken words. These gestures help to visualize the imagery and are the most pictorial of the nonverbal gestures. These are mostly used to illustrate directions. The Italians, Greeks, and Spaniards use more illustrators than the Americans. Arabs, South Americans, and Egyptians use animated illustrators. Belgians, Finns, and those from Asian cultures use fewer illustrators. The Arabs do not gesture or eat with the left hand as it is perceived as unclean. Members of some Asian countries refrain from patting the head, as the head is considered sacred.

Regulators are vocalics, kinesics, and oculesics to regulate the flow of conversation. As with emblems, they are also culture specific. Interruptions, for example, are regulators as is the use of silence. Brazilians interrupt twice as much as the British or Americans. In Bulgaria, when people nod their heads, it means no, but in other parts of the world, nodding means yes. The French also like to interrupt with interjections such as an exclamation, a remark, a protest, or even laughter. Pauses and filler cues such as "uh huh" (British) or "hai hai" (Japanese) are also regulators as is eye contact. Regulators, like other nonverbal gestures, have the potential to create misunderstandings when used across cultures.

Adaptors are essential postural changes at a low level of awareness. Seldom intentional, adaptors are often true indicators of what a person is thinking because people perform these movements at a subconscious level. For example, a slumped posture conveys boredom and disinterest, while an erect posture suggests enthusiasm and vitality. Similarly, leaning forward suggests keen listening and active involvement while leaning away indicates disinterest and boredom. Other examples of adaptors include fiddling with one's hair (low involvement), chewing fingernails (anxiety), tapping one's foot and leg (impatience), playing with jewelry (nervousness), and cracking knuckles (awkwardness).

Extent of eye contact and its implication in various cultures

Minimal or very less eye contact:	Far East Asian countries
Moderate eye contact:	Thailand, India, Pakistan, Korea, Africa
Firm eye contact:	United States, most parts of northern Europe, Turkey
Intense eye contact:	Saudi Arabia, Italy, Spain, Greece, parts of South America

Meaning of raised eyebrows in various cultures

Germans	Brilliant!
Arabs and Chinese	Disagreement

Impression Formation

Impression formation occurs throughout the process of communication. An individual's personality, physical attributes, profession, and behavior create an impression on the receiver. Positive impression formation is often related to the person's posture, style of walking, voice modulation, eye contact, dress, and accessories. However, norms regarding what constitutes professionalism vary across cultures. While some types of business attire are universally acceptable in all cultures, the same may not hold true for eye contact, voice modulation, and posture. In the United States, for example, assertiveness is a valued trait but this may not hold true for many South Asian countries. A positive impression in these countries is associated with passive behavior (especially when lower in hierarchy), a reserved communication style, and minimal display of gestures.

Interpreting Nonverbal Messages

Nonverbal messages must be interpreted in totality and not in isolation because most messages have more than one possible interpretation. Nonverbal messages are often rooted in cultural contexts. For example, it may appear perfectly normal in many cultures to lightly pat a child's head, but the gesture has a negative connotation in Thailand. Similarly, in some cultures, direct eye contact is preferred, while in others, a direct gaze is considered offensive. South European countries are more physically demonstrative than the north European countries.

In a negotiation process, the Americans erroneously concluded that the Chinese were in agreement with their proposal. Every time the Americans expressed a viewpoint, they were met with silence and an impassive gaze. Because there was no overt resistance, the Americans felt confident about their proposal. The confidence was misplaced, however.

Handshakes

It is important to consider the effects of cultural differences when interpreting handshake cues. For example, in the Middle East, the grip is more gentle than executive in nature. In most Asian countries, direct eye contact is avoided when shaking hands. It is considered suspicious in the United States and in Latin American countries when people avoid eye contact while shaking hands. In Islamic countries, it is taboo to shake hands with women. Women also avoid touching gestures such as the shoulder pat. In the United States, women are accustomed to using the executive grip when shaking hands with both men and women. In India, businessmen also prefer the executive grip; however, only a few women use it; most women prefer the gentle touching of the fingers or the *limp fish* handshake, which can be misinterpreted in other cultures as a sign of weakness. In many countries including India, shoulder pats, kissing on the cheek, embraces, or other types of touching are considered a violation of one's personal space, especially between strangers. In Japan, the custom is to bow, although visiting dignitaries need not do so. U.S. President Obama was criticized by the U.S. media for bowing too low to the point of depicting extreme servility to his Japanese counterpart (see picture in the following text):

President Obama: Bowing too low?

Source: The Telegraph (2009).

U.S. President George Bush in 1992 toured Australia and gave a peace sign in the form of a *V* gesture to a group of farmers in Canberra. He apparently wanted to appease the farmers who were protesting U.S. farm subsidies. The signal backfired; the outward facing *V* sign in Australia is an insulting and hostile gesture.

Source: Tarpley and Chaitkin (2004).

North Americans, for example, value privacy; therefore they have fairly wide proxemic requirements in contrast to Latin Americans who have little concept of privacy. The British maintain greater distance than the French, who are a more high-contact culture than the former. Similarly, an Arab's concept of personal space is very different from that of an American (see the following illustration). As with other types of nonverbal communication, space and distance are open to misinterpretation and misunderstandings. A too-close proximity is often viewed as invading the privacy and space of another person. People tend to react, become defensive in their behavior, and actually move away from the person who they perceive as invading their space.

An Arab greeting an American

Preferred distances between people belonging to different cultures:

Least   Moderate   Most

Arabs, Latin Americans, Greeks, Turks, French, Italians, Indians, Japanese, Chinese, Thai, British, Germans, Dutch, Americans

Hall distinguishes two types of spatial arrangements that can convey different types of meaning and hinder effective communication: the sociofugal space (greater distance between the manager and the subordinates expressed by placement of furniture and room arrangement), and the sociopetal arrangement (minimal distance between the manager and subordinates resulting from room and furniture arrangement).

Japanese office seating arrangements are designed to facilitate control and quick interpersonal communication. The manager sits in a far corner to supervise ably the subordinates who sit facing each other, each with a small desk. The manager's desk is slightly bigger than that of the subordinates. In the conference room, the seating is strictly hierarchical, with the manager sitting at the head of the table and the subordinates sitting in decreasing order of hierarchy.

Source: Nishiyama (2000).

Touching

Touching is a universal emotional behavior, though it differs widely in social contexts across cultures. Touching in the workplace can be indicative of positive emotions such as appreciation, support, affection, inclusion, and liking. Touching is also said to facilitate self-disclosure. In a multicultural workforce, opportunities for conflicts are imminent because each culture has its own norms regarding touching behavior.

With respect to touching, cultures may be divided into contact and noncontact cultures. In the workplace, touching behavior can be triggered by professional concerns (handshakes to greet people, the need to pat the back of a junior member to motivate or congratulate him or her); by concerns relating to politeness (light kiss on the cheek); or friendship (hugging, caressing). In many countries such as the United States, touching behavior at the workplace has become a matter of litigation. A senior who pokes his subordinate to emphasize a point is viewed as a bully; a casual pat on the arm may be (mis)construed as sexual misconduct or harassment.

For example, at the G-8 Summit in St. Petersburg in 2006, U.S. President George Bush stepped behind the German Chancellor, Angela Merkel, and gave her shoulders a brief massage. Visibly surprised and plainly uncomfortable, Merkel threw up her arms to avoid Bush's hands. The event was captured by the press and attracted a lot of negative attention on websites and other social media. In Germany, surprisingly, the reaction was mute and one of indifference. The debate was branded as more of an American rather than a German issue. Needless to say, in the United States, an offense of this type could result in litigation (See the previous illustration).

In another incident, Iranian President Mahmoud Ahmadinejad was criticized severely by the Islamic clerics for hugging the mother of Venezuelan President Hugo Chavez at his funeral in Caracas. Under Islamic law, it is strictly forbidden for a man to have physical contact with a member of the female gender, who is not closely related to him.

George Bush and Angela Merkel: Too close for comfort?

Source: Warren (2006).

> "Shaking hands with a non-mahram (non-family member) woman, whether young or old, and under any circumstances, is not allowed. Hugging or expressing emotions is improper for the dignity of the president of a country such as the Islamic Republic of Iran," Mohammad Taghi Rahbar told Iran's Mehr News Agency.
>
> *Source*: Associated Press (2013).

Members of contact cultures maintain closer distance, face each other, and tend to touch each other while conversing. Members of noncontact cultures tend to maintain distance with each other and rarely touch each other during conversation. These differences can create communication problems. The latter's behavior may appear cold and distant to those from high-contact cultures who in turn may perceive them as pushy and aggressive.

> In 2009, there was an apparent breach of protocol when Mrs. Obama briefly put her hand on the back of Queen Elizabeth II as they chatted at a reception. British etiquette is rigid about protocol (touching the Queen is a strict no-no).
>
> *Source*: Chua-Eoan (2009).

Handling a business card in some cultures such as Japan is akin to a touching gesture. The card has to be held in both hands and read carefully for its contents. It is considered discourteous to write anything on the card, fold it, or put in the pocket or bag without glancing at it.

Summary

1. It is vital to increase one's understanding of global norms of etiquette before attempting to do business beyond boundaries.

2. Nonverbal communication is a product of culture and tends to be interpreted in a culture-specific way. Deciphering nonverbal communication is a crucial skill for anyone working across cultures.

3. Technically, the study of body language includes kinesics, oculesics, proxemics, haptics, vocalics, and chronemics.

4. People use kinesics and oculesics to manage their conversations with each other.

5. Kinesics comprises emblems, illustrators, regulators, and adaptors, and each of these has a specific communication objective.

6. In a multicultural workplace, people may send negative micromessages to members of minority or ethnic groups (people who are perceived to be different from the majority), even if their verbal messages are polite and courteous. This form of communication complicates relationships and provides an unconscious source of misunderstandings across cultures. It also has the potential to affect performance and output.

Key Terms

- Conscious and subliminal messages
- Kinesics, oculesics, haptic, chronemics, and vocalics
- Illustrators, regulators, and adaptors

References

Associated Press. *Mahmoud Ahmadinejad under fire for hugging Hugr Chavez's mother,* 2013, http://nbclatino.com/2013/03/12/ahmadinejad-under-fire-for-hugging-hugo-chavezs-mother/, (accessed March 13, 2013).

Chua-Eoan, H. "The Queen and Mrs. Obama: A Breach in Protocol." *Time magazine*, April 1, 2009, http://www.time.com/time/world/article/0,8599,1888962,00.html#ixzz2TLgr19v2

Nishiyama, K. "Barriers to International Business Communication." In *Doing Business with Japan: Successful Strategies for Intercultural Communication.* Honolulu, HI: University of Hawaii press, 2000.

Tarpley, W.G.; and A. Chaitkin. *George Bush: The Unauthorized Biography*, 651. San Diego, CA: Progressive Press paperback edition, 2004. Web link to Chapter -XXV- Thyroid Storm, January 3, 1992.

The Telegraph. *Barack Obama Criticised for 'treasonous' Bow to Japanese Emperor*, November 16, 2009, http://www.telegraph.co.uk/news/worldnews/barackobama/6580190/Barack-Obama-criticised-for-treasonous-bow-to-Japanese-emperor.html

Warren, J. "The Politics of Good Touch, Bad Touch." *The New York Times*, July 23, 2006, http://www.nytimes.com/2006/07/23/fashion/sundaystyles/23touch.html?_r=0; http://www.worldalmanac.com/blog/2007/01/22/bush-merkel.jpg

Campus Event: Nonverbal Communication Real-World Lab

1. Attend a campus event where there is a speaker and audience members. Be sure to grab a program or take a selfie to show you were there. Attach your program from the event to the following worksheet or upload your selfie from the event to your online course management system. If you are unable to take a selfie and there is no program, write detailed observation notes to show you were there.

2. When at the event, do your best to take in the details of the situation. Pay attention to verbal and nonverbal communication cues.

3. Answer the questions on the worksheet.

Name: _____

Title/name of event attended: _____

Date attended: _____

Describe the event you attended in a couple of paragraphs by answering the following questions:

1. What type of event did you attend and how did that influence the nonverbal communication of the people at the event? (e.g., formal presentations usually have audience members facing a stage with one or two people talking, less formal presentations may also have audience members chatting with one another).

_____

_____

_____

_____

_____

_____

_____

2. How was the room set up and how did the room set up influence the communication?

_____

_____

_____

3. Who was talking? Who wasn't talking?

_____

_____

_____

4. How were the people who were talking and not talking still communicating via nonverbal communication?

_____

_____

_____

5. What nonverbal behaviors did you notice in the audience members (e.g., Were they making eye contact with one another? The speaker? Describe their kinesics, haptics, etc.)? List and describe the nonverbal behaviors you noticed there.

_____

_____

_____

6. If applicable, what nonverbal behaviors did you notice the presenters doing?

_____

_____

_____

7. Did you notice any miscommunications between the speakers? If yes, describe what happened. How could it have been avoided?

_____

_____

_____

8. Did the speakers take turns smoothly? How?

_____

_____

_____

9. Did you see any touching at the event? Did it seem socially appropriate? Why or why not?

_____

_____

_____

10. What did you notice and what did you learn? Show you can use the terms you have been reading about in this book.

_____

_____

_____

CHAPTER 4

Listening

Introduction to the Chapter

Listening and communication are intimately tied. You cannot do one well without the other. This chapter defines listening with a focus on presence and active listening. You will learn the four major components of effective listening: being present, listening nonjudgmentally, inviting the communication to continue, and waiting for the speaker to finish before forming your response. The author asks you to consider how it feels when you are not being listened to and how to use listening to your advantage in the workplace.

The Importance of Listening

By Leslie Shore

....

I only wish I could find an institute that teaches people how to listen. Business people need to listen at least as much as they need to talk. Too many people fail to realize that real communication goes in both directions.

—Lee Iacocca

I magine a world where every world leader, parent, teacher, manager, and friend has become an effective listener. What would a world populated with truly effective listeners be like? How would it be different? In this kind of world, conversations would not lead to arguments; discussions would not escalate into altercations; and everyone would thoroughly listen to what a speaker had to say in order to understand what was said the *first* time it was spoken.

Defining "Listening"

Many people believe that hearing and listening are the same, but they are not. Hearing is merely the physical reception of sound. Listening is the process of attaching meaning to sound through knowledge and experience.

Hearing is Passive and Automatic

Unless our hearing is impeded for some reason (hearing impairment, protective devices or ear plugs, background noise or distractions), we hear sounds whether we're trying to receive them or not. *Listening, on the other hand, is active and intentional.* It involves three functions: hearing, processing the message, and reacting to it either through words or body language. Listening does not occur automatically. It's the result of a conscious choice we make, as we can make a conscious decision *not* to listen.

We often spend only enough time and energy to hear without taking the time to listen. Whether in our personal or professional life, we now do more multitasking, experience more technology interruptions, and fall victim to far more stress caused by an overly packed schedule than ever before. But understanding the difference between hearing and listening is an important prerequisite for listening effectively, and listening effectively is the key to success in all areas of life.

The Importance of Listening

Why is listening so important? Though the answer to this question may seem obvious, it really isn't. Ready answers might be ...

"So I can do the job right."
"So I can learn from the person talking."
"So I can see what is bothering my teenager."
"So I can be on top of my game at work."

Although these answers are right, they only scratch the surface. We are working and living today in a "knowledge economy." Personal and professional success leans heavily on how much we can learn about our friends and family, our jobs, the organizations where we work, and ourselves. Applying that knowledge to new situations through our *effective* listening skills helps us not only to increase our own knowledge but to handle ourselves in the world around us as well.

Learning to listen effectively calls for developing a certain set of skills, and it's important to acknowledge to ourselves that, even though our skills may be well developed, they can weaken without practice. Regardless of current capabilities, all listeners can continue to improve through practice, practice, practice.

Listening and Self-Esteem

Before we consider the multitude of benefits we get from listening effectively, a good place for us to start our journey is by looking at ourselves and the kind of listeners we are *now*. The reality is that the reasons for becoming a more effective listener reach deep down into our own self-esteem needs and those of the people we're listening to.

Take a look at the two questions asked of hundreds of participants in [Leslie Shore's] Listening Effectiveness Seminar and the responses they described.

*How do you feel when you know you are **not** being listened to?*

Ignored	Disrespected
Frustrated	Unimportant
Not valued	Irritated

Angry	Disconnected
Alone	Insecure
Invisible	Disappointed

We can see that many of the sentiments expressed above relate directly to a speaker's emotional well-being. Not being listened to creates significant negative emotions in us, often leaving us feeling unwelcome, unsafe, unappreciated, and devalued, all of which strike at the core of one's self-esteem. We may have experienced these negative feelings when we were talking to someone who was not listening, and the feeling of not really having been heard could easily have sent us to our most insecure places.

As listeners, therefore, we hold a tremendous amount of power in deciding how a conversation will proceed. Only through thoughtfully paying attention to the speaker can creative, forward-thinking responses and lively conversation take place. If we're not attentive, not only does the speaker feel devalued, but we put significant limits on our own capacity to learn and grow.

We give speakers a number of visual clues that let them know we're not really listening:

- Failing to make eye contact
- Using closed or defensive body language
- Engaging in other activities that take concentration, like looking at a monitor, or texting on a cell phone
- Not nodding as a silent response, or saying "I see" or "Ah-ha"

Now let's look at listening from a different perspective. Note the responses to another question from my Listening Effectiveness Seminar.

*How do you feel when you know you **are** being listened to?*

Valued	Appreciated
Loved	Content
Involved	Intelligent
Welcome	Rescued
Relaxed	Secure

These were the words the participants used, but what others could we add? Just imagine how instrumental we might be in raising a person's self-esteem if we could change the visual and other cues we give speakers and create an engaging environment for the speaker, one that makes the most out of the exchange we are involved in.

If the feelings above are how positive we feel when we're being listened to, think about the positive role we could play if we let speakers know we were listening to them.

Exploring Effective Listening

When we listen *effectively*, we are activating a skill. We understand the content and meaning of what the speaker is saying and are able to put what was said into our own words. We can then show the speaker, through our responses, that we've understood the intent and the content of the message from the speaker's perspective.

When we listen effectively:

- Cooperation is increased because speakers can see that their input is valued.
- Better decisions are made because information is accumulated from multiple sources.
- Conflict is lessened because misunderstandings and misconceptions are avoided or caught more quickly.
- Costly errors are prevented because we've heard and processed information and had feedback from all stakeholders.
- The speaker's level of openness increases, allowing for deeper conversations and connection.

There are four major components to effective listening:

- Being present
- Taking in information from others while being nonjudgmental
- Acknowledging the speaker in a way that invites communication to continue
- Waiting for the period at the end of the speaker's sentence before formulating a reply

If we use all four components simultaneously, we're listening effectively! What follows is a quick look at each component.

Being Present

Being "present" is a simple concept, but a difficult one to achieve. Being present is the act of being in the present moment in our mind and body, not thinking about the past or the future, but *being in the moment* with the person we are listening to. Being present means we're not comparing the speaker or

the message with anything or anyone else, and we're not wishing we could be somewhere else. Being present means practicing self-control and suppressing the urge to convey our own thoughts. Being present means not focusing on ourselves, but concentrating on understanding what the speaker has to say instead. Effective listeners, those who are in the moment and focused on the speaker, receive, welcome, and remain free to accept the communication as it's offered.

> As a manager, I am required to constantly interact with others every day. When I come home at the end of the day, I want nothing more than to read my emails and browse the web for the latest news. I want nothing more than to sit in silence without the requirement to listen.
>
> My wife, however, wants nothing more than to tell me about her day, and so the listening challenge begins. Yes, being an effective listener does require sacrifice.
>
> While I have previously heard her talk, I realize now that I have not really listened. I have allowed the preoccupation with my daily routine to get in the way of my ability to be present to what my wife's thoughts and emotions are.
>
> Unfortunately, this selfishness is not confined to my personal life. I can also be preoccupied at work with finalizing a proposal, sending an email, or any of the other myriad tasks I must accomplish within a day.
>
> My commitment to release myself from such preoccupations is an absolute requirement if I am to become an effective listener.
>
> Robert

Taking in Information from Others While Being Nonjudgmental

Listening to what others have to say can be a difficult task. As we will find out, being judgmental is one of the major barriers standing in the way of effective listening. If we are to receive a speaker's intended message in unadulterated form, it is essential that we remove judgment from our listening process while the speaker is speaking. On-the-spot judgments about what we're hearing don't benefit us or the speaker. When we're reactive or defensive,

we cannot listen. We need to set aside our egos, our biases, and our inner thoughts so that we don't filter the speaker's message until we've had time to consider it. This type of listening is highly reflective; it allows us to process the speaker's communication first before we use our own experience and knowledge to create a reply.

> I consider my coworker to have a higher socio-economic status than I have in terms of income, education, and occupation. Because of this, I simply cannot listen to what she says without bias. When she talks about having to "budget" since enrolling her infant in a nursery school, I immediately assume that she has no idea of what it is really like to have to live on a budget. Don't get me wrong. I know that she has worked hard to get where she is today, but I always dismiss what she talks about based on my preconceived opinion of her socio-economic status.
> Jessi

Acknowledging the Speaker in a Way That Invites Communication to Continue

When we show no visible reaction to what we're hearing, it can be easy for the speaker to assume that we're either not listening, not understanding what we're hearing, or not comfortable with the message we're getting. This kind of misunderstanding stops the free flow of information. No matter what reasons we may have for not reacting outwardly, we are responsible for our listening. We need to acknowledge the speaker in a way that tells the speaker we *are* listening.

Speakers can interpret facial expressions in any number of ways (interested, quizzical, earnest, bored). They can also read our body language in the form of posture, gestures, and head movements. Simply making comments along the lines of "wow," "ah-ha," "hmm," or "I see" acknowledge the speaker and let him or her know that we're listening. Without acknowledgment, speakers can feel invisible and not listened to; but with appropriate acknowledgment, they can tell that their message is coming across and how we're receiving it.

Waiting for the Period at the End of the Speaker's Sentence before Formulating a Reply

As a marriage counselor, I hear the same stories over and over again and find it difficult to stay engaged. My normal form of acknowledgment is a raised eyebrow, a nod, or a simple, "I understand." But I find that when I don't actively acknowledge my clients as they are speaking, they shut down quickly. They assume correctly that I am not listening to them carefully. I've recently realized I can do more to remodel my listening behavior in a way my clients could use in their relationships.

Diane

The most difficult component of listening effectively seems to be *waiting for the period at the end of the sentence before formulating a reply.* Kenneth Wells, the former CEO of General Motors, writes, "A good listener tries to understand what the other person is saying. In the end he may disagree sharply; but because he disagrees, he wants to know exactly what it is he is disagreeing with" (1956).

The only way we can know *what* we are disagreeing *with* is to listen all the way through to the end of the sentence or the thought that has been expressed. When we begin working on a reply before the speaker is finished, we lose both the complete information being offered and an understanding of the kind of emotion present in the speaker's delivery. We unilaterally decide that what we're thinking about as a reply is more important than what the listener has been saying. We are fully engaged in the process of putting our own thoughts and ourselves first without giving the speaker a complete hearing. Many misunderstandings and communication conflicts can arise when the listener is too involved in preparing a response to completely listen to what's been said.

When we deliberate as a group, I think I may not be completely invested in listening to people as they are speaking to me. Meaning, I am often thinking about my response to what is being said, not listening intently to what is being presented. Holding my responses and suspending my own thoughts until the end of the presented information is challenging. I occasionally catch myself creating responses before the speaker is completely finished.

Josh

Keys to Effective Listening

The key to becoming an effective listener lies in recognizing that there are barriers standing in the way of our ability to listen fully. Using our knowledge of how to deal with these barriers can become an important pathway to our personal and professional success. We need only to look at technology and our own sensory skills of seeing and hearing to recognize some of these barriers to listening effectively. Information overload like telephones ringing, emails popping  up, and text message alerts beeping, creates a formidable barrier to our effective listening. It can border on impossible to focus entirely on what's being said to us when there's so much noise around. But there are many other kinds of barriers too—all of them fighting for our attention and concentration and challenging our ability to listen effectively.

Because listening is a single-minded, reasoning task, multitasking and listening effectively at the same time are mutually exclusive. From Eyal Ophir, a researcher at Stanford University's Communication Between Humans and Interactive Media Lab, we have learned that "The human mind is not really built for processing multiple streams of information. The ability to process a second stream of information is really limited" (2009).

In order to develop mastery over barriers like information overload, and to acknowledge our inability to process multiple streams of information, we must first understand that we are continually being challenged by two kinds of listening barriers: *external* and *internal*. Each type of barrier can prevent us from listening effectively; once we recognize them for what they are, we can use our awareness to develop an improvement plan that will benefit both our personal and our occupational goals.

As we move forward, the reader will never see terms like "good," "bad," "better," or "worse" to describe the level of the listening skills we have now. The listeners we are now are the result of who our models have been in the past. We didn't choose our parents, the extended family we were born into, or the culture we came from. Our listening skills have been largely determined by what we have learned so far from those skills modeled by family, friends, teachers, bosses, and other people who have influenced our life. But with this book, we have an opportunity to examine not only how we're listening today, but how we can create a new listening model for the future.

Putting Effective Listening into Action

Now that we know *why* we need to listen effectively, we need to discover *what* can get in the way. Current culture seems to contribute to our being passive listeners rather than active ones. We've been conditioned to rely on the speaker of the message to motivate us to listen; we've put the burden on the speaker instead of taking responsibility ourselves. Yet it's up to us as the listeners, rather than the speaker, *to work with each spoken message we receive as we are receiving it* in order to benefit from it. To do that, we need to understand the nature of the barriers that might be getting in our way.

Even though we want to listen effectively, barriers tend to stop us from being the best listeners we can be. They may stem directly from how we were listened to by parents and teachers while we were growing up, or they may come from experiences we have had as adults in the working world. Our barriers to listening effectively normally go undetected; however, once we're aware of them, we can choose to temporarily push them aside.

In the next three chapters, we will familiarize ourselves with the kinds of external, internal, and technology-driven barriers that impede effective listening, and we'll also look at steps we can take to overcome them.

Bibliography

Eyal Ophir, Clifford Nass, and Anthony D. Wagner PNAS September 15, 2009. 106 (37) 15583–15587; https://doi.org/10.1073/pnas.0903620106

Wells, Kenneth. 1956. *Guide to Good Leadership*. Chicago: Science Research Associates.

Listening and Conflict Real-World Lab

Name: _____

Date: _____

Think about a recent conflict you experienced with a relational partner. This could be a conflict with a parent, friend, roommate, coworker, and so on.

    Once you have a conflict episode in mind, answer the questions:

1. Describe the conflict in two to three paragraphs including who was involved, what the conflict was about, and what was said.

_____

_____

_____

_____

_____

_____

_____

_____

_____

_____

_____

_____

_____

_____

_____

_____

_____

_____

_____

_____

2. Define active listening.

_____

_____

_____

3. Did both parties use active listening? If no, why not? What could they have done instead?

_____

_____

_____

_____

_____

_____

4. What was the outcome of the conflict?

_____

_____

_____

_____

_____

5. Do you think the conflict was healthy for the relationship? Why or why not?

_____

_____

_____

_____

_____

_____

6. What does listening have to do with conflict?

_____

_____

_____

_____

_____

_____

CHAPTER 5

Social Roles and Expectations

Introduction to the Chapter

Social perception describes how humans see and make sense of the world. It was shocking to me to learn that I do not see things as they are. Instead, I see the world through the lens of my past experiences, my expectations of others, and my goals. Have you ever heard the phrase, "You see what you want to see?" This chapter explains why that statement is true, at least in part. In this chapter you will learn about organizational structures in your brain that keep track of everything you know about certain types of people, events, and situations. For example, how do you know what to do when you enter a restaurant? Most of us know to go to the host stand, wait to be seated, and walk with the host to the table. Then we are given a menu. Next, we choose what we want to eat and a server comes by to take our order. Hopefully you recognize this pattern. Our brains store away information like "what to do at a restaurant" so that we do not have to figure it out every time we want to dine out. Our brains do the same for understanding people and social situations. The mental shortcuts our brains create to make these interactions easier can sometimes get us into trouble. For example, we often make mistakes when making attributions about others. Attributions are the way we make sense of why others behave and do the things they do. We also use attributions to make sense of our own behavior. You will learn about these concepts and more in this chapter. I suggest reading this chapter in two parts. The first part is the start of the chapter through the various types of heuristics. Next, read the section on attribution theory through the end of the chapter.

Social Perception and Cognition

By John DeLamater, Daniel Myers, and Jessica Collett

....

Introduction

It is 10 p.m., and the admitting physician at the psychiatric hospital is interviewing a respectable-looking man who has asked for treatment. "You see," the patient says, "I keep hearing voices." After taking a full history, the physician diagnoses the man with schizophrenia and assigns him to an inpatient unit. The physician is well trained and makes the diagnosis with apparent ease. Yet to diagnose someone's mental condition correctly is a difficult problem in social perception. The differences between paranoia, schizophrenia, depression, and normality are not always easy to discern.

A classic study conducted by Rosenhan (1973) demonstrates this problem. Eight pseudo-patients who were actually research investigators gained entry into mental hospitals by claiming to hear voices. During the intake interviews, the pseudo-patients gave true accounts of their backgrounds, life experiences, and present (quite ordinary) psychological condition. They falsified only their names, occupations, and their complaint of hearing voices. Once in the psychiatric unit, the pseudo-patients immediately stopped simulating symptoms of schizophrenia. They reported that the voices had ceased and talked normally with other patients. The other patients began to suspect that the investigators were not really mentally ill, but the staff continued to believe they were. The nurses and orderlies made note of the pseudo-patients' "strange" behavior, including a tendency to line up very early for meals and to spend significant amounts of time writing in their notebooks. Although such behavior would not be seen as odd for healthy researchers with little else to do, the staff considered it evidence of mental illness. Because of these enduring beliefs, upon discharge, the pseudo-patients were still diagnosed with schizophrenia, although now it was "schizophrenia in remission."

A man voluntarily checking into a psychiatric hospital may pose a confusing problem for the hospital staff. Is he really "mentally ill" and in need of hospitalization, or is he "healthy"? Is he no longer able to function in the outside world? Or is he merely faking and trying to get a break from his work or his family?

To try to answer these questions, the admitting physician gathers information about the person and classifies it as indicating illness or health. Then the doctor combines these facts to form a general diagnosis (paranoia, schizophrenia, or depression) and determines what treatment the person needs. While performing these actions, the doctor is engaging in **social perception**. Broadly defined, social perception refers to constructing an understanding of the social world from the data we get through our senses. More narrowly defined, it refers to the processes by which we form impressions of other people's traits and personalities.

In making her diagnosis, the physician not only forms an impression about the traits and characteristics of the new patient, but she also tries to understand the causes of that person's behavior. She tries, for instance, to figure out whether the patient acts as he does because of some internal dispositions or because of external pressures from the environment. Social psychologists term this process attribution. In attribution, we observe others' behavior and then infer backward to causes—intentions, abilities, traits, motives, and situational pressures—that explain why people act as they do.

Social perception and attribution are not passive activities. We do not simply register the stimuli that impinge on our senses; rather, our expectations and cognitive structures influence what we notice and how we interpret it. This is closely tied to the dual-process model introduced in Chapter 1. The intake physician at the psychiatric hospital, for example, does not expect to encounter researchers pretending to be mentally ill; instead, she expects to meet people who are mentally ill. Thus, even before the interaction begins, the doctor has categorized the patient as mentally ill. With that categorization firmly in place, the doctor falls victim to **confirmation bias**, focusing on information relevant to that condition and ignoring or downplaying information that is inconsistent with a diagnosis of mental illness (Nickerson, 1998). In other words, her interpretation is influenced by her expectation that the patient is a real patient. Most of the time, the impressions we form of others are sufficiently accurate to permit smooth interaction. After all, few people who are admitted to psychiatric hospitals are researchers faking mental illness. Yet social perception and attribution can be unreliable. Even highly trained observers can misperceive, misjudge, and reach the wrong conclusions.

In February 1999, police officers in New York City were attempting to track down a serial rapist. Sketches of the rapist had been circulated to the police, and so they had some idea what the rapist looked like. Four White officers patrolling the Bronx encountered Amadou Diallo, a Black man, and thought he resembled the sketches of the rapist. As Diallo was entering his apartment building, the police officers ordered him to stop. Diallo stopped and began to reach for his wallet to produce his identification. The police officers interpreted this action quite differently, however. Believing he was reaching for a gun, the officers opened fire. They fired a total of 41 shots, and Diallo died immediately. Diallo was not the rapist and had no criminal record—the officers' snap judgments were wrong.

The image of a Black man in a bad neighborhood, reaching into his pocket as he was being stopped by the police, provided too many dangerous cues that caused the officers to act immediately. Many have wondered whether the police officers would have been slower to act if Diallo had been White. Did race help activate a dangerous image in the police officers' minds and encourage them to respond aggressively? Thirteen years later, the shooting of an unarmed Trayvon Martin prompted similar questions. George Zimmerman, a neighborhood watch coordinator, shot Martin, a 17-year-old African American, during a confrontation in Zimmerman's gated community. Just moments before the shooting, Zimmerman called the local police department because he was concerned about Martin's behavior: "There is a really suspicious guy.... This guy looks like he's up to no good. Or he's on drugs or something. It's raining and he's just walking around, looking about" (CNN, March 20, 2012). The case received national attention and left many asking whether it was racially motivated. Did an African American teen in a hoodie elicit different reactions from what he would have if he been wearing something else? If Martin had been White, would Zimmerman have interpreted his actions—"walking through [the neighborhood], looking about"—as less threatening?

Studies conducted in laboratory settings confirm this type of dynamic. In one study, subjects were asked to act as police officers and decide whether to shoot at suspected criminals. The suspected criminals were either holding a gun (in which case the officer should shoot) or were holding a neutral object such as a cell phone (in which case the officer should not shoot). The results showed that the subjects were more likely to mistakenly shoot a suspect holding a cell phone if the suspect was Black. Similarly, they were also more likely to mistakenly hold back from shooting a suspect holding a gun if the suspect was White (Plant, Peruche, & Butz, 2005). Research replicated with actual police officers had similar results (Plant & Peruche, 2005).

This chapter focuses on these processes of social perception and attribution and addresses the following questions:

1. How do we make sense of the flood of information that surrounds us? How do we categorize that information and use it in social situations?

2. Why do we rely so much on notions about personality and group stereotypes? What problem does this practice solve, and what difficulties does it create?

3. How do we form impressions of others? That is, how do we integrate the information into a coherent, overall impression?

4. How do we ascertain the causes of other people's behavior and interpret the origins of actions we observe? For instance, when we judge someone's behavior, how do we know whether to attribute the behavior to that person's internal dispositions or to the external situation affecting that person?

5. What sorts of errors do we commonly make in judging the behavior of others, and why do we make such errors?

Schemas

The human mind is a sophisticated system for processing information. One of our most basic mental processes is **categorization**—our tendency to perceive stimuli as members of groups or classes rather than as isolated, unique entities. For instance, at the theater, we see a well-groomed woman on stage wearing a short dress and dancing on her toes; rather than viewing her as a novel entity, we immediately categorize her as a "ballerina."

How do we go about assigning people or things to categories? For instance, how do we know the woman should be categorized as a ballerina and not as an "actress" or a "cheerleader"? To categorize some person, we usually compare that person to our prototype of the category. A **prototype** is an abstraction that represents the "typical" or quintessential instance of a class or group—as least to us. It is the best example of the category. Perhaps your prototypical quarterback is Tom Brady. Others may have a different prototype for the same category, like Joe Montana or Peyton Manning. Although he was an outstanding quarterback, few might think of Donovan McNabb as a prototypical quarterback, in part because of his race. Although the number is growing, there have been very few Black quarterbacks in the history of the NFL. Usually, prototypes are specified in terms of a set of common attributes among members of a category. For example, the prototype of a "quarterback" may be someone who is tall, White, athletic, intelligent, and who has had a successful career, perhaps even winning a Super Bowl.

Categorizing people, objects, situations, events, and even the self becomes complicated because the categories we use are not isolated from one another; rather, they link together and form a structure. For instance, we may think of a person (Jonathan) not only as having various attributes (tall, wealthy) but also as bearing certain relations to other persons or entities (friend of Kareem, stronger than Bill, owner of a Lexus). These other persons or entities will themselves have attributes (Kareem: thin, athletic, Black; Bill: short, fat, balding; Lexus: silver, two-door, new). They also have relations with still other persons and entities (Kareem: coworker of Bill, husband of Lisa; Bill: friend of Lisa, owner of a Prius). In this way, we build a cognitive structure consisting of persons, attributes, and relations.

Social psychologists use the term **schema** to denote a well-organized structure of cognitions about some social entity such as a person, group, role, or event. Schemas usually include information about an entity's attributes and about its relations with other entities. To illustrate, suppose Chandra, who is somewhat cynical about politics, has a schema about the role of "member of Congress." In Chandra's schema, the member of Congress will insist he or she serves the needs of his constituents but will actually vote for the special interests of those who contributed most to his campaign, will run TV advertisements containing half-truths at election time, will spend more time in Washington, DC, than in his home district, will put avoiding scandal above ethics, will vote for large pay raises and retirement benefits for himself, and, above all, will never do anything to lessen his own power.

Someone else, of course, may hold a less cynical view of politics than Chandra and have a different schema about the role of "member of Congress." But, like Chandra's, this schema will likely incorporate such elements as the congressional representative's typical activities, relations, motives, and tactics. Whatever their exact content, schemas enable us to organize and remember facts, to make inferences that go beyond the facts immediately available, and to assess new information (Fiske & Linville, 1980; Wilcox & Williams, 1990).

Types of Schemas

There are several distinct types of schemas, including person schemas, self-schemas, group schemas, role schemas, and event schemas (Eckes, 1995; Taylor & Crocker, 1981).

Person schemas are cognitive structures that describe the personalities of others. Person schemas can apply either to specific individuals (such as Barack Obama, Lady Gaga, your father) or to types of individuals (such as introvert, class clown, sociopath). Person schemas organize our conceptions of others' personalities and enable us to develop expectations about others' behavior.

Self-schemas are structures that organize our conception of our own characteristics (Catrambone & Markus, 1987; Markus, 1977). For instance, if you conceive of yourself as independent (as opposed to dependent), you may see yourself as individualistic, unconventional, and assertive. To behave in a manner consistent with your self-schema, you may refuse to accept money from your parents, refuse to ask others for help with schoolwork, take a part-time job, or dye your hair an unusual color. Self- schemas are discussed in detail in Chapter 4.

Group schemas—also called stereotypes—are schemas regarding the members of a particular social group or social category (Hamilton, 1981). Stereotypes indicate the attributes and behaviors considered typical of members of that group or social category. These are rigid conceptions and widely shared by members of a culture or community. American culture uses a wide variety of stereotypes about different races (Blacks, Asians), religious groups (Protestants, Catholics, Jews), and ethnic groups (Arabs, Irish, Latinos, Italians).

Role schemas indicate which attributes and behaviors are typical of persons occupying a particular role in a group. Chandra's conception of the role of a congressional representative illustrates a role schema. Role schemas exist for most occupational roles—nurses, cab drivers, store managers, and the like—but they also exist for other kinds of roles in groups: group leader, captain of a sports team. Role schemas are often used to understand and predict the behaviors of people who occupy particular roles.

Event schemas (also called *scripts*) are schemas regarding important, recurring social events (Abelson, 1981; Hue & Erickson, 1991; Schank & Abelson, 1977). In our society, these events include weddings, funerals, graduation ceremonies, job interviews, cocktail parties, and hook-ups. An event schema specifies the activities that constitute the event, the predetermined order or sequence for these activities, and the persons (or role occupants) participating in the event. Scripts can be revealed by asking people to describe what typically happens during an event.

One type of script of interest to both social psychologists and college students alike is a hook-up script (Cohen & Wade, 2012). Hooking up—or engaging in a casual physical encounter—has replaced dating on many college campuses (Simon & Gagnon, 2003). As shown in Table 5.1, when asked to describe a "typical" hook-up, students tend to agree on a number of important characteristics (Paul & Hayes, 2002): Hook-ups tend to occur between strangers or acquaintances. Although someone may go out intending to hook-up, in most cases hooking up with a particular person is not planned. Men usually initiate the encounter, and the couples tend to meet one another at parties. Alcohol or drugs are often involved, and hook-up partners seldom talk about what is happening (or what has happened, after the hook-up ends). Although most hookups are one-time encounters, couples will occasionally engage in multiple hook-ups with the same person (Bogle, 2007). However, unlike a couple who is dating exclusively, a couple who is hooking-up—even repeatedly—has no obligations toward one another. The component of the hook-up script in which there is the least agreement among young people is what exactly "hooking up" implies (Glenn & Marquardt, 2001). Hooking up can range from kissing to intercourse. This ambiguity is one of the reasons the

Table 5.1 Illustrative Descriptions of a Typical Hook-up (quotes from student questionnaires)

	From a 20-Year-Old Woman	From a 21-Year-Old Man
Who is involved?	A guy and a girl who are somewhat attracted to each other but are strangers. It can also be a guy and a girl who are acquaintances and under the right conditions hook-up.	Any two people who find each other attractive or just there.
What leads to the hook-up? Is planning involved? Who instigates the hook-up?	The two may talk, flirt, dance together, drink together, make glances at each other. They are close to each other. Planning can be involved if one person scopes out the other or plans certain things to say. Usually the guy instigates the hook-up, but sometimes it is mutual instigation.	Sometimes investigation is done. One of the people may inquire about the other person in hopes of initiating the hook-up. Most often, however, the hook-up just kind of happens. The girl lets it be known (with eye contact or extremely friendly behavior) that she wants it, and generally the guy must then go and give it to her.
Where does it happen?	In rooms, at clubs, at parties. It can happen in a stairwell.	Anywhere possible. Most often on a couch or in adjacent chairs. Maybe in a bed if you're lucky.
Is alcohol or other drugs involved?	Sometimes, actually often. From my experiences, hook-ups always happen at parties. … Many situations involve alcohol and drugs because people lose inhibition and wear beer goggles, increasing the likelihood of hooking up.	Alcohol is almost always involved. This helps the guy with his confidence to initiate the hook-up.

	From a 20-Year-Old Woman	From a 21-Year-Old Man
What sexual behaviors take place? Are precautions taken to prevent transmission of sexually transmitted diseases (STDs)?	It depends. Some people just kiss. Others go further into oral sex and sexual intercourse. Usually in oral sex, precautions aren't taken to prevent the transmission of STDs. Sometimes in sex, condoms are used. In situations with alcohol and drugs, condoms are often forgotten.	Condoms are sometimes used if intercourse takes place. But a lot of hook-ups go to oral sex, in which case no preventative measures are used.
What communication takes place between the hook-up partners? Do they talk about what is happening?	Usually not a lot. They mainly just hook up or communicate with sexual noises.	Sometimes partners may say, "I can't believe I'm doing this. I don't even know you!" But this is generally only the females, and the males are just hoping this will not put a premature end to the hook-up.

These representative highlights demonstrate the consistency among students' event schemas for hook-ups and illustrate the tremendous agreement (and some differences) between men and women.
Source: Adapted from Paul & Hayes, 2002.

term "hooking up" appeals to young people, particularly women. Because it has a casual tone and could imply simply kissing or heavy petting, using the term can save women from potential damage to their reputations that may come from being seen as too promiscuous. Although people might sometimes ask for details, when a friend tells us that they attended a cousin's wedding or hooked up with a co-ed this past weekend, we usually fill in the gaps based on knowledge from our event schemas (and schemas for cousins and co-eds).

Schematic Processing

Why Do We Use Schemas?

Although schemas may produce reasonably accurate judgments much of the time, they do not always work. Wouldn't it be better for us to rely less on schemas, perhaps to avoid the kind of tragic mistake the police made with Amadou Diallo or to not jump to conclusions about a friend's promiscuity (or chastity)? Perhaps, but we come to rely on schemas because they give us a way to efficiently organize, understand, and react to the complex world around us. It is simply impossible to process all the information present in each interaction. We have to find a way to focus on what is most important in defining the situation and the persons involved so we can respond appropriately. Schemas help us do this in several ways: (1) they influence our capacity to recall information by making certain kinds of facts more salient and easier to remember, (2) they help us process information faster, (3) they guide our inferences and judgments about people and objects, and (4) they allow us to reduce ambiguity by providing a way to interpret ambiguous elements in the situation. Once we have applied a schema to the situation, our decisions about how to interact in it become much more straightforward (Mayer, Rapp, & Williams, 1993).

Schematic Memory

Human memory is largely reconstructive. That is, we do not usually remember all the precise details of what transpired in a given situation—we are not a camera capturing a video, instantly recording all the images and sounds. Instead, we typically remember some of what happened, enough to identify the appropriate schema and then rely on that schema to fill in other details. Schemas organize information in memory and, therefore, affect what we remember and what we forget (Hess & Slaughter, 1990; Sherman, Judd, & Park, 1989). When trying to recall something, people often remember better those facts that are consistent with their schemas. For instance, one study (Cohen, 1981) investigated the impact of an occupational role schema on recall. Participants viewed a video of a woman celebrating her birthday by having dinner with her husband at home. Half the participants were told the woman was a librarian; the other half were told she was a waitress in a local diner.

Some characteristics of the woman were consistent with the schema of a librarian: She wore glasses, had spent the day reading, liked classical music, and received a romantic novel as a gift. Other characteristics of the woman, however, were consistent with the schema of a waitress: She drank beer, had a bowling ball in the room, ate chocolate birthday cake, flirted with her husband, and received a nightgown as a gift. Later, when participants tried to recall details of the video, they recalled most accurately those facts consistent with the woman's occupational label. That is, participants who thought she was a librarian remembered facts consistent with the librarian schema, whereas those who thought she was a waitress remembered facts consistent with the diner-waitress schema.

What about memory for material inconsistent with schemas? Several studies have tested the recall of three types of information: material consistent with schemas, material contradictory to schemas, and material irrelevant to schemas. The results show that people recall both schema-consistent and schema-contradictory material better than schema-irrelevant material (Cano, Hopkins, & Islam, 1991; Higgins & Bargh, 1987). People recall schema-contradictory material better when the schema itself is concrete (for example, spends money wisely, often tells lies, brags about her accomplishments) rather than abstract (for example, practical, dishonest, egotistical).

Schematic Inference

Schemas affect the inferences we make about persons and other social entities (Fiske & Taylor, 1991). That is, they supply missing facts when gaps exist in our knowledge. If we know certain facts about a person but are ignorant about others, we fill in the gaps by inserting suppositions consistent with our schema for that person. For example, knowing your roommate is head of the campus PETA (People for the Ethical Treatment of Animals) chapter, you can infer he will not want to spend time with your new friend who enjoys hunting. Of course, the use of schemas can lead to erroneous inferences. If the schema is incomplete or does not correctly mirror reality, some mistakes are likely. For instance, the police officers who confronted Amadou Diallo applied a schema that was incorrect. Their schema for "a Black man who puts his hand in his pocket as he is being confronted by the police" includes the element that the suspect would be reaching for a gun in his pocket. From this, they inferred that he would try to shoot at them, and they reacted according to that erroneous inference.

Schemas—especially well-developed schemas—can also help us infer new facts. For instance, if a physician diagnoses a patient as having the flu, he can make inferences about how the patient contracted the disease, which symptoms might be present, what side effects or complications might arise, and what treatment will be effective. For another person who has no schema regarding this disease, these inferences would be virtually impossible.

Schematic Judgment

Schemas can influence our judgments or feelings about persons and other entities. The schemas themselves may be organized in terms of evaluative dimensions; this is especially true of person schemas. For example, Chandra's schemas for members of Congress had a negative valence, predisposing her to view any congressperson unfavorably. The complexity of a schema—or the variety of attributes included in a schema—also affects our evaluations of other persons. The complexity of schemas is directly tied to diversity of experience with the group (Crisp & Turner, 2011). The more members of a group we interact with, the less uniform we see group members (perhaps their personality, values, and so forth), and the more complex our schema of the group is. Conversely, less complex schemas lead to more extreme judgments and evaluations. This is called the **complexity-extremity effect**.

For instance, in one study (Linville & Jones, 1980), White college students evaluated a person applying for admission to law school. Depending on treatment, the applicant was either White or Black and had an academic record that was either strong or weak. The results showed an interaction effect between academic record and race. Participants rated a weak Black applicant more negatively than a weak White applicant, but they rated a strong Black applicant more positively than a strong White applicant. Judgments about Black applicants were more extreme—in both directions—than those about White applicants because the participants' schema for their own in-group (White) was more complex than their schema for the out-group (Black). Because these White students had more experience with a variety of Whites, it was difficult to infer competence based solely on this quality, and the schema was more complex. Further research (Linville, 1982) shows that the complexity-extremity effect also holds for other attributes, such as age. College students have less complex schemas for older persons than for persons their own age, so they are more extreme in judgments of older persons.

Drawbacks of Schematic Processing

Although schemas provide certain advantages, they also entail some corresponding disadvantages. First, people are overly accepting of information that fits consistently with a schema. In fact, some research suggests that perceivers show a confirmatory bias (also called a confirmation bias) when collecting new information relevant to schemas (Higgins & Bargh, 1987; Snyder & Swann, 1978). That is, when gathering information, perceivers tend to ask questions that will elicit information supportive of the schemas rather than questions that will elicit information contradictory to the schemas. Consider the intake process of Rosenhan's study at the mental hospital. The doctors asked particular questions of the researchers, assuming they were mentally ill, that biased responses toward confirmation of that belief. The nurses and orderlies interpreted information about pseudo-patients' behavior in ways that confirmed their schemas and ignored or downplayed information suggesting that the pseudo-patients were actually not ill, because it contradicted their existing schemas.

Second, when faced with missing information, people fill in gaps in knowledge by adding elements that are consistent with their schemas. Sometimes these added elements turn out to be erroneous or factually incorrect. When this happens, it will, of course, create inaccurate interpretations or inferences about people, groups, or events. As an example, research on eyewitness accounts of crimes finds that witnesses draw on event schemas of "typical crimes" when recalling specific incidents. This can distort memories in schema-consistent ways, leading to misinformation in reporting (Holst & Pezdek, 1992). Furthermore, as witnesses share their accounts of events, listeners who were not privy to the scene are likely to interpret events in ways that are influenced by their own existing beliefs (Allport & Postman, 1947). This introduces further distortion, like a children's game of telephone.

When schematic categories are not salient, we view persons as individuals and their behaviors as unique. However, when we view persons as category members, we tend to interpret their behavior as stereotypic and representative of the entire category or group. Comic courtesy of xkcd.com

Third, because people are often reluctant to discard or revise their schemas, they occasionally apply schemas to persons or events even when the schemas do not fit the facts very well. Forced misapplication of a schema may lead to incorrect characterization and inferences, and this in turn can produce inappropriate or inflexible responses toward other persons, groups, or events. A teacher who believes a child is lazy because she is not getting the class reading done may be less inclined to engage with the child in class or encourage the child's parents to have her tested for dyslexia or ADD (attention deficit disorder).

Person Schemas and Group Stereotypes

Person Schemas

As noted earlier, person schemas are cognitive structures that describe the personalities of other individuals. There are several distinct types of person schemas. Some person schemas are very specific and pertain to particular people. For example,

Sarah is a 17-year-old high school student, and Joan is her mother. After years of interacting with Joan, Sarah has an elaborate schema of her mother. She can usually predict how Joan will react to new situations, information, or problems and plan accordingly. Similarly, we often have individual schemas for public figures (for instance, Oprah Winfrey, former talk show host, actor, advocate for women, Black, extremely wealthy) or for famous historical figures (for instance, Abraham Lincoln, political leader during the Civil War, honest, determined, opposed to slavery, committed to holding the Union together).

Other person schemas are very abstract and focus on the relations among personality traits. A schema of this type is an **implicit personality theory**—a set of unstated assumptions about which personality traits are correlated with one another (Anderson & Sedikides, 1991; Grant & Holmes, 1981; Sternberg, 1985). These theories tend to also include beliefs about the behaviors associated with various personality traits (Skowronski & Carlston, 1989). If you learn that a child is gifted, do you automatically assume the child has other attributes? Recent research explored the beliefs that teachers in Germany associate with giftedness (Baudson & Preckel, 2013). When a student was described as "gifted," teachers were more likely to also perceive the student as emotionally deficient. Although teachers believed gifted students would be more open to new experiences than students of average ability, they also saw them as more introverted, less emotionally stable, and less agreeable. These beliefs are considered implicit, or automatic, because we seldom subject our person schemas to close examination and are usually not explicitly aware of the schemas' contents. Therefore, the teachers were likely unaware of their biased judgments of gifted students and how these implicit assumptions were influencing their behavior toward the students in class.

Implicit Personality Theories and Mental Maps

As do all schemas, implicit personality theories enable us to make inferences that go beyond the available information. Instead of withholding judgment, we use them to flesh out our impressions of a person about whom we have little information. For instance, if we learn someone has a warm personality, we might infer she is also likely to be sociable, popular, good-natured, and so on. If we hear that somebody else is pessimistic, we may infer he is humorless, irritable, and unpopular, even though we lack evidence that he actually has these traits.

We can depict an implicit personality theory as a mental map indicating the way traits are related to one another. Figure 5.1 displays such a mental map. This figure, based on judgments made by college students, shows how various personality traits

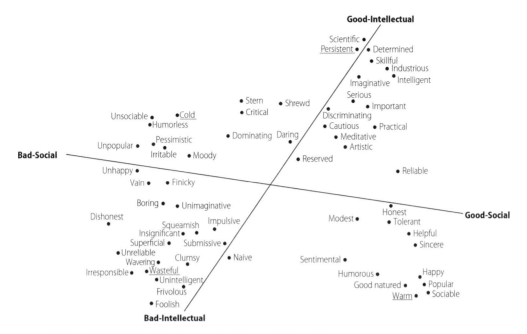

Figure 5.1 Relationships Among Attributes: A Mental Map

Each of us has an implicit theory of personality—a theory about which personality attributes tend to go together and which do not. We can represent our theories of personality in the form of a mental map. The closer attributes are located to each other on our mental map, the more we assume these attributes will appear together in the same person. The mental map shown above was created based on the mental maps of American college students. Adapted from Rosenberg, Nelson, & Vivekanandan, 1968

stand in relation to one another (Rosenberg, Nelson, & Vivekananthan, 1968). Traits thought to be similar are located close together within our mental map, meaning we expect people who have one trait to have the other. Traits thought to be dissimilar are located far apart, meaning we believe they rarely occur together in one person.

If your mental map resembles the one portrayed in Figure 5.1, you think that people who are wasteful are also likely to be unintelligent and irresponsible (see the lower left part of the map). Similarly, you think that people who are persistent are also likely to be determined and skillful (the upper right part of the map).

Early research, like that presented in Figure 5.1, believed that the two distinct evaluative dimensions traits fell upon were social and intellectual. For instance, the traits "warm" and "cold" differ mainly on the social dimension, whereas "frivolous" and "industrious" differ on the intellectual dimension (Rosenberg & Sedlak, 1972). Traits usually tend to be either good on both dimensions (like "important") or bad on both dimensions (like "unreliable," explaining a common bias in impression formation). We tend to judge persons who have several good traits as generally good and persons who have several bad traits as generally bad. Once we have a global impression of someone as, say, generally good, we assume that other positive traits (located nearby in the mental map) also apply. This tendency for our general or overall liking for a person to influence our subsequent assessment of more specific traits of that person is called the **halo effect** (Lachman & Bass, 1985; Thorndike, 1920). The halo effect produces bias in impression formation; it can lead to inaccuracy in our ratings of others' traits and performances (Cooper, 1981; Fisicaro, 1988).

In the decades since Rosenberg's mental map was published, social psychologists have worked to refine the dimensions and test impression formation across different cultures and groups. There is growing consensus that the two universal dimensions are better conceived of as warmth and competence (rather than social and intellectual). As early research (Asch, 1946, discussed later in this chapter) found, warmth is a highly influential trait in impression formation, and it appears to take precedence over competence, both in how rapidly it is judged and how much weight it carries in impressions (Fiske, Cuddy, & Glick 2007). Immediately upon encountering someone else, we must determine whether they are more likely to harm or help us. To do so, we gauge their level of warmth because it is the dimension that is tied to our perceptions of another's intent. The warmth dimension captures traits like friendliness, helpfulness, and sincerity. The competence dimension, however, is related to ability and includes traits like intelligence, creativity, and skill. Although everyone lends primacy to the warmth dimension in forming impressions, women and individuals from collectivist cultures appear particularly cued in to warmth (Abele, 2003).

Our impressions influence the emotions we feel toward others. We are likely to pity those who we consider high on warmth but low on competence and envy those who are high on competence and low on warmth. We admire those who we believe are high on both dimensions and hold contempt for those who are seen as low on both (Cuddy, Fiske, & Glick, 2007). Similar emotions are directed toward groups that we classify using the same two dimensions. We envy the rich (high-competence, low-warmth), admire the middle-class (high-competence, high-warmth), pity the elderly (low-competence, high-warmth), and have contempt for welfare recipients (low-competence, low-warmth).

Group Stereotypes

- "Politicians are liars and cheaters, with no compassion for ordinary people."
- "Asian women are 'tiger moms,' demanding perfection from their kids."
- "People on welfare are lazy, wasteful, and unemployed."
- "Arabs and Muslims are terrorists who hate America."
- "Jocks might be strong and athletic, but they're stupid and arrogant."

An unfortunate reality in our society is that we have all heard remarks like these—categorical, extreme, inaccurate characterizations. Each of these is an example of a group schema or stereotype. A **stereotype** is a set of characteristics attributed to all members of some specified group or social category (McCauley, Stitt, & Segal, 1980; Taylor, 1981). Just like other types of schemas, stereotypes simplify the complex social world. Rather than encouraging us to treat each member of a group individually, stereotypes encourage us to think about and treat all politicians, welfare recipients, or jocks the same way. By helping us quickly place people into categories, stereotypes enable us to form impressions of people and predict their behavior with only minimal information—the groups to which they belong.

Stereotypes, however, involve overgeneralization. They lead us to think that all members of a particular group or social category possess certain attributes. Although stereotypes might contain a kernel of truth—some members of the stereotyped group may have some of the imputed characteristics—it is almost never the case that all members have those characteristics. For this reason, stereotypes often lead to inaccurate inferences. Consider, for instance, all the feminists you know. Perhaps one of them is—as the stereotype suggests—a radical who would like to have the gender binary completely eradicated, and maybe another is lesbian. It is certainly false, however, that all your feminist acquaintances are as politically active or eschew relationships—romantic or otherwise—with men. It is also false that all feminists are women.

We can hardly avoid making a snap judgment about the personalities of these individuals, but are we right? We draw on stereotypes to form impressions about people merely by knowing the group to which they belong. © Renphoto/iStock

Throughout our daily lives, we are constantly categorizing people who we encounter into existing groups to conserve mental attention. Walking down the street, we pass men and women, Blacks and Whites, young people and the elderly. Without much conscious thought, we sort these strangers into groups based on distinguishing characteristics and then draw on group schemas (stereotypes) to decide how to respond to these others without giving our actions much consideration (Fiske & Neuberg, 1990). We tend to not notice the work that our minds are doing until we encounter someone who does not neatly fit into one of our group schemas: an individual whose gender, race, or age is ambiguous. In these situations, because we need to gather additional information, processing takes longer and becomes more conscious. If it is difficult to determine a person's gender from a cursory glance, we may look for other nonverbal or vocal clues. If we are unable to classify someone—a running joke on *Saturday Night Live* with the infamous, gender-ambiguous character, Pat—we grow increasingly uncomfortable. Thinking back to moments when we sought such clarification and considering how seldom such moments occur demonstrates the ubiquity of categorization and stereotypes in our everyday lives.

Although stereotypes are overgeneralizations, we still constantly use them and are often unaware of their impact on our judgments of others (Hepburn & Locksley, 1983; Bornstein & Pittman, 1992). And although there is nothing inherent in stereotypes that requires them to be negative, many stereotypes do contain negative elements. Of course, some stereotypes are positive ("Asians excel at math"; "Blacks are gifted athletes"), but many others disparage or diminish the group stereotyped. Stereotypes can have many negative effects, especially when they are used to limit access to important social roles—for example, when an individual applies for a job or for admission to college.

To explore the effect of gender stereotypes on women's underrepresentation in science, a group of scientists recently asked science faculty at research-intensive universities to rate the materials of a student applying for a lab manager position (Moss-Racusin et al., 2012). The scientists used an experimental design and created fake applications that were randomly assigned a masculine (John) or feminine (Jennifer) name. Other than the name, the application materials sent out were identical. Both men and women faculty who received John's application rated the applicant as significantly more competent and hireable than those who received Jennifer's (identical) application. Faculty also reported that they would offer a higher starting salary and more mentoring to John than to Jennifer. None of the faculty actively disliked women. In fact, faculty perceived Jennifer as a more likeable applicant than John. However, the pervasive gender stereotypes of women being less competent at science unintentionally influenced the raters' evaluations. This is just one study of many suggesting that stereotypes can negatively affect work-related outcomes (see also Correll, Benard & Paik, 2007).

Stereotypes can also have less direct effects on members of stereotyped groups through a process called **stereotype threat** (Steele, 1997, 2010). When a member of a group believes there is a real threat of being judged based on group stereotypes, this can negatively affect their performance and actually cause an individual to perform more poorly than he or she would when not under stereotype threat. Box 5.1 explains how stereotype threat reduces the performance of some students

When people act on their stereotypes, this can produce many negative effects for those who are the subjects of these stereotypes. Members of racial groups may be denied jobs or promotions because of the stereotypes employers hold of their racial group (Pager, Western, & Bonikowski, 2009). As damaging as these direct uses of stereotypes can be, researchers have recently discovered a second, less direct negative effect of stereotypes called *stereotype threat* (Steele, 1997, 1999).

Stereotype threat occurs when a member of a group suspects that he or she will be judged based on a common stereotype that is held of that group. For example, one stereotype of women is that they are less proficient at mathematics than men are. If a woman enters a situation in which her mathematical ability is being judged and she believes the judgment will be negatively affected by the stereotype about women's mathematical ability, even without any conscious thought about the stereotype, her performance on the exam may suffer (Spencer, Steele, & Quinn, 1999). To test for this kind of effect, Steele and Aronson (1995) gave Stanford University students a very difficult test using questions from the Graduate Record Examination in literature. The difficulty of the test provided a stereotype threat for Black students because poor performance would confirm a stereotype that they were not as able as White students. Even though the White and Black students were matched on ability, the Black students scored much lower than the White students. However, when researchers told the students that the test was part of a study to understand how people solved problems and that it did not measure ability, the stereotype threat was removed and the Black and White students did equally well.

Why does performance deteriorate when stereotype threat is present? Isn't it possible that the desire to disprove the stereotype might cause students to try harder and thereby cause them to do even better than they normally would? In a follow-up study, students took the exam on a computer, so the researchers could time how long the students took with each question. The results showed that under conditions of stereotype threat, Black students

(Continued)

were exerting extra effort and were overthinking the questions. They reread questions, changed their answers, and generally became less efficient at taking the test (Steele, 1999). This result also made sense of a finding that stereotype threat affected academically strong students more than academically weak students—for those students who saw academics as an important part of their self-concept, the threat was much more meaningful than for those who cared less about academics (Steele, 2010).

The negative effects of stereotype threat are not limited to women or racial minorities, nor is it exclusively seen in academic spheres. In a novel application of stereotype threat, social psychologists tested racial stereotypes about athletic performance (Stone, Lynch, Sjomeling, & Darley, 1999). Black and White students were recruited to take an athletic test (simply ten rounds of miniature golf) in the laboratory. Black students who were told that this task was a diagnostic of "natural athletic ability" performed significantly better than those who were told that the task measured "sports intelligence." White participants, however, performed better in the "sports intelligence" condition than the "natural athletic ability" condition. Although stereotypes about Whites are generally more favorable than those about Blacks, students were aware of the stereotype that favors Blacks over Whites in athletic ability, and this caused differences in performance. Another study found that when primed with a stereotype of older people's propensity for memory problems, older adults performed worse on a recall test than either younger people or older adults who had not had a threat induced by a prime (Hess, Auman, Colcombe, & Rahhal, 2003).

Outside the laboratory, it may be possible to reduce stereotype threat and to even the playing field. One way of doing this is to convince students who may be experiencing stereotype threat that the test being used is not biased. This is not easy to do given current deeply held beliefs about the unfairness of testing and the pervasiveness of racial stereotypes. However, Cohen, Steele, and Ross (1999) found that they could reduce stereotype threat by informing students that the evaluations of their performance would use very high standards and that they believed the students could perform up to those standards. Such an approach lets the student know that assessment is based on standards rather than stereotypes and that the student will not be viewed stereotypically. Another approach is to have individuals shift away from viewing themselves stereotypically by giving them the opportunity to construct a narrative of their selves that is about other positive attributes and values rather than the stereotyped characteristic. Simply asking individuals to write their primary values and why these are important to them before engaging in a threatening situation can improve performance (Steele, 2010).

on academic tasks and standardized tests and can also influence success among other groups in other domains.

Common Stereotypes

As the foregoing examples suggest, in American society, some widely known stereotypes pertain to ethnic, racial, and gender groups. Ethnic (national) stereotypes held by Americans might include, for example, the view that Mexicans are undocumented immigrants who struggle to speak English, the French are cultured and romantic, and Vietnamese people are hardworking and friendly. Investigators have studied ethnic, racial, and gender stereotypes for many years, and the results show that the content of stereotypes changes over time (Diekman, Eagly, Mladinic, & Ferreira, 2005). For instance, few of us now believe—as many once did—that the typical Native American is a drunk, the typical African American is superstitious, or the typical Chinese American is conservative and inscrutable. Stereotypes may not have disappeared over time, but they have changed form (Dovidio & Gaertner, 1996).

Just as stereotypes about ethnic and racial groups are commonly held in our society, so also are stereotypes about gender groups. Usually, our first judgment when meeting people involves classifying them as men or women. This classification is likely to activate an elaborate stereotype. This stereotype depicts men as more independent, dominant, competent, rational, competitive, assertive, and stable in handling crises. It characterizes women as more emotional, sensitive, expressive, gentle, helpful, and patient (Ashmore, 1981; Martin, 1987; Minnigerode & Lee, 1978). Research on the nature of these gender stereotypes is discussed in Box 5.2.

Box 5.2   Test Yourself: Gender Schemas and Stereotypes

One of the most consistent findings on stereotypes is that many people believe men and women have different personality traits. What are the traits believed to be typical of each sex? Where do these sex stereotypes come from?

Studies of sex stereotyping have established a number of characteristics that people associate differently with men and women. In the chart opposite, 20 characteristics are listed that are consistently associated with men or women. To see how aware you are of these stereotypes, fill out the chart by indicating which of the traits listed are thought to be more typical of men and which are more typical of women. Also indicate if you consider each trait as a desirable or undesirable characteristic.

(Continued)

The Bem Sex Role Inventory (BSRI; Bem, 1974) is a widely used measure of sex-role stereotyping and self-perceptions. Although there has been some weakening of the distinctions between stereotypes of men and women over time, gender differences endure (Bergen & Williams, 1991; Holt & Ellis, 1998). The first five traits in the chart (*defends beliefs* to *individualistic*) are seen as more typical of men, whereas the next five (*cheerful* to *childlike*) are considered more typical of women. Although there are subtle differences, the first seven traits are seen as desirable for both men and women. The next three (*gullible, shy,* and *childlike*), however, are rated as both feminine and generally undesirable (Colley, Mulhern, Maltby, & Wood, 2009). The next five (*affectionate* to *compassionate*) are seen as feminine and more desirable for women than for men, and the last five (*assertive* to *has leadership abilities*) are considered more desirable for men than for women. In general, research finds that traits associated with men are more desirable than those associated with women (Broverman et al., 1972). Did your evaluations of trait desirability favor the male stereotyped traits? If not, you may fit in with the trend among educated respondents toward valuing some traditionally feminine traits more positively and some more traditionally masculine traits more negatively (Der-Karabetian & Smith, 1977; Lottes & Kuriloff, 1994; Pleck, 1976). If this trend continues, even if sex stereotypes persist, women may be evaluated less negatively than before.

Trait	Most Typical of		Desirable	
	Men	Women	Yes	No
Defends beliefs				
Athletic				
Strong personality				
Makes decisions easily				
Individualistic				
Cheerful				
Loyal				
Gullible				
Shy				
Childlike				
Affectionate				
Flatterable				
Tender				
Eager to soothe hurt feelings				
Compassionate				
Assertive				
Competitive				
Independent				
Dominant				
Has leadership abilities				

Within gender, stereotypes are linked to subtle cues like titles and surnames. For instance, research conducted in the 1980s found that women labeled "Ms." were seen as more achieving, more masculine, and less likable than women labeled "Mrs." (Dion & Schuller, 1991). These impressions were consistent with the high-competence, low-warmth stereotype of feminists in general (Fiske, Cuddy, Glick, & Xu, 2002), who were often associated with the term. However, today's college students are more likely to see "Ms." as related to marital status rather than concerns about sexism and, therefore, rate "Ms." as positively as "Mrs." or "Miss" (Lawton, Blakemore, & Vartanian, 2003).

Perhaps a more contemporary example related to the nuances of titles is the use of hyphenated surnames. Research finds that women who hyphenate their surnames after marriage are assumed to be well-educated and more likely to have a career as well as more friendly, good-natured, industrious, and intellectually curious than married women who do not hyphenate. Men with hyphenated surnames are also perceived as good-natured, as well as more nurturing and more committed to their marriages than married men who do not hyphenate (Forbes, Adams-Curtis, White & Hamm, 2002).

Gender, ethnicity, and race are only a handful of the groups that are stereotyped in our culture. People also stereotype groups defined by occupation, age, political ideology, mental illness, hobbies, musical tastes, majors, school attended, and so on (Miller, 1982; Rahn, 1993; Rothbart 1996; Rentfrow & Gosling, 2007).

Origins of Stereotypes

How do various stereotypes originate? Some theorists suggest that stereotypes arise out of direct experience with some members of the stereotyped group (Campbell, 1967). We may once have known an Italian who was passionate, someone from Japan who was polite, or a southerner who was bigoted. We then build a stereotype by generalizing—that is, we infer that all members of a group share the attribute we know to be characteristic of some particular members.

Other theorists (Eagly & Steffen, 1984) suggest that stereotypes derive in part from a biased distribution of group members into social roles. Consider professional athletes. After professional sports integrated, Blacks quickly dominated a number of popular sports. In the late 1990s, 60% of professional football players and 85% of professional basketball players were African American (Sailes, 1998). The impressive athletic performances meant that Blacks also dominated the sports coverage in newspapers and on television (Davis & Harris, 1998). Roles have associated characteristics—professional sports players are athletically gifted—and eventually those characteristics are attached to the persons occupying the roles.

The overwhelming athletic success and related images contributed to and helped maintain the stereotype that Blacks are athletically superior to other racial groups. If a social group is concentrated in roles with negative characteristics, an unflattering stereotype of that group may emerge that ascribes the negative characteristics of the role to members of the group.

Stereotyping may also be a natural outcome of social perception (McGarty, Yzerbyt & Spears, 2002). When people have to process and remember a lot of information about many others, they store this information in terms of group categories rather than in terms of individuals (Taylor, Fiske, Etcoff, & Ruderman, 1978). In trying to remember what went on in a classroom discussion, you may recall that several women spoke and a Black person expressed a strong opinion, although you cannot remember exactly which women spoke or who the Black person was. Because people remember behavior by group category rather than by individual, they attach the behavior to the groups (Rothbart, Fulero, Jensen, Howard, & Birrell, 1978). Remembering that women spoke and a Black person expressed a strong opinion, you might infer that in general, women are talkative and Blacks are opinionated. You would not form these stereotypes if you recalled these attributes as belonging to individuals rather than remembering them as attached to group membership.

Errors Caused by Stereotypes

Because stereotypes are overgeneralizations, they foster various errors in social perception and judgment. First, stereotypes lead us to assume that all members of a group are alike and possess certain traits. Yet individual members of a group obviously differ in many respects. One person wearing a hard hat may shoulder you into the stairwell on a crowded bus; another may offer you his seat. Second, stereotypes lead us to assume that all the members of one group differ from all the members of another group. Stereotypes of football players and ballet dancers may suggest, for instance, that these groups have nothing in common. But both groups contain individuals who are athletic, hardworking, intelligent, and so on. If we see the two groups as nonoverlapping, we neglect to realize that there are ballet dancers who also play football.

Although stereotypes can produce inaccurate inferences and judgments in simple situations, they are especially likely to do so in complex situations when our minds are attending to a lot of stimuli. This is because we rely on stereotypes for efficiency (Sherman, Lee, Bessenoff & Frost, 1998). If an observer uses a stereotype as a central theme around which to organize information relevant to a decision, he or she may neglect information that is inconsistent with the stereotype

(Bodenhausen & Lichtenstein, 1987). A process like this can contribute to bias in educational admissions or hiring decisions, like with the faculty ratings of lab assistant applications discussed earlier. With a large amount of material to be read and significant detail in each, our minds take shortcuts wherever they can. The stereotype that favors men with regard to scientific competence (and disfavors women) may overshadow specific evidence of competence from the applications.

Research also indicates that people of higher status have a tendency to use stereotypes more than people of lower status do. This seems to occur because people of higher status have more people competing for their attention and, thus, have more incentive to use shortcuts. They may also be able to afford to make more mistakes because of their power (Goodwin, Gubin, Fiske, & Yzerbyt, 2000). This dynamic occurs even when subjects are randomly assigned to higher- and lower-status roles (Richeson & Ambady, 2003).

Although stereotypes involve overstatement and overgeneralization, they resist change even in the face of concrete evidence that contradicts them. This occurs because people tend to accept information that confirms their stereotypes and ignore or explain away information that disconfirms them (Lord, Lepper, & Mackie, 1984; Snyder, 1981; Weber & Crocker, 1983). Suppose, for example, that Omar stereotypes gay men as effeminate, nonathletic, and artistic. If he stumbles into a gay bar, he is especially likely to notice the men in the crowd who fit this description, thereby confirming his stereotype. But how does he construe any rough-looking, athletic men who are there? It is possible that these individuals might challenge his stereotype, but reconstructing schemas is a lot of work, and Omar is more likely to find a way around this challenge. He might scrutinize those who don't fit his stereotype for hidden signs of effeminacy. He might underestimate their number or even assume they are straight. He may also engage in **subtyping**, a process through which perceivers create subcategories of stereotyped groups who serve as exceptions to the rule without threatening the overarching stereotype (e.g., these are "atypical gay men"). Through cognitive strategies like these, people explain away contradictory information and preserve their stereotypes.

Impression Formation

Information about other people comes to us from various sources. We may read facts about someone. We may hear something from a third party. We may witness acts by the other. We may interact directly with the other and form an impression of that person based on his or her appearance, dress, speech style, or background. We even infer personality characteristics from people's facial features (Hassin & Trope, 2000; Zebrowitz et al., 1998). Regardless of how we get information about someone, we as perceivers must find a way to integrate these diverse facts into a coherent picture. This process of organizing diverse information into a unified impression of the other person is called **impression formation**. It is fundamental to person perception.

Trait Centrality

In a classic experiment, Asch (1946) used a straightforward procedure to show that some traits have more impact than others on the impressions we form. Undergraduates in one group received a list of seven traits describing a hypothetical person. These traits were *intelligent, skillful, industrious, warm, determined, practical,* and *cautious.* Undergraduates in a second group received the same list of traits but with one critical difference: The trait "warm" was replaced by "cold." All participants then wrote a brief paragraph indicating their impressions and completed a checklist to rate the stimulus person on such other characteristics as *generous, wise, happy, good-natured, humorous, sociable, popular, humane, altruistic,* and *imaginative.*

The findings led to several conclusions. First, the students had no difficulty performing the task. They were able to weave the trait information into a coherent whole and construct a composite sketch of the stimulus person. Second, substituting the trait "warm" for the trait "cold" produced a large difference in the overall impression the students formed. When the stimulus person was "warm," the students typically described him as happy, successful, popular, and humorous. But when he was "cold," they described him as self-centered, unsociable, and unhappy. Third, the terms "warm" and "cold" had a larger impact than other traits on the overall impression formed of the stimulus person. This was demonstrated, for instance, by a variation in which the investigator repeated the basic procedure but substituted the pair "polite" and "blunt" in place of "warm" and "cold." Whereas describing the stimulus person as warm rather than cold made a great difference in the impressions formed by the students, describing him as polite rather than blunt made little difference.

We say that a trait has a high level of **trait centrality** when it has a large impact on the overall impression we form of that person. In Asch's study, the warm/cold trait displayed more centrality than the polite/blunt trait because differences in warm/cold produced larger differences in participants' ratings.

A follow-up study (Kelley, 1950) replicated the warm/cold finding in a more realistic setting. Students in sections of a psychology course read trait descriptions of a guest lecturer before he spoke. These descriptions contained adjectives similar to those Asch used (that is, *industrious, critical, practical, determined*), but they differed regarding the warm/cold variable. For half the students, the description contained the trait "warm"; for the other half, it contained "cold." The lecturer subsequently arrived at the classroom and led a discussion for about 20 minutes. Afterward, the students were asked to report their impressions of him. The results showed large differences between the impressions formed by those who read he was "warm" and those who read he was "cold." Those who had read he was "cold" rated him as less considerate, sociable, popular, good-natured, humorous, and humane than those who had read he was "warm." Because all students saw the same guest instructor in the classroom, the differences in their impressions could stem only from the use of "warm" or "cold" in the profile they had read.

How could a single trait embedded in a profile have such an impact on impressions of someone's behavior? Several theories have been advanced, but one plausible explanation holds that the students used a schema—a mental map—indicating what traits go with being warm and what traits go with being cold. Looking again at Figure 5.1, we note the locations of the attributes "warm" and "cold" on the map and the nature of the other attributes close by. If the mental maps used by the participants in the Asch (1946) and Kelley (1950) studies resembled Figure 5.1, it becomes immediately clear why they judged the warm person as more sociable, popular, good-natured, and humorous; these traits are close to "warm" and remote from "cold" on the mental map.

First Impressions

You have surely noticed the effort individuals make to create a good impression when interviewing for a new job, entering a new group, or meeting an attractive potential date. This effort reflects the widely held belief that first impressions are especially important and have an enduring impact. In fact, this belief is supported by a body of systematic research. Observers forming an impression of a person give more weight to information received early in a sequence than to information received later. This is called the **primacy effect** (Luchins, 1957).

What accounts for the impact of first impressions? One explanation is that after forming an initial impression of a person, we interpret subsequent information in a way that makes it consistent with our initial impression. Having established that your new roommate is neat and considerate, you interpret the dirty socks on the floor as a sign of temporary forgetfulness rather than as evidence of sloppiness and lack of concern. Thus, the schema into which an observer assimilates new information influences the interpretation of that information (Zanna & Hamilton, 1977).

A second explanation for the primacy effect holds that we attend very carefully to the first bits of information we get about a person, but we pay less attention once we have enough information to make a judgment. It is not that we interpret later information differently; we simply use it less. This explanation assumes that whatever information we attend to most has the biggest effect on our impressions (Dreben, Fiske, & Hastie, 1979).

What happens if we make an effort to attend to all information equally? In such cases, recent information exerts the strongest influence on our impressions (Crano, 1977), an occurrence known as the **recency effect** (Jones & Goethals, 1971; Steiner & Rain, 1989). Jurors, for example, are asked to take the perspective that an individual on trial is innocent until proven guilty and instructed to weigh all the evidence presented at trial. Research shows the sequencing of the presentation of that evidence is important. Two groups witnessing identical courtroom arguments came to different verdicts based on whether it was the prosecution or defense who presented last (Furnham, 1986). When the defendant's case came second, perceptions of innocence increased significantly. A recency effect may also occur when so much time has passed that we have largely forgotten our first impression or when we are judging characteristics that change over time, like performance or moods. Perceivers' own moods also influence what information they attend to. Those in good moods seem to favor early information, while the primacy effect is eliminated for those who are experiencing a bad mood (Forgas, 2011).

In one study investigating the relative impact of primacy and recency effects on impression formation (Jones et al., 1968), participants observed the performance of a college student on an SAT-type aptitude test. In one condition, the student started successfully on the first few items but then her performance deteriorated steadily. In a second condition, the student started poorly and then gradually improved. In both conditions, the student answered 15 out of 30 test items correctly. After observing one or the other performance, participants rated the student's intelligence and tried to predict how well she would do on the next 30 items. Although the student's overall performance was the same in both conditions (15 of 30 correct), participants rated the student as more intelligent when she started well and then tailed off than when she started poorly and then improved. Observers also predicted higher scores for the student on the next series when the student started well than when she started poorly. Clearly, participants gave more weight to the student's performance on the first few items—a primacy effect.

Impressions as Self-Fulfilling Prophecies

Whether correct or not, the impressions we form of people influence our behavior toward them. Recall, for instance, the study in which students read that their guest instructor was "warm" or "cold" before meeting him (Kelley, 1950). Not only did the students form different impressions of the instructor, but they also behaved differently toward him. Those who believed the instructor was "warm" participated more in the class discussion than those who believed he was "cold." In a classic study, Rosenthal and Jacobson (1968) found that teachers act differently toward students who they expect to succeed—giving them more time, attention, and approval than other students—thereby creating more opportunity for those students to rise to the teachers' expectations and unintentionally disadvantaging the children for whom the teachers have lower expectations.

When our behavior toward people reflects our impressions of them, we cause them to react in ways that confirm our original impressions. When this happens, our impressions become **self-fulfilling prophecies** (Darley & Fazio, 1980). For example, if we ignore someone because we think she is dull, she will probably withdraw and add nothing interesting to the conversation, living up to our initial impressions. Because our own actions evoke appropriate reactions from others, our initial impressions—whether correct or incorrect—are often confirmed by the reactions of others.

The self-fulfilling prophecy can influence desirability in dating. In a recent study, researchers took the actual dating profiles of 100 men (both unattractive and attractive) from an online dating website and separated the photos from the text (Brand, Bonatsos, D'Orazio, & DeShong 2012). Fifty women then rated both the photos and the profile texts independently. Even without the photos attached, the women rated the attractive men's profile texts as more attractive than those of the unattractive men. The researchers argued that the confidence these men had established in their earlier dating history was the key factor. Having been treated as more attractive in previous interactions, these men came to act in a way that was more appealing even long after those previous dating experiences had ended.

Heuristics

In most social situations, our impressions could be guided by a number of different schemas. How do we make decisions on how to characterize these situations? The answer comes in the form of another type of mental shortcut called a **heuristic** (Tversky & Kahneman, 1974). Heuristics provide a quick way of selecting schemas that—although far from infallible—often help us make an effective choice amid considerable uncertainty.

Availability

One factor that determines how likely we are to choose a particular schema is how long it has been since we have used that particular schema. If we have recently used a particular schema, it is easier for us to call up that schema for use in the current situation. There are other reasons why certain schemas are more available to us. If, for instance, certain examples of categorizations are easier to remember, schemas consistent with those examples are more likely to be called up and used. Suppose you were asked whether there are more words in the English language that begin with the letter *r* or if there are more words in which the third letter is an *r*. Most people find it much easier to think of examples of words that begin with *r*, and thus, the ease of producing examples makes it seem as if there are more words that begin with *r* (Tversky & Kahneman, 1974). These words are more easily available to us, and thus, they cause us to overestimate their frequency of occurrence (Manis, Shedler, Jonides, & Nelson, 1993).

Representativeness

A second heuristic we often use is called the representativeness heuristic (Tversky & Kahneman, 1974). In this case, we take the few characteristics we know about someone or something and determine whether that person or object is likely to be a member of a particular category (Dawes, 1998; Thomsen & Borgida, 1996). We use this type of heuristic when we judge the musical tastes of others (Lonsdale & North, 2012). The closer one is to a stereotypical country music fan—based on age (older), race (White), religion (Christian), and political beliefs (conservative)—the more likely we are to believe they listen to country music (Lonsdale, 2009). This heuristic holds even when less than half of the Whites (43%) in the United States consider themselves country music fans—and even with almost 10% of country fans people of color—because people tend to discount statistical information in the face of the representativeness heuristic (Kahneman & Tversky, 1973; National Endowment for the Arts, 2008).

Anchoring and Adjustment

When faced with making a judgment on something we know very little about, we grasp any cues we can find to help us make a decent guess. Oftentimes, we will use some particular standard as a starting point and then try to determine whether we should guess higher or lower than that starting point. Such a starting point is called an *anchor*, and our modification relative to the anchor is called *adjustment* (Mussweiler, Strack, & Pfeiffer, 2000; Tversky & Kahneman, 1974). Suppose you were asked on an exam to provide the population of Chicago. If you did not know that population but you did know the population of New York City, you might use the population of New York as an anchor and, thinking that Chicago must be somewhat smaller than New York, adjust the New York value downward to produce your guess.

When using this heuristic, however, we do not always have meaningful anchors. If a number is in our head for any reason, we are likely to use it as an anchor even if it has nothing whatsoever to do with the situation we are facing (Cadinu & Rothbart, 1996; Wilson, Houston, Etling, & Brekke, 1996). Suppose an employer is conducting an annual evaluation of employees and has the power to give employees a raise of anywhere from 0 to 40 percent depending on their performance. If the boss just attended a retirement party for someone who worked in the firm for 30 years, he or she may unconsciously use this value as an anchor and end up giving relatively high raises. If, however, the boss just attended the birthday party of a five-year-old niece, five may be used as the anchor, and although the boss may adjust up from five, the raises are likely to be considerably lower than if 30 were used as the anchor. These kinds of anchoring effects tend to occur even if we are explicitly warned not to allow arbitrary anchors to affect our decisions (Griffin, Gonzalez, & Varey, 2001).

Perhaps most often, we use ourselves as an anchor when judging social situations (Markus, Smith, & Moreland, 1985). We have a tendency to do this even when we know we are unusual. If you are a very generous person who always tips at least 25 percent at a restaurant and are asked whether your friend Emily is miserly or charitable, you would be likely to use your own rather unusual behavior as an anchor and report that she is tightfisted because you know she typically tips "only" 20 percent.

Attribution Theory

When we interact with other people, we observe only their actions and the visible effects those actions have. As perceivers, we often want to also know why others act as they do. To figure this out, we must usually make inferences beyond what we observe. For instance, if a coworker performs a favor for us, why is she doing it? Is she doing it because she is fundamentally a generous person? Or is she manipulative and pursuing some ulterior motive? Does her social role require her to do it? Have other people pressured her into doing it? To act effectively toward her and to predict her future behavior, we must first figure out why she behaves as she does.

The term **attribution** refers to the process an observer uses to infer the causes of another's behavior: "Why did that person act as he or she did?" In attribution, we observe another's behavior and infer backward to its causes—to the intentions, abilities, traits, motives, and situational pressures that explain why people act as they do. Theories of attribution focus on the methods we use to interpret another person's behavior and to infer its sources (Kelley & Michela, 1980; Lipe, 1991; Ross & Fletcher, 1985).

Dispositional versus Situational Attributions

Fritz Heider (1944, 1958), whose work was an early stimulus to the study of attribution, noted that people in everyday life use commonsense reasoning to understand the causes of others' behavior. They act as "naive scientists" and use something resembling the scientific method in attempting to discern causes of behavior. Heider maintained that regardless of whether their interpretations about the causes of behavior are scientifically valid, people act on their beliefs. For this reason, social psychologists must study people's commonsense explanations of behavior and events so we can understand their behavior.

The most crucial decision observers make is whether to attribute a behavior to the internal state(s) of the person who performed it—this is termed a **dispositional attribution**—or to factors in that person's environment—a **situational attribution**. For example, consider the attributions an observer might make when learning that her neighbor is unemployed. She might judge that he is out of work because he is lazy, irresponsible, or lacking in ability. These are dispositional attributions, because they attribute the causes of behavior to his internal states or characteristics. Alternatively, she might attribute his unemployment to the scarcity of jobs in his line of work, to employment discrimination, to the depressed condition of the economy, or to the evils of the capitalist system. These are situational attributions because they attribute his behavior to external causes.

What determines whether we attribute an act to a person's disposition or to the situation? One important consideration is the strength of situational pressures on the person. These pressures may include normative role demands as well as rewards or punishments applied to the person by others in the environment. For example, suppose we see a judge give the death penalty to a criminal. We might infer that the judge is tough (a dispositional attribution). However, suppose we learn that the law in that state requires the death penalty for the criminal's offense. Now we would see the judge not as tough but as responding to role pressures (a situational attribution).

This logic has been formalized as the **subtractive rule**, which states that when making attributions about personal dispositions, the observer subtracts the perceived impact of situational forces from the personal disposition implied by the behavior itself (Trope & Cohen, 1989; Trope, Cohen, & Moaz, 1988). Thus, considered by itself, the judge's behavior (imposing the death penalty) might imply that she is tough in disposition. The subtractive rule, however, states that the observer must subtract the effect of situational pressures (the state law) from the disposition implied by the behavior itself. When the observer does this, he or she may conclude the judge is not especially tough or overly inclined to impose the death penalty. In other words, using the subtractive rule in this situation served to weaken the dispositional attribution and strengthen the situational attribution.

There are other times, however, when applying the subtractive rule (by accounting for the situational influences) actually strengthens or augments the dispositional attribution—not unlike what happens when we subtract a negative number in arithmetic. This happens, for instance, when someone engages in an activity that his or her environment discourages or punishes. If we learn that the judge in the previous example gave the death penalty even though she was the first to give the death penalty for such a crime or that the jury suggested a lesser punishment or that she would face difficulty being reelected because of her decision, these situational factors would strengthen our dispositional attribution. She is more than tough; she is harsh.

Another factor that may influence our attributions is our attention to situational pressures and structural constraints. Social science students, whose coursework and training encourages them to think beyond the individual and to consider social structure, are more likely to blame the system for individuals' problems with unemployment and poverty than are either business or engineering students (Guimond, Begin, & Palmer, 1989; Guimond & Palmer, 1990). Some might argue that this is a selection effect; students who embrace system-blame are somehow drawn toward the social sciences. However, Figure 5.2 shows that students begin college with quite similar levels of system-blame, and it is over time that differences emerge. In a sense, as students are socialized into the norms of their disciplines, they acquire a particular view of the social world and reality—a type of cultural lens.

Culture plays an important role in the attribution process. One important cultural difference has to do with how individualist or collectivist a culture is (Norenzayan & Nisbett, 2000; Triandis, 1995). Individualist cultures emphasize the individual and value individual achievement; collectivist cultures emphasize the welfare of the family, ethnic group, and perhaps work group over the interests of individuals. This difference in emphasis turns out to have a substantial impact on the orientation toward dispositional versus situational attributions for behavior. Individualist cultures focus on the individual—thus, their members are predisposed to make individualist or dispositional attributions. In collectivist cultures, the focus on groups draws some attention to context—thus, members of these cultures are more likely to include situational elements in their attributions.

In one study, researchers compared attributions made by students from an individualist society (the United States) with those made by students from a collectivist society (Saudi Arabia). Participants in the study were 163 students recruited from

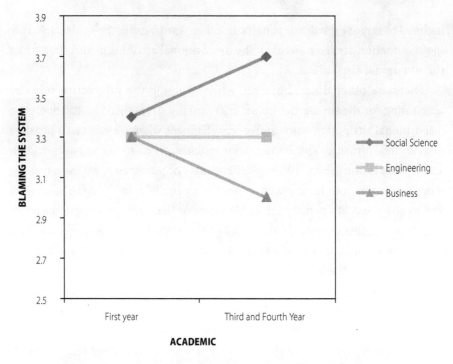

Figure 5.2 Situational Attributions for Poverty and Unemployment, by Field of Study and Academic Year

Students enter college with similar levels of "system-blame" for poverty and unemployment. College classes increase the likelihood of making situational attributions among social science students and decrease such attributions among business students. Because engineering classes are unlikely to engage discussions of poverty or unemployment, engineering students' views remain unaffected over the course of study. Adapted from Guimond & Palmer, 1990.

U.S. universities and 162 students from a university in Saudi Arabia (Al-Zahrani & Kaplowitz, 1993). Each student was presented with vignettes describing eight situations—four involving achievement and four involving morality. Students were asked to assign responsibility for the outcome to each of several factors. Consistent with the hypothesis, the results showed that across the eight situations, U.S. students assigned greater responsibility to internal dispositional factors than did Saudi students.

Inferring Dispositions from Acts

Although Heider's analysis and the subtractive rule are useful in identifying some conditions under which observers make dispositional attributions, they do not explain which specific dispositions observers will ascribe to a person. Suppose, for instance, that you are on a city street during the Christmas season and you see a young, well-dressed man walking with a woman. Suddenly, the man stops and tosses several coins into a Salvation Army pot. From this act, what can you infer about the man's dispositions? Is he generous and altruistic? Or is he trying to impress the woman? Or is he perhaps just trying to clear out some nuisance change from his coat pocket?

When we try to infer a person's dispositions, our perspective is much like that of a detective. We can observe only the act (a man gives coins to the Salvation Army) and the effects of that act (the Salvation Army receives more resources, the woman smiles at the man, the man's pocket is no longer cluttered with coins). From this observed act and its effects, we must infer the man's dispositions.

According to one prominent theory (Jones, 1979; Jones & Davis, 1965), we perform two major steps when inferring personal dispositions. First, we try to deduce the specific intentions that underlie a person's actions. In other words, we try to figure out what the person originally intended to accomplish by performing the act. Second, from these intentions we try to infer what prior personal disposition would cause a person to have such intentions. If we think the man intended to benefit the Salvation Army, for example, we infer the disposition "helpful" or "generous." However, if we think the man had some other intention, such as impressing his girlfriend, we do not infer he has the disposition "helpful." Thus, we attribute a disposition that reflects the presumed intention.

Several factors influence observers' decisions regarding which effect(s) the person is really pursuing and, hence, what dispositional inference is appropriate. These factors include the commonality of effects, the social desirability of effects, and the normativeness of effects (Jones & Davis, 1965).

Commonality

If any given act produced one and only one effect, then inferences of dispositions from acts would always be clear-cut. Because many acts have multiple effects, however, observers attributing specific intentions and dispositions find it informative to observe the actor in situations that involve choices between alternative actions.

Suppose, for example, that a person can engage either in action 1 or in action 2. Action 1, if chosen, will produce effects a, b, and c. Action 2 will produce effects b, c, d, and e. As we can see, two of these effects (b and c) are common to actions 1 and 2. The remaining effects (a, d, and e) are unique to a particular alternative; these are noncommon effects. The unique (noncommon) effects of acts enable observers to make inferences regarding intentions and dispositions, but the common effects of two or more acts provide little or no basis for inferences (Jones & Davis, 1965).

Thus, observers who wish to discern the specific dispositions of a person try to identify effects that are unique to the action chosen. Research shows that the fewer non-common effects associated with the chosen alternative, the greater the confidence of observers about their attributions (Ajzen & Holmes, 1976).

Social Desirability

In many situations, people engage in particular behaviors because those behaviors are socially desirable. Yet people who perform a socially desirable act show us only that they are "normal" and reveal nothing about their distinctive dispositions. Suppose, for instance, that you observe a guest at a party thank the hostess when leaving. What does this tell you about the guest? Did she really enjoy the party? Or was she merely behaving in a polite, socially desirable fashion? You cannot be sure—either inference could be correct. Now suppose instead that when leaving, the guest complained loudly to the hostess that she had a miserable time at such a dull party. This would likely tell you more about her because observers interpret acts low in social desirability as indicators of underlying dispositions (Miller, 1976).

Normative Expectations

When inferring dispositions from acts, observers consider the normativeness of behavior. Normativeness is the extent to which we expect the average person to perform a behavior in a particular setting. This includes conformity to social norms and to role expectations in groups (Jones & McGillis, 1976). Actions that conform to norms are uninformative about personal dispositions, whereas actions that violate norms lead to dispositional attributions. An observer could be confident that a Michigan fan who cheered for his team while sitting in the middle of Notre Dame's student section is much more passionate about football (a dispositional attribution) than if the same fan was acting similarly in the heart of the Michigan student section.

Covariation Model of Attribution

Up to this point, we have examined how observers make attributions regarding a person's behavior in a single situation. Sometimes, however, we have multiple observations of a person's behavior. That is, we have information about a person's behavior in a variety of situations or in a given situation vis-à-vis different partners. Multiple observations enable us to make many comparisons, and these, in turn, facilitate causal attribution.

How do perceivers use multiple observations to arrive at a conclusion about the cause(s) of a behavior? Extending Heider's ideas, Kelley (1967, 1973) suggests that when we have multiple observations of behavior, we analyze the information essentially in the same way a scientist would. That is, we try to figure out whether the behavior occurs in the presence or absence of various factors (actors, objects, contexts) that are possible causes. Then to identify the cause(s) of the behavior, we apply the **principle of covariation**: We attribute the behavior to the factor that is both present when the behavior occurs and absent when the behavior fails to occur—the cause that covaries with the behavior.

To illustrate, suppose you are at work one afternoon when you hear your boss loudly criticizing another worker, Zach. To what would you attribute your boss'sbehavior? There are at least three potential causes: the actor (the boss), the object of the behavior (Zach), and the context or setting in which the behavior occurs. For example, you might attribute the loud criticism to your boss' confrontational personality (a characteristic of the actor), to Zach's slothful performance (a characteristic of the object), or to some particular feature of the context.

Kelley (1967) suggests that when using the principle of covariation to determine whether a behavior is caused by the actor, object, or context, we rely on three types of information: consensus, consistency, and distinctiveness.

Consensus refers to whether all actors perform the same behavior or only a few do. For example, do all the other employees at work criticize Zach (high consensus), or is your boss the only person who does so (low consensus)?

Consistency refers to whether the actor behaves in the same way at different times and in different settings. If your boss criticizes Zach on many different occasions, her behavior is high in consistency. If she has never before criticized Zach, her behavior is low in consistency.

Distinctiveness refers to whether the actor behaves differently toward a particular object than toward other objects. If your boss criticizes only Zach and none of the other workers, her behavior is high in distinctiveness. If she criticizes all workers, her behavior toward Zach is low in distinctiveness.

The causal attribution that observers make for a behavior depends on the particular combination of consensus, consistency, and distinctiveness information that people associate with that behavior. To illustrate, Table 5.2 reviews the scenario in which your boss criticizes Zach. The table displays three combinations of information that might be present in this situation. These combinations of information are interesting because studies have shown they reliably produce different attributions regarding the cause of the behavior (Cheng & Novick, 1990).

As Table 5.2 indicates, observers usually attribute the cause of a behavior to the actor (the boss) when the behavior is low in consensus, low in distinctiveness, and high in consistency. In contrast, observers usually attribute a behavior to the object (Zach) when the behavior is high in consensus, high in distinctiveness, and high in consistency. Finally, observers usually attribute a behavior to the context when consistency is low.

Table 5.2 Why Did the Boss Criticize Zach?
. . . .

Situation: At work today, you observe your boss criticizing and yelling at another employee, Zach.

Question: Why did the boss criticize Zach?

1. Kelley's (1973) model indicates that attributions are made to the actor (boss) when consensus is low, distinctiveness is low, and consistency is high.

   Example: Suppose no other persons criticize Zach (low consensus). The boss criticizes all the other employees (low distinctiveness). The boss criticized Zach last month, last week, and yesterday (high consistency).

   Attribution: The perceiver will likely attribute the behavior (criticism) to the boss. ("The boss is a very critical person.")

2. The model indicates that attributions are made to the stimulus object (Zach) when consensus is high, distinctiveness is high, and consistency is high.

   Example: Suppose everyone at work criticizes Zach (high consensus). The boss does not criticize anyone else at work, only Zach (high distinctiveness). The boss criticized Zach last month, last week, and yesterday (high consistency).

   Attribution: The perceiver will likely attribute the behavior (criticism) to Zach. ("Zach is a lazy, careless worker.")

3. The model indicates that attributions are made to the context or situation when consistency is low.

   Example: Suppose the boss has never criticized Zach before (low consistency).

   Attribution: The perceiver will likely attribute the behavior (criticism) to a particular set of contextual circumstances rather than to Zach or the boss per se. ("Zach made a remark this morning that the boss misinterpreted.")

Several studies show that, at least in general terms, people use consensus, consistency, and distinctiveness information in the way Kelley theorized (Hewstone & Jaspars, 1987; McArthur, 1972; Pruitt & Insko, 1980), although consensus seems to have a weaker effect on attributions than the other two aspects of covariation (Winschild & Wells, 1997). Of course, in any given situation, the combination of available information may differ from the three possibilities shown in Table 5.2. In such cases, attributions are more complicated, more ambiguous, and less certain. We usually assign less weight to a given cause if other plausible causes are also present (Kelley, 1972; Morris & Larrick, 1995).

Bias and Error in Attribution

According to the picture presented thus far, observers scrutinize their environment, gather information, form impressions, and interpret behavior in rational, if sometimes unconscious, ways. In actuality, however, observers often deviate from the logical methods described by attribution theory and fall prey to biases. These biases may lead observers to misinterpret events and to make erroneous judgments. This section considers several major biases and errors in attribution.

Overattribution to Dispositions

At the time of the Cuban Missile Crisis, the Cuban leader Fidel Castro was generally unpopular, even feared, in the United States. In an interesting study done shortly after the crisis, Jones and Harris (1967) asked participants to read an essay written by another student. Depending on the experimental condition, the essay either strongly supported the Cuban leader or strongly opposed him. Moreover, the participants received information about the conditions under which the student wrote the essay. They were told either that the essay was written by a student who was assigned by the instructor to take a pro-Castro or anti-Castro stand (no-choice condition) or that the essay was written by a student who was free to choose whichever position he or she wanted to present (choice condition). The participants' task was to infer the writer's true underlying attitude about Castro. In the conditions in which the writer had free choice, participants inferred that the content of the essay reflected the writer's true attitude about Castro. That is, they saw the pro-Castro essay as indicating pro-Castro attitudes and the anti-Castro essay as indicating anti-Castro attitudes. In the conditions in which the writer was assigned the topic and had no choice, participants still thought the content of the essay reflected the writer's true attitude about Castro, although they were less sure that this was so. Participants made these internal attributions even though it was possible the writer held an opinion directly opposite of that expressed in the essay. In effect, participants overestimated the importance of internal dispositions (attitudes about Castro) and underestimated the importance of situational forces (role obligations) in shaping the essay.

The tendency to overestimate the importance of personal (dispositional) factors and to underestimate situational influences is called the **fundamental attribution error** (Higgins & Bryant, 1982; Ross, 1977; Small & Peterson, 1981). This tendency was first identified by Heider (1944), who noted that most observers ignore or minimize the impact of role pressures and situational constraints on others and interpret behavior as caused by people's intentions, motives, or attitudes. This bias toward dispositional factors was labeled "fundamental" because it was documented in study after study over the years and assumed to be universal (for instance, Allison, Mackie, Muller, & Worth, 1993; Jones, 1979; Ross, 2001; Sabini, Siepmann, & Stein, 2001). However, more recent research suggests that the bias is less universal than it originally seemed. The tendency was mistakenly considered fundamental because early social psychological research relied almost exclusively on American and Western European participants in surveys and experiments. Members of these cultures have a more independent view of the self (Markus & Kitayama, 1991) than those in Eastern cultures, who were seldom studied. Contemporary social psychologists, now more attentive to cultural differences, find that members of collectivist cultures (e.g., China, India, Taiwan) tend to favor situational explanations over dispositional ones—the reverse of the fundamental attribution error (Smith & Bond, 1994). Although the term remains the same, through cross-cultural research social psychologists realize that the bias is not as fundamental as it once seemed.

Overemphasizing the importance of disposition is especially dangerous when it causes us to overlook the advantages of power built into social roles. For instance, we may incorrectly attribute the successes of the powerful to their superior personal capabilities, or we may incorrectly attribute the failures of persons without power to their personal weaknesses.

Focus-of-Attention Bias

A closely related error is the tendency to overestimate the causal impact of whomever or whatever we focus our attention on; this is called the **focus-of-attention bias**. A striking demonstration of this bias appears in a study by Taylor and Fiske (1978). The study involved six participants who observed a conversation between two persons (Speaker 1 and Speaker 2). Although all six participants heard the same dialogue, they differed in the focus of their visual attention. Two observers sat behind Speaker 1, facing Speaker 2; two sat behind Speaker 2, facing Speaker 1; and two sat on the sides, equally focused on the two speakers. Measures taken after the conversation showed that observers thought the speaker they faced not only had more influence on the tone and content of the conversation but also had a greater causal impact on the other speaker's behavior. Observers who sat on the sides and were able to focus equally on both speakers attributed equal influence to them.

We perceive the stimuli that are most salient in the environment—those that attract our attention—as most causally influential. Thus, we attribute most causal influence to people who are noisy, colorful, vivid, or in motion. We credit the person who talks the most with exercising the most influence; we blame the person who we see run past us when we hear a rock shatter a window. Although salient stimuli may be causally important in some cases, we overestimate their importance (Krull & Dill, 1996; McArthur & Post, 1977).

The students are visually focused on the professor, whereas the professor is visually focused on the students. These visual perspectives influence attributions. If a lecture is not going well, the professor may blame the class's inattention and apathy, but the students are more likely to blame the professor and his lack of teaching ability or enthusiasm. © Dirk Anschütz/Corbis

The focus-of-attention bias provides one explanation for the fundamental attribution error. The person behaving is the active entity in the environment. If we watch our math professor struggle with a problem on the board, the professor is what captures our attention. In fact, many of the contextual influences on the actor (for example, things that happened earlier in the day or a pounding headache) may be completely invisible to us (Gilbert & Malone, 1995) or simply less salient (the distracting murmur from our classmates) as we focus on the professor. Because many of us are socialized to direct our attention more to people who act than to the context, we attribute more causal importance to people (the math professor is nervous or incapable) than to their situations.

Actor-Observer Difference

Actors and observers make different attributions for behavior. Observers tend to attribute actors' behavior to the actors' internal characteristics, whereas actors believe their own behavior is due more to characteristics of the external situation (Jones & Nisbett, 1972; Watson, 1982). This tendency is known as the **actor-observer difference**. Thus, although other customers in a market may attribute the mix of items in your grocery cart (beer, vegetables, candy bars) to your personal characteristics (hard-drinking, vegetarian, chocolate addict), you will probably attribute it to the requirements of your situation (preparing for a party) or the qualities of the items (nutritional value or special treat).

In one demonstration of the actor-observer difference (Nisbett, Caputo, Legant, & Maracek, 1973), male students wrote descriptions explaining why they liked their girlfriends and why they chose their majors. Then, as observers, they explained why their best friend liked his girlfriend and chose his major. When explaining their own actions, the students emphasized external characteristics like the attractive qualities of their girlfriends and the interesting aspects of their majors. However, when explaining their friends' behavior, they downplayed external characteristics and emphasized their friends' internal dispositions (preferences and personalities).

Two explanations for the actor-observer difference in attribution are that actors and observers have different visual perspectives and different access to information.

Visual Perspectives

The actor's natural visual perspective is to look at the situation, whereas the observer's natural perspective is to look at the actor. Thus, the actor-observer difference reflects a difference in the focus of attention. Both the actor and the observer attribute more causal influence to what they focus on. Consider the students and math professor from the focus-of-attention example above. The students in the example may think of their math professor as incapable because she is the students' visual focus. The professor, who cannot see herself and whose visual attention is turned toward the classroom, blames the disrespectful behavior of the students in her class.

Storms (1973) reasoned that if the actor-observer difference in attributions was due simply to a difference in perspective, it might be possible to reverse the actor-observer difference by making the actor see the behavior from the observer's viewpoint and the observer see the same behavior from the actor's viewpoint. To give each the other's point of view, Storms videotaped a conversation between two people, using two separate cameras. One camera recorded the interaction from the visual perspective of the actor, the other from the perspective of the observer. Storms then showed actors the videotape made from the observer's perspective, and he showed observers the videotape made from the actor's perspective. As predicted, reversing the visual perspectives reversed the actor-observer difference in attribution; finding ways to make individuals more self-aware can, therefore, reduce the actor-observer bias (Fejfar & Hoyle, 2000).

Information

A second explanation for the actor-observer difference is that actors have information about their own past behavior and the context relevant to their behavior that observers lack (Johnson & Boyd, 1995). Thus, for example, observers may assume that certain behaviors are typical of an actor when in fact they are not. This would cause observers to make incorrect dispositional attributions. An observer who sees a clerk return an overpayment to a customer may assume the clerk always behaves this way—resulting in a dispositional attribution of honesty. However, if the clerk knows he has often cheated customers in the past, he would probably not interpret his current behavior as evidence of his honest nature. Consistent with this, research shows that observers who have a low level of acquaintance with the actor tend to form more dispositional attributions and fewer situational attributions than those who have a high level of acquaintance with the actor (Prager & Cutler, 1990).

Even when observers have some information about an actor's past behavior, they often do not know how changes in context influence the actor's behavior. This is because observers usually see an actor only in limited contexts. Suppose that students observe a professor delivering witty, entertaining lectures in class week after week. The professor knows that in other social situations he is shy and withdrawn, but the students do not have an opportunity to see this. As a result, the observers (students) may infer dispositions from apparently consistent behavior that the actor (the professor) knows to be inconsistent across a wider range of contexts.

Motivational Biases

Up to this point, we have considered attribution biases based on cognitive factors. That is, we have traced biases to the types of information that observers have available, acquire, and process. Motivational factors—a person's needs, interests, and goals—are another source of bias in attributions.

When events affect a person's self-interests, biased attribution is likely. Specific motives that influence attribution include the desire to defend deep-seated beliefs, to enhance one's self-esteem, to increase one's sense of control over the environment, and to strengthen the favorable impression of oneself that others have.

The desire to defend cherished beliefs and stereotypes may lead observers to engage in biased attribution. Observers may interpret actions that correspond with their stereotypes as caused by the actor's personal dispositions. For instance, they may attribute a female executive's outburst of tears during a crisis to her emotional instability because that corresponds to their stereotype about women. At the same time, people attribute actions that contradict stereotypes to situational causes. If the female executive manages the crisis smoothly, the same people may credit this to the effectiveness of her male assistant. When observers selectively attribute behaviors that contradict stereotypes to situational influences, these behaviors reveal nothing new about the persons who perform them. As a result, the stereotypes persist (Hamilton, 1979). Social psychologists refer to our tendency to view our initial assumption as correct despite evidence to the contradictory as **belief perseverance** (Ross, Lepper & Hubbard, 1975).

Motivational biases may also influence attributions for success and failure. People tend to take credit for acts that yield positive outcomes, whereas they deflect blame for bad outcomes and attribute them to external causes (Bradley, 1978; Campbell & Sedikides, 1999; Ross & Fletcher, 1985). This phenomenon, referred to as the **self-serving bias**, is illustrated clearly by athletes' reporting of the results of competitions (Lau & Russell, 1980; Ross & Lumsden, 1982). Whereas members of winning teams take credit for winning ("We won"), members of losing teams are more likely to attribute the outcome to an external cause—their opponent ("They won," not "We lost"). Students are similar. In a study in which college students were asked to explain the grades they received on three examinations (Bernstein, Stephan, & Davis, 1979), students who received As and Bs attributed their grades much more to their own effort and ability than to good luck or easy tests. However, students who received Cs, Ds, and Fs attributed their grades largely to bad luck and the difficulty of the tests. Other studies show similar effects (Reifenberg, 1986).

Various motives may contribute to this self-serving bias in attributions of performance. For instance, attributing success to personal qualities and failure to external factors enables us to enhance or protect our self-esteem. Regardless of the outcome, we can continue to see ourselves as competent and worthy. Moreover, by avoiding the attribution of failure to personal qualities, we maximize our sense of control. This in turn supports the belief that we can master challenges successfully if we choose to apply ourselves because we possess the necessary ability.

Attributions for Success and Failure

Given motivational biases, how do observers (and actors) decide which of these is the "real" cause of success or failure? For students, football coaches, elected officials, and anyone else whose fate rides on evaluations of their performance, attributions for success and failure are vital. As observers realize, however, attributions of this type are problematic. Whenever someone succeeds at a task, a variety of explanations can be advanced for the outcome. For example, a student who passes a test could credit her own intrinsic ability ("I have a lot of intelligence"), her effort ("I really studied for that exam"), the easiness of the task ("The exam could have been much more difficult"), or even luck ("They just happened to test us on the few articles I read").

These four factors—ability, effort, task difficulty, and luck—are general and apply in many settings. When observers look at an event and try to figure out the cause of

Table 5.3 Perceived Causes of Success and Failure

Degree of Stability	Locus of Control	
	Internal	**External**
Stable	Ability	Task difficulty
Unstable	Effort	Luck

Source: Adapted from Weiner, Heckhausen, Meyer, and Cook, 1972.

success or failure, they must consider two things. First, they must decide whether the outcome is due to causes within the actor (an internal or dispositional attribution) or due to causes in the environment (an external or situational attribution). Second, they must decide whether the outcome is a stable or an unstable occurrence. That is, they must determine whether the cause is a permanent feature of the actor or the environment or whether it is labile and changing. Only after observers make judgments regarding internality-externality and stability-instability can they reach conclusions regarding the cause(s) of the success or failure.

As various theorists (Heider, 1958; Weiner, 1986; Weiner et al., 1971) have pointed out, the four factors aforementioned—ability, effort, task difficulty, and luck—can be grouped according to internality-externality and stability-instability. Ability, for instance, is usually considered internal and stable. That is, observers usually construe ability or aptitude as a property of the person (not the environment), and they consider it stable because it does not change from moment to moment. In contrast, effort is internal and unstable. Effort or temporary exertion is a property of the person that changes depending on how hard he or she tries. Task difficulty depends on objective task characteristics, so it is external and stable. Luck or chance is external and unstable. Table 5.3 displays these relations.

Determinants of Attributed Causes

Whether observers attribute a performance to internal or external causes depends on how the actor's performance compares with that of others. We usually attribute extreme or unusual performances to internal causes. For example, we would judge a tennis player who wins a major tournament as extraordinarily able or highly motivated. Similarly, we would view a player who has an unusually poor performance as weak in ability or unmotivated. In contrast, we usually attribute average or common performances to external causes. If defeat comes to a player halfway through the tournament, we are likely to attribute it to tough competition or perhaps bad luck.

Whether observers attribute a performance to stable or unstable causes depends on how consistent the actor's performance is over time (Frieze & Weiner, 1971). When performances are very consistent, we attribute the outcome to stable causes. Thus, if a tennis player wins tournaments consistently, we would attribute this success to her great talent (ability) or perhaps to the uniformly low level of her opponents (task difficulty). When performances are very inconsistent, however, we attribute the outcomes to unstable causes rather than stable ones. Suppose, for example, that our tennis player is unbeatable one day and a pushover the next. In this case, we would attribute the outcomes to fluctuations in motivation (effort) or to random external factors such as wind speed, court condition, and so on (luck).

Consequences of Attributions

Attributions for performance are important because they influence both our emotional reactions to success and failure and our future expectations and aspirations. For instance, if we attribute a poor exam performance to lack of ability, we may despair of future success and give up studying; this is especially likely if we view ability as given and not controllable by us. Alternatively, if we attribute the poor exam performance to lack of effort, we may feel shame or guilt, but we are likely to study harder and expect improvement. If we attribute the poor exam performance to bad luck, we may experience feelings of surprise or bewilderment, but we are not likely to change our study habits, because the situation will not seem controllable; despite this lack of change, we might nevertheless expect improved grades in the future. Finally, if we attribute our poor performance to the difficulty of the exam, we may become angry, but we do not strive for improvement (McFarland & Ross, 1982; Valle & Frieze, 1976; Weiner, 1985, 1986).

Summary

Social perception is the process of using information to construct understandings of the social world and form impressions of people.

Schemas

A schema is a well-organized structure of cognitions about some social entity. (1) There are several distinct types of schemas: person schemas, self-schemas, group schemas (stereotypes), role schemas, and event schemas (scripts). (2) Schemas organize information in memory and, therefore, affect what we remember and what we forget. Moreover, they guide our inferences and judgments about people and objects.

Person Schemas and Group Stereotypes

(1) One important type of person schema is an implicit personality theory—a set of assumptions about which personality traits go together with other traits. These schemas enable us to make inferences about other people's traits. We can depict an implicit personality theory as a mental map. (2) A stereotype is a fixed set of characteristics attributed to all members of a given group. American culture includes stereotypes for ethnic, racial, gender, and many other groups. Because stereotypes are overgeneralizations, they cause errors in inference; this is especially true in complex situations.

Impression Formation

(1) Research on trait centrality using the "warm/cold" variable illustrates how variations in a single trait can produce a large difference in the impression formed by observers of a stimulus person. (2) Information received early usually has a larger impact on impressions than information received later; this is called the primacy effect. (3) Impressions become self-fulfilling prophecies when we behave toward others according to our impressions and evoke corresponding reactions from them. (4) Impressions are informed by schemas that are selected through mental shortcuts called heuristics.

Attribution Theory

Through attribution, people infer an action's causes from its effects. (1) One important issue in attribution is locus of causality—dispositional (internal) versus situational (external) attributions. Observers follow the subtractive rule when making attributions to dispositions or situations. (2) To attribute specific dispositions to an actor, observers observe an act and its effects and then try to infer the actor's intention with respect to that act. Observers then attribute the disposition that corresponds best with the actor's inferred intention. (3) Observers who have information about an actor's behaviors in many situations make attributions to the actor, object, or context. The attribution made depends on which of these causes covaries with the behavior in question. Observers assess covariation by considering consensus, consistency, and distinctiveness information.

Bias and Error in Attribution

(1) Observers frequently overestimate personal dispositions as causes of behavior and underestimate situational pressures; this bias is called the fundamental attribution error. (2) Observers also overestimate the causal impact of whatever their attention is focused on. (3) Actors and observers have different attribution

tendencies. Actors attribute their own behavior to external forces in the situation, whereas observers attribute the same behavior to the actor's personal dispositions. (4) Motivations—needs, interests, and goals—lead people to make self-serving, biased attributions. People defend deep-seated beliefs by attributing behavior that contradicts their beliefs to situational influences. People defend their self-esteem and sense of control by attributing their failures to external causes and taking personal credit for their successes.

Attributions for Success and Failure

Observers attribute success or failure to four basic causes—ability, effort, task difficulty, and luck. They attribute consistent performances to stable rather than to unstable causes, and they attribute average performances to external rather than internal causes.

Critical Thinking Skill: Understanding Stereotyping

Although our culture makes it seem as though there are vast differences between men and women, the scientific data show a very different picture. Men and women are actually quite similar on most, though not all, psychological characteristics, including behaviors such as math performance and leadership (Hyde, 2005). If men and women are so similar, why do people like to believe they are so different?

The answers lie in stereotypes and motives for stereotyping. As noted in the chapter, a stereotype is a generalization about a group of people (e.g., men) that distinguishes those people from another group (e.g., women). Gender stereotypes abound. Women are talkative, and men have little to say. Women are submissive, whereas men are dominant. Women are best suited for the humanities and social sciences, whereas men excel at science and math. When we collect rigorous scientific data, it turns out that some stereotypes are fairly accurate and some are not. For example, it turns out that although men tend to dominate task-oriented groups and women acquiesce (Ridgeway, 2011), gender differences in talkativeness is tiny (Leaper & Smith, 2004) and girls and boys perform equally on standardized math tests (Hyde et al., 2008) (see also Box 5.1).

If so many stereotypes turn out not to be accurate, why do people continue to stereotype? Although this chapter introduced cognitive efficiency as a possible explanation, another motivation is self-enhancement.

We make ourselves feel better by denigrating people from another group. For example, if we say or think, "Teenagers are so irresponsible," by implication we, as adults, are much more responsible. Although when people stereotype for cognitive efficiency, the stereotypes can be positive or negative, when people stereotype for self-enhancement purposes, the stereotypes tend to be negative.

How does this illuminate potential reasons for gender stereotyping? Answer this question before you proceed to the next paragraph.

When people engage in gender stereotyping, sometimes it is for cognitive efficiency. Assuming that a man is interested in sports allows us to know what to ask him when we see him. Other times, people engage in gender stereotyping for self-enhancement purposes. A man might say, "You women are so emotional," which makes him feel emotionally in control and masculine. Or a woman might say, "Men are just clueless about how other people feel," making her feel good about her skills at reading others' emotions.

Good critical thinking involves understanding why people stereotype and acknowledging that stereotypes are often not accurate. The next time you hear someone (or yourself!) making a stereotyped comment (whether based on gender, race, age, or other differences), ask yourself two questions: (1) What is the person's/your goal in stereotyping? and (2) Is this an accurate stereotype that is supported by scientific data?

References

Abele, A. E. (2003). The dynamics of masculine-agentic and feminine-communal traits: Findings from a prospective study. *Journal of Personality and Social Psychology*, *85*, 768–776.

Abelson, R. P. (1981). The psychological status of the script concept. *American Psychologist*, *36*, 715–729.

Ajzen, I., & Holmes, W. H. (1976). Uniqueness of behavioral effects in causal attribution. *Journal of Personality*, *44*, 98–108.

Allison, S. T., Mackie, D. M., Muller, M. M., & Worth, L. T. (1993). Sequential correspondence biases and perceptions of change: The Castro studies revisited. *Personality and Social Psychology Bulletin*, *19*, 151–157.

Allport, G. W., & Postman, L. J. (1947). *The psychology of rumor*. New York: Holt, Rinehart & Winston.

Al-Zahrani, S. S. A., & Kaplowitz, S. A. (1993). Attributional biases in individualistic and collectivistic cultures: A comparison of Americans with Saudis. *Social Psychology Quarterly*, *56*, 223–233.

Anderson, C. A., & Sedikides, C. (1991). Thinking about people: Contribution of a typological alternative to associationistic and dimensional models of person perception. *Journal of Personality and Social Psychology*, *60*, 203–217.

Asch, S. E. (1946). Forming impressions of personality. *Journal of Abnormal and Social Psychology, 41,* 258–290.

Ashmore, R. D. (1981). Sex stereotypes and implicit personality theory. In D. L. Hamilton (Ed.), *Cognitive processes in stereotyping and intergroup behavior* (pp. 37–81). Hillsdale, NJ: Erlbaum.

Baudson, T. G., & Preckel, F. (2013). Teachers' implicit personality theories about the gifted: An experimental approach. *School Psychology Quarterly, 28*(1), 37–46.

Bem, S. (1974). The measurement of psychological androgyny. *Journal of Consulting and Clinical Psychology, 42,* 155–162.

Bergen, D., & Williams, J. (1991). Sex stereotypes in the United States revisited: 1972–1988. *Sex Roles, 24,* 413–423.

Bernstein, W. M., Stephan, W. G., & Davis, M. H. (1979). Explaining attributions for achievement: A path analytic approach. *Journal of Personality and Social Psychology, 37,* 1810–1821.

Bodenhausen, G. V., & Lichtenstein, M. (1987). Social stereotypes and information processing strategies: The impact of task complexity. *Journal of Personality and Social Psychology, 52,* 871–880.

Bogle, K. A. (2007). The shift from dating to hooking up in college: What scholars have missed. *Sociology Compass, 1*(2), 775–788.

Bornstein, R. (1992). Subliminal mere exposure effects. In R. Bornstein & T. Pittman (Eds.), *Perception without awareness: Cognitive, clinical, and social perspectives* (pp. 101–210). New York: Guilford Press.

Bradley, G. W. (1978). Self-serving biases in the attribution process: A reexamination of the fact or fiction question. *Journal of Personality and Social Psychology, 36,* 56–71.

Brand, R. J., Bonatsos, A., D'Orazio, R., & DeShong, H. (2012). What is beautiful is good, even online: Correlations between photo attractiveness and text attractiveness in men's online dating profiles. *Computers in Human Behavior, 28*(1), 166–170.

Broverman, I., Vogel, S., Broverman, D., Clarkson, F., & Rosenkrantz, P. (1972). Sex-role stereotypes: A current appraisal. *Journal of Social Issues, 28*(2), 59–78.

CNN. (2012, March 20). 911 calls paint picture of chaos after Florida teen is shot. http://news.blogs.cnn.com/2012/03/20/911-calls-paint-picture-of-chaos-after-florida-teen-is-shot/.

Cadinu, M. R., & Rothbart, M. (1996). Self-anchoring and differentiation processes in minimal group settings. *Journal of Personality and Social Psychology, 70,* 661–677.

Campbell, D. T. (1967). Stereotypes in the perception of group differences. *American Psychologist, 22,* 817–829.

Campbell, W. K., & Sedikides, C. (1999). Self-threat magnifies the self-serving bias: A meta-analysis integration. *Review of General Psychology, 3,* 23–43.

Cano, I., Hopkins, N., & Islam, M. R. (1991). Memory for stereotype-related material: A replication study with real-life social groups. *European Journal of Social Psychology*, *21*, 349–357.

Catrambone, R., & Markus, H. (1987). The role of self-schemas in going beyond the information given. *Social Cognition*, *5*, 349–368.

Cheng, P. W., & Novick, L. R. (1990). A probabilistic contrast model of causal induction. *Journal of Personality and Social Psychology*, *58*, 545–567.

Cohen, E. G. (1980). Design and redesign of the desegregated school: Problems of status, power, and conflict. In W. G. Stephan & J. Feagin (Eds.), *School desegregation*. (pp. 251–280). New York: Academic Press.

Cohen, G., Steele, C. M., & Ross, L. D. (1999). The mentor's dilemma: Providing critical feedback across the racial divide. *Personality and Social Psychology Bulletin*, *25*, 1302–1318.

Cohen, M. J., & Wade, T. J. (2012). Individual differences in first and fourth year college women's short term mating strategy preferences and perceptions. *Psychology*, *3*(11), 966–973.

Colley, A., Mulhern, G., Maltby, J., & Wood, A. M. (2009). The short form BSRI: Instrumentality, expressiveness and gender associations among a United Kingdom sample. *Personality and individual differences*, *46*(3), 384–387.

Cooper, W. H. (1981). Ubiquitous halo. *Psychological Bulletin*, *90*, 218–244.

Correll, S. J., Benard, S., & Paik, I. (2007). Getting a job: Is there a motherhood penalty? *American Journal of Sociology*, *112*(5), 1297–1339.

Crano, W. D. (1977). Primacy versus recency in retention of information and opinion change. *Journal of Social Psychology*, *101*(1), 87–96.

Cuddy, A. J., Fiske, S. T., & Glick, P. (2007). The BIAS map: Behaviors from intergroup affect and stereotypes. *Journal of Personality and Social Psychology*, *92*(4), 631–648.

Darley, J. M., & Fazio, R. H. (1980). Expectancy confirmation processes arising in the social interaction sequence. *American Psychologist*, *35*, 867–881.

Davis, L. R., & Harris, O. (1998). Race and ethnicity in US sports media. *MediaSport*, 154–169.

Dawes, R. M. (1998). Behavioral decision making and judgement. In D. Gilbert, S. Fiske, & G. Lindzey (Eds.), *The handbook of social psychology* (4th ed., Vol. 1, pp. 497–548). New York: McGraw-Hill.

Der-Karabetian, A., & Smith, A. (1977). Sex-role stereotyping in the United States: Is it changing? *Sex Roles*, *3*, 193–198.

Diekman, A. B., Eagly, A. H., Mladinic, A., & Ferreira, M. C. (2005). Dynamic stereotypes about women and men in Latin America and the United States. *Journal of Cross-Cultural Psychology*, *36*, 209–226.

Dion, K. L., & Schuller, R. A. (1991). The Ms. stereotype: Its generality and its relation to managerial and marital status stereotypes. *Canadian Journal of Behavioural Science, 23,* 25–40.

Dovidio, J. F., & Gaertner, S. L. (1996). Affirmative action, unintentional racial biases, and intergroup relations. *Journal of Social Issues, 52*(4), 51–75.

Dreben, E. K., Fiske, S. T., & Hastie, R. (1979). The independence of evaluative and item information: Impression and recall order effects in behavior-based impression formation. *Journal of Personality and Social Psychology, 37,* 1758–1768.

Eagly, A., & Steffen, V. J. (1984). Gender stereotypes stem from distribution of women and men into social roles. *Journal of Personality and Social Psychology, 46,* 735–754.

Eckes, T. (1995). Features of situations: A two-mode clustering study of situation prototypes. *Personality and Social Psychology Bulletin, 21,* 366–374.

Fejfar, M. C., & Hoyle, R. H. (2000). Effect of private self-awareness on negative affect and self-referent attribution. *Personality and Social Psychology Review, 4,* 132–142.

Fisicaro, S. A. (1988). A reexamination of the relation between halo error and accuracy. *Journal of Applied Psychology, 73,* 239–244.

Fiske, S. T., Cuddy, A. J., & Glick, P. (2007). Universal dimensions of social cognition: Warmth and competence. *Trends in Cognitive Sciences, 11*(2), 77–83.

Fiske, S. T., Cuddy, A. J., Glick, P., & Xu, J. (2002). A model of (often mixed) stereotype content: Competence and warmth respectively follow from perceived status and competition. *Journal of Personality and Social Psychology, 82*(6), 878–902.

Fiske, S. T., & Linville, P. (1980). What does the schema concept buy us? *Personality and Social Psychology Bulletin, 6,* 543–557.

Fiske, S. T., & Neuberg, S. L. (1990). A continuum model of impression formation, from category-based to individuating processes: Influence of information and motivation on attention and interpretation. In M. P. Zanna (Ed.), *Advances in experimental social psychology* (Vol. 23, pp. 1–74). San Diego, CA: Academic Press.

Fiske, S. T., & Taylor, S. E. (1991). *Social cognition* (2nd ed.). New York: McGraw-Hill.

Forbes, G. B., Adams-Curtis, L. E., White, K. B., & Hamm, N. R. (2002). Perceptions of married women and married men with hyphenated surnames. *Sex Roles, 46*(5–6), 167–175.

Forgas, J. P. (2011). Can negative affect eliminate the power of first impressions? Affective influences on primacy and recency effects in impression formation. *Journal of Experimental Social Psychology, 47*(2), 425–429.

Frieze, I., & Weiner, B. (1971). Cue utilization and attributional judgments for success and failure. *Journal of Personality, 39,* 591–605.

Furnham, A. (1986). The robustness of the recency effect: Studies using legal evidence. *Journal of General Psychology, 113*(4), 351–357.

Gilbert, D. T., & Malone, P. S. (1995). The correspondence bias. *Psychological Bulletin, 117*, 21–38.

Glenn, N., & Marquardt, E. (2001). *Hooking up, hanging out, and hoping for Mr. Right.* New York: Institute for American Values. www.americanvalues.org/search/item.php?id=18.

Goodwin, S. A., Gubin, A., Fiske, S. T., & Yzerbyt, V. Y. (2000). Power can bias impression processes: Stereotyping subordinates by default and by design. *Group Processes and Intergroup Relations, 3*, 227–256.

Grant, P. R., & Holmes, J. G. (1981). The integration of implicit personality schemas and stereotype images. *Social Psychology Quarterly, 44*, 107–115.

Griffin, D., Gonzalez, R., & Varey, C. (2001). The heuristics and biases approach to judgment under uncertainty. In A. Tesser & N. Schwartz (Eds.), *Blackwell handbook of social psychology: Intraindividual processes.* (pp. 207–235). Oxford, UK: Blackwell.

Guimond, S., Begin, G., & Palmer, D. L. (1989). Education and causal attributions: The development of "person-blame" and "system-blame" ideology. *Social Psychology Quarterly, 52*(2), 126–140.

Guimond, S., & Palmer, D. L. (1990). Type of academic training and causal attributions for social problems. *European Journal of Social Psychology, 20*(1), 61–75.

Hamilton, D. L. (1979). A cognitive-attributional analysis of stereotyping. In L. Berkowitz (Ed.), *Advances in experimental social psychology* (Vol. 12, pp. 53–85). New York: Academic Press.

Hamilton, D. L. (1981). Stereotyping and intergroup behavior: Some thoughts on the cognitive approach. In D. L. Hamilton (Ed.), *Cognitive processes in stereotyping and intergroup behavior* (pp. 333–353). Hillsdale, NJ: Erlbaum.

Hassin, R., & Trope, Y. (2000). Facing faces: Studies on the cognitive aspects of physiognomy. *Journal of Personality and Social Psychology, 78*, 837–852.

Heider, F. (1944). Social perception and phenomenal causality. *Psychological Review, 51*, 258–374.

Heider, F. (1958). *The psychology of interpersonal relations.* New York: Wiley.

Hepburn, C., & Locksley, A. (1983). Subjective awareness of stereotyping: Do we know when our judgments are prejudiced? *Social Psychology Quarterly, 45*, 311–318.

Hess, T. M., Auman, C., Colcombe, S. J., & Rahhal, T. A. (2003). The impact of stereotype threat on age differences in memory performance. *Journals of Gerontology Series B: Psychological Sciences and Social Sciences, 58*(1), P3–P11.

Hess, T. M., & Slaughter, S. J. (1990). Schematic knowledge influences on memory for scene information in young and older adults. *Developmental Psychology, 26*, 855–865.

Hewstone, M., & Jaspars, J. (1987). Covariation and causal attribution: A logical model of the intuitive analysis of variance. *Journal of Personality and Social Psychology, 53*, 663–672.

Higgins, E. T., & Bargh, J. A. (1987). Social cognition and social perception. *Annual Review of Psychology, 38,* 369–425.

Higgins, E. T., & Bryant, S. L. (1982). Consensus information and the fundamental attribution error: The role of development and in-group versus out-group knowledge. *Journal of Personality and Social Psychology, 47,* 422–435.

Holst, V. F., & Pezdek, K. (1992). Scripts for typical crimes and their effects on memory for eyewitness testimony. *Applied Cognitive Psychology, 6*(7), 573–587.

Holt, C. L., & Ellis, J. B. (1998). Assessing the current validity of the Bem Sex-Role Inventory. *Sex Roles, 39*(11–12), 929–941.

Hue, C., & Erickson, J. R. (1991). Normative studies of sequence strength and scene structure of 30 scripts. *American Journal of Psychology, 104,* 229–240.

Hyde, J., Lindberg, S., Linn, M., Ellis, A., & Williams, C. (2008). Gender similarities characterize math performance. *Science, 321,* 494–495.

Hyde, J. S. (2005). The gender similarities hypothesis. *American Psychologist, 60*(6), 581–592.

Johnson, J. T., & Boyd, K. R. (1995). Dispositional traits versus the content of experience: Actor/observer differences in judgments of the "authentic self." *Personality and Social Psychology Bulletin, 21,* 375–383.

Jones, E. E. (1979). The rocky road from acts to dispositions. *American Psychologist, 34,* 107–117.

Jones, E. E., & Davis, K. E. (1965). From acts to dispositions. In L. Berkowitz (Ed.), *Advances in experimental social psychology* (Vol. 2, pp. 219–266). New York: Academic Press.

Jones, E. E., & Goethals, G. R. (1971). *Order effects in impression formation: Attribution context and the nature of the entity.* Morristown, NJ: General Learning Press.

Jones, E. E., & Harris, V. A. (1967). The attribution of attitudes. *Journal of Experimental Social Psychology, 3,* 1–24.

Jones, E. E., & McGillis, D. (1976). Correspondent inferences and the attribution cube: A comparative reappraisal. In J. H. Harvey, W. J. Ickes, & R. F. Kidd (Eds.), *New directions in attribution research* (Vol. 1, pp. 389–420). Hillsdale, NJ: Erlbaum.

Jones, E. E., & Nisbett, R. (1972). The actor and observer: Divergent perceptions of the causes of behavior. In E. E. Jones, D. E. Kanouse, H. H. Kelley, R. E. Nisbett, S. Valins, & B. W. Weiner (Eds.), *Attribution: Perceiving the causes of behavior.* (pp. 79–94). Morristown, NJ: General Learning Press.

Jones, E. E., Rock, L., Shaver, K. G., Goethals, G. R., & Ward, L. M. (1968). Pattern of performance and ability attribution: An unexpected primacy effect. *Journal of Personality and Social Psychology, 10,* 317–340.

Kahneman, D., & Tversky, A. (1973). On the psychology of prediction. *Psychological Review, 80,* 237–251.

Kelley, H. H. (1950). The warm-cold variable in first impressions. *Journal of Personality*, *18*, 431–439.

Kelley, H. H. (1967). Attribution theory in social psychology. In D. Levine (Ed.), *Nebraska symposium in motivation, 1967*. (pp. 192–238). Lincoln: University of Nebraska Press.

Kelley, H. H. (1972). Causal schemata and the attribution process. In E. Jones, D. Kanouse, H. Kelley, R. Nisbett, S. Valms, & B. Weiner (Eds.), *Attribution: Perceiving the causes of behavior*. (pp. 151–176). Morristown, NJ: General Learning Press.

Kelley, H. H. (1973). The process of causal attribution. *American Psychologist*, *28*, 107–128.

Kelley, H. H., & Michela, J. L. (1980). Attribution theory and research. *Annual Review of Psychology*, *31*, 457–501.

Krull, D. S., & Dill, J. C. (1996). On thinking first and responding fast: Flexibility in social inference processes. *Personality and Social Psychology Bulletin*, *22*, 949–959.

Lachman, S. J., & Bass, A. R. (1985). A direct study of halo effect. *Journal of Psychology*, *119*, 535–540.

Lau, R. R., & Russell, D. (1980). Attributions in the sports pages. *Journal of Personality and Social Psychology*, *39*, 29–38.

Lawton, C. A., Blakemore, J. E. O., & Vartanian, L. R. (2003). The new meaning of Ms.: Single, but too old for Miss. *Psychology of Women Quarterly*, *27*(3), 215–220.

Leaper, C., & Smith, T. E. (2004). A meta-analytic review of gender variations in children's language use: talkativeness, affiliative speech, and assertive speech. *Developmental Psychology*, *40*(6), 993–1027.

Lipe, M. G. (1991). Counterfactual reasoning as a framework for attribution theories. *Psychological Bulletin*, *109*, 456–471.

Lonsdale, A. J. (2009). The social psychology of music and musical taste. Doctoral dissertation, Heriot Watt University, UK. www.ros.hw.ac.uk/handle/10399/2275.

Lonsdale, A. J., & North, A. C. (2012). Musical taste and the representativeness heuristic. *Psychology of Music*, *40*(2), 131–142.

Lord, C. G., Lepper, M. R., & Mackie, D. (1984). Attitude prototypes as determinants of attitude-behavior consistency. *Journal of Personality and Social Psychology*, *46*, 1254–1266.

Lottes, I. L., & Kuriloff, P. J. (1994). The impact of college experience on political and social attitudes. *Sex Roles*, *31*, 31–54.

Luchins, A. S. (1957). Experimental attempts to minimize the impact of first impressions. In C. I. Hovland (Ed.), *The order of presentation in persuasion*. (pp. 62–75). New Haven, CT: Yale University Press.

Manis, M., Shedler, J., Jonides, J., & Nelson, T. E. (1993). Availability heuristic in judgments of set size and frequency of occurrence. *Journal of Personality and Social Personality*, *65*, 448–457.

Markus, H. (1977). Self-schemas and processing information about the self. *Journal of Personality and Social Psychology, 35,* 63–78.

Markus, H., & Zajonc, R. B. (1985). The cognitive perspective in social psychology. In G. Lindzey & E. Aronson (Eds.), *Handbook of social psychology* (3rd ed., Vol. 1, pp. 137–230). New York: Random House.

Markus, H. R., & Kitayama, S. (1991). Culture and the self: Implications for cognition, emotion, and motivation. *Psychological Review, 98,* 224–253.

Martin, C. L. (1987). A ratio measure of sex stereotyping. *Journal of Personality and Social Psychology, 52,* 489–499.

Mayer, J. D., Rapp, H. C., & Williams, L. (1993). Individual differences in behavioral prediction: The acquisition of personal-action schemata. *Personality and Social Psychology Bulletin, 19,* 443–451.

McArthur, L. Z. (1972). The how and what of why: Some determinants and consequences of causal attribution. *Journal of Personality and Social Psychology, 22,* 171–193.

McArthur, L. Z., & Post, D. L. (1977). Figural emphasis and person perception. *Journal of Experimental Social Psychology, 13,* 520–535.

McCauley, C., Stitt, C. L., & Segal, M. (1980). Stereotyping: From prejudice to prediction. *Psychological Bulletin, 87,* 195–208.

McFarland, C., & Ross, M. (1982). The impact of causal attributions on affective reactions to success and failure. *Journal of Personality and Social Psychology, 43,* 937–946.

McGarty, C., Yzerbyt, V. Y., & Spears, R. (Eds.). (2002). *Stereotypes as explanations: The formation of meaningful beliefs about social groups.* Cambridge University Press.

Miller, A. G. (1976). Constraint and target effects on the attribution of attitudes. *Journal of Experimental Social Psychology, 12,* 325–339.

Miller, A. G. (Ed.). (1982). *In the eye of the beholder: Contemporary issues in stereotyping.* New York: Praeger.

Minnigerode, F., & Lee, J. A. (1978). Young adults' perceptions of sex roles across the lifespan. *Sex Roles, 4,* 563–569.

Morris, M. W., & Larrick, R. P. (1995). When one cause casts doubt on another: A normative analysis of discounting in causal attribution. *Psychological Review, 102,* 331–355.

Moss-Racusin, C. A., Dovidio, J. F., Brescoll, V. L., Graham, M. J., & Handelsman, J. (2012). Science faculty's subtle gender biases favor male students. *Proceedings of the National Academy of Sciences, 109*(41), 16474–16479.

Mussweiler, T., Strack, F., & Pfeiffer, T. (2000). Overcoming the inevitable anchoring effect: Considering the opposite compensates for selective accessibility. *Personality and Social Psychology Bulletin, 26,* 1142–1150.

National Endowment for the Arts. (2008). Survey of public participation in the arts 2008 [MRDF]. Washington, DC: National Endowment for the Arts [producer]. Princeton, NJ: Cultural Policy and the Arts National Data Archive [distributor].

Nickerson, R. S. (1998). Confirmation bias: A ubiquitous phenomenon in many guises. *Review of General Psychology*, *2*(2), 175–220.

Nisbett, R. E., Caputo, C., Legant, P., & Maracek, J. (1973). Behavior as seen by the actor and as seen by the observer. *Journal of Personality and Social Psychology*, *27*, 154–164.

Norenzayan, A., & Nisbett, R. E. (2000). Culture and causal cognition. *Current Directions in Psychological Science*, *9*, 132–135.

Pager, D., Western, B., & Bonikowski, B. (2009). Discrimination in a low-wage labor market a field experiment. *American Sociological Review*, *74*(5), 777–799.

Paul, E. L., & Hayes, K. A. (2002). The casualties of casual sex: A qualitative exploration of the phenomenology of college students' hookups. *Journal of Social and Personal Relationships*, *19*(5), 639–661.

Plant, E. A., & Peruche, B. M. (2005). The consequences of race for police officers' responses to criminal suspects. *Psychological Science*, *16*(3), 180–183.

Plant, E. A., Peruche, B. M., & Butz, D. A. (2005). Eliminating automatic racial bias: Making race nondiagnostic for responses to criminal suspects. *Journal of Experimental Social Psychology*, *41*(2), 141–156.

Pleck, J. H. (1976). The male sex role: Definitions, problems, and sources of change. *Journal of Social Issues*, *32*(3), 155–164.

Prager, I. G., & Cutler, B. L. (1990). Attributing traits to oneself and to others: The role of acquaintance level. *Personality and Social Psychology Bulletin*, *16*, 309–319.

Pruitt, D. G., & Insko, C. A. (1980). Extension of the Kelley attribution model: The role of comparison-object consensus, target-object consensus, distinctiveness, and consistency. *Journal of Personality and Social Psychology*, *39*, 39–58.

Rahn, W. M. (1993). The role of partisan stereotypes in information processing about political candidates. *American Journal of Political Science*, *37*(2), 472–496.

Reifenberg, R. J. (1986). The self-serving bias and the use of objective and subjective methods for measuring success and failure. *Journal of Social Psychology*, *126*, 627–631.

Rentfrow, P. J., & Gosling, S. D. (2007). The content and validity of music-genre stereotypes among college students. *Psychology of Music*, *35*(2), 306–326.

Richeson, J. A., & Ambady, N. (2003). Effects of situational power on automatic racial prejudice. *Journal of Experimental Social Psychology*, *39*, 177–183.

Ridgeway, C. L. (2011). *Framed by gender: How gender inequality persists in the modern world*. New York: Oxford University Press.

Rosenberg, S. V., Nelson, C., & Vivekananthan, P. S. (1968). A multidimensional approach to the structure of personality impressions. *Journal of Personality and Social Psychology, 9,* 283–294.

Rosenberg, S. V., & Sedlak, A. (1972). Structural representations in implicit personality theory. In L. Berkowitz (Ed.), *Advances in experimental social psychology* (Vol. 6, pp. 235–297). New York: Academic Press.

Rosenhan, D. L. (1973). On being sane in insane places. *Science, 179,* 250–258.

Rosenthal, R., & Jacobson, L. (1968). *Pygmalion in the classroom: Teacher expectation and pupils' intellectual development.* New York: Rinehart and Winston.

Ross, L. (1977). The intuitive psychologist and his shortcomings: Distortion in the attribution process. In L. Berkowitz (Ed.), *Advances in experimental social psychology* (Vol. 10, pp. 173–220). New York: Academic Press.

Ross, L., Lepper, M. R., & Hubbard, M. (1975). Perseverance in self-perception and social perception: biased attributional processes in the debriefing paradigm. *Journal of Personality and Social Psychology, 32*(5), 880–892.

Ross, L. D. (2001). Getting down to fundamentals: Lay dispositionism and the attributions of psychologists. *Psychological Inquiry, 12,* 37–40.

Ross, M., & Fletcher, G. (1985). Attribution and social perception. In G. Lindzey & E. Aronson (Eds.), *The handbook of social psychology* (3rd ed., pp. 73–122). Reading, MA: Addison-Wesley.

Ross, M., & Lumsden, H. (1982). Attributions of responsibility in sports settings: It's not how you play the game but whether you win or lose. In H. Hiebsch, H. Brandstatter & H. H. Kelley (Eds.), *Social psychology.* East Berlin: Deutscher Verlag der Wissenschaften.

Rothbart, M. (1996). Category-exemplar dynamics and stereotype change. *International Journal of Intercultural Relations, 20*(3), 305–321.

Rothbart, M., Fulero, S., Jensen, C., Howard, J., & Birrell, B. (1978). From individual to group impressions: Availability heuristics in stereotype formation. *Journal of Experimental Social Psychology, 14,* 237–255.

Sabini, J., Siepmann, M., & Stein, J. (2001). The really fundamental attribution error in social psychological research. *Psychological Inquiry, 12,* 1–15.

Sailes, G. A. (1998). The African American athlete: Social myths and stereotypes. In G. A. Sailes (Ed.), *African Americans in sport: Contemporary themes* (pp. 183–198). New Brunswick: NJ: Transaction.

Schank, R. C., & Abelson, R. P. (1977). *Scripts, plans, goals and understanding.* Hillsdale, NJ: Erlbaum.

Sherman, J. W., Lee, A. Y., Bessenoff, G. R., & Frost, L. A. (1998). Stereotype efficiency reconsidered: Encoding flexibility under cognitive load. *Journal of Personality and Social Psychology, 75*(3), 589–606.

Sherman, S. J., Judd, C. M., & Park, B. (1989). Social cognition. *Annual Review of Psychology*, *40*, 281–326.

Simon, W., & Gagnon, J. H. (2003). Sexual scripts: Origins, influences and changes. *Qualitative Sociology*, *26*(4), 491–497.

Skowronski, J. J., & Carlston, D. E. (1989). Negativity and extremity biases in impression formation: A review of explanations. *Psychological Bulletin*, *105*, 131–142.

Small, K. H., & Peterson, J. (1981). The divergent perceptions of actors and observers. *Journal of Social Psychology*, *113*, 123–132.

Smith, P. B., & Bond, M. H. (1994). *Social psychology across cultures: Analysis and perspectives*. Needham Heights, MA: Allyn and Bacon.

Snyder, M. (1981). On the self-perpetuating nature of social stereotypes. In D. L. Hamilton (Ed.), *Cognitive processes in stereotyping and intergroup behavior*. (pp. 183–212). Hillsdale, NJ: Erlbaum.

Snyder, M., & Swann, W. B. (1978). Hypothesis-testing processes in social interaction. *Journal of Personality and Social Psychology*, *36*, 1202–1212.

Spencer, S. J., Steele, C. M, & Quinn, D. M. (1999). Stereotype threat and women's math performance. *Journal of Experimental Social Psychology*, *35*, 4–28.

Steele, C. M. (1997). A threat in the air: How stereotypes shape the intellectual identities and performance of women and African-Americans. *American Psychologist*, *52*, 613–629.

Steele, C. M. (1999, August). Thin ice: "Stereotype threat" and Black college students. *Atlantic Monthly*, *284*(2), 44–47, 50–54.

Steele, C. M. (2010). *Whistling Vivaldi: And other clues to how stereotypes affect us*. New York: W. W. Norton.

Steele, C. M., & Aronson, J. (1995). Stereotype threat and the intellectual test performance of African-Americans. *Journal of Personality and Social Psychology*, *69*, 797–811.

Steiner, D. D., & Rain, J. S. (1989). Immediate and delayed primacy and recency effects in performance evaluation. *Journal of Applied Psychology*, *74*, 136–142.

Sternberg, R. J. (1985). Implicit theories of intelligence, creativity, and wisdom. *Journal of Personality and Social Psychology*, *49*, 607–627.

Stone, J., Lynch, C. I., Sjomeling, M., & Darley, J. M. (1999). Stereotype threat effects on Black and White athletic performance. *Journal of Personality and Social Psychology*, *77*(6), 1213–1227.

Storms, M. D. (1973). Videotape and attribution process: Reversing actors' and observers' points of view. *Journal of Personality and Social Psychology*, *27*, 165–175.

Taylor, S. E. (1981). A categorization approach to stereotyping. In D. L. Hamilton (Ed.), *Cognitive processes in stereotyping and intergroup behavior* (pp. 83–114). Hillsdale, NJ: Erlbaum.

Taylor, S. E., & Crocker, J. (1981). Schematic bases of social information processing. In E. T. Higgins, C. P. Herman, & M. P. Zanna (Eds.), *Social cognition: The Ontario symposium* (Vol. 1, pp. 89–134). Hillsdale, NJ: Erlbaum.

Taylor, S. E., & Fiske, S. T. (1978). Salience, attention, and attribution: Top of the head phenomena. In L. Berkowitz (Ed.), *Advances in experimental social psychology* (Vol. 11, pp. 249–288). New York: Academic Press.

Taylor, S. E., Fiske, S. T., Etcoff, N. L., & Ruderman, A. J. (1978). The categorical and contextual bases of person memory and stereotyping. *Journal of Personality and Social Psychology, 36*, 778–793.

Thomsen, C. T., & Borgida, E. (1996). Throwing out the baby with the bathwater? Let's not overstate the overselling of the base rate fallacy. *Behavioral and Brain Sciences, 19*, 39–40.

Thorndike, E. L. (1920). A constant error in psychological ratings. *Journal of Applied Psychology, 4*, 25–29.

Triandis, H. C. (1995). *Individualism and collectivism.* Boulder, CO: Westview Press.

Trope, Y., & Cohen, O. (1989). Perceptual and inferential determinants of behavior-correspondent attributions. *Journal of Experimental Social Psychology, 25*(2), 142–158.

Trope, Y., Cohen, O., & Maoz, Y. (1988). The perceptual and inferential effects of situational inducements on dispositional attribution. *Journal of Personality and Social Psychology, 55*(2), 165–177.

Tversky, A., & Kahneman, D. (1974). Judgment under uncertainty: Heuristics and biases. *Science, 185*, 1124–1131.

Valle, V. A., & Frieze, I. H. (1976). Stability of causal attributions as a mediator in changing expectations for success. *Journal of Personality and Social Psychology, 35*, 579–589.

Watson, D. (1982). The actor and the observer: How are their perceptions of causality divergent? *Psychological Bulletin, 92*, 682–700.

Weber, R., & Crocker, J. (1983). Cognitive processes in the revision of stereotypic beliefs. *Journal of Personality and Social Psychology, 45*, 961–977.

Weiner, B. (1985). An attributional theory of achievement motivation and emotion. *Psychological Review, 92*, 548–573.

Weiner, B. (1986). *An attributional theory of motivation and emotion.* New York: Springer Verlag.

Weiner, B., Frieze, I., Kukla, A., Reed, L., Rest, B., & Rosenbaum, R. M. (1971). *Perceiving the causes of success and failure.* Morristown, NJ: General Learning Press.

Weiner, B., Heckhausen, H., Meyer, W. U., & Cook, R. E. (1972). Causal ascriptions and achievement behavior: A conceptual analysis of effort and reanalysis of locus of control. *Journal of Personality and Social Psychology, 21*, 239–248.

Wilcox, C., & Williams, L. (1990). Taking stock of schema theory. *Social Science Journal, 27,* 373–393.

Wilson, T. D., Houston, C. E., Etling, K. M., & Brekke, N. C. (1996). A new look at anchoring effects: Basic anchoring and its antecedents. *Journal of Experimental Psychology: General, 125,* 387–402.

Winschild, P. D., & Wells, G. L. (1997). Behavioral consensus information affects people's inferences about population traits. *Personality and Social Psychology Bulletin, 23,* 148–156.

Zanna, M. P., & Hamilton, D. L. (1977). Further evidence for meaning change in impression formation. *Journal of Experimental Social Psychology, 13,* 224–238.

Zebrowitz, L. A., Andreoletti, C., Collins, M. A., Lee, S. Y., & Blumenthal, J. (1998). Bright, bad, babyfaced boys: Appearance stereotypes do not always yield self-fulfilling prophecy effects. *Journal of Personality and Social Psychology, 75,* 1300–1320.

Attributions Journal Real-World Lab

Name: _____

Date: _____

Keep a diary of your day and note behaviors of others that surprised you. You could look at the behaviors of your classmates, roommates, friends, and so on. Surprising behaviors do not have to be shocking; they just have to be unexpected. For example, did someone unexpectedly get up in the middle of class and leave? This is probably an unexpected behavior. Write about at least five behaviors on the worksheet. "Watch" your brain make sense of these unexpected behaviors. Then decide whether your initial attribution was based on personality/disposition or situation. Finally, describe whether you modified your original attribution, and if you did, why. Did you gain more information or give them the benefit of the doubt once you thought it through?

For each behavior entry, include the following:

1. The behavior you witnessed and why it was surprising
2. What your brain did to make sense of the behavior (e.g., Did it compare the behavior to past experiences with the person? Did it think something was wrong or off?)
3. Whether you made a situational or personality/dispositional attribution and why

Behavior 1:

1. _____

2. _____

3. _____

Behavior 2:

1. _____

2. _____

3. _____

Behavior 3:

1. _____

2. _____

3. _____

Behavior 4:

1. _____

2. _____

3. _____

Behavior 5:

1. _____

2. _____

3. _____

1. How did stereotypes influence the attributions you made? If they didn't, explain instead how you've used stereotypes when interacting with stranger(s) recently.

_____

_____

_____

CHAPTER 6

Communication Goals
Message Effectiveness and Persuasion

Introduction to the Chapter

People use persuasion techniques every day without realizing it. Think about the last time you talked your friends into seeing the movie you wanted to see, asked your parents for money, or talked your professor into giving you a deadline extension. Chances are, sometimes you reach your goal and successfully get that extension on your paper deadline but other times your persuasion attempts fail. In this chapter, you will learn how persuasion works and why you are successfully able to persuade others some of the time. You might even learn how to increase your chances of successfully persuading others. This chapter introduces the concept of compliance gaining, or getting others to do something they weren't planning to do before (for example, your professor giving you that paper extension). You will learn how researchers have come to understand persuasion and compliance gaining through interesting research experiments. You will also learn 16 different compliance-gaining techniques ranging from moral appeals to threatening others. Finally, you'll learn about contextual factors like cultural and individual differences that affect which persuasion strategies work best in different situations.

Selections from "Interpersonal Persuasion"

By Richard M. Perloff

B ernae Gunderson, a paralegal specialist from St. Paul, has no difficulty deciphering the fine print of legal documents. Still, she was puzzled by materials
she received from her mortgage company. They didn't jibe with the home equity
loan she and her husband had been promised. Mrs. Gunderson called the company,
First Alliance Corporation, asked questions about monthly payments and fees, and
was promptly reassured that her understanding of the loan was indeed correct.
What Mrs. Gunderson was not told—but soon would discover—was that First
Alliance had tacked on $13,000 in fees to the loan, and the interest rate rose a full
percentage point every 6 months (Henriques & Bergman, 2000).

First Alliance, it turned out, used deceptive sales procedures to promote its
services. Sued by regulators in five states, the company recruited unsuspecting
borrowers using a high-level con game and elaborate sales pitch that was designed
to snooker people into paying higher fees and interest rates than were justified by
market factors. The company's loan officers were required to memorize a 27-page
selling routine that included the following gambits:

- Establish rapport and a common bond. Initiate a conversation about jobs,
  children, or pets. Say something funny to get them laughing.
- To soften the financial blow, when talking about dollar amounts, say "merely,"
  "simply," or "only."
- If the customer asks questions about fees, just reply, "May I ignore your
  concern about the rate and costs if I can show you that these are minor issues
  in a loan?"
- If all else fails and the sale appears to be lost, say, "I want to apologize for being
  so inept a loan officer. I want you to know that it's all my fault, and I'm truly
  sorry. Just so I don't make the same mistake again, would you mind telling me
  what I did that was wrong? Didn't I cover that?" (And get right back into it.)

(Henriques & Bergman, 2000, p. C12).

There is nothing wrong with using persuasion techniques to make a sale. The problem is that First Alliance trained its loan officers to deceive customers about its services. They lied about the terms of home equity loans and refused to come clean when people like Bernae Gunderson raised questions. They were experts in using strategies of interpersonal persuasion. Unfortunately, they exploited their knowledge, manipulating individuals into signing off on deals that were unduly expensive and unfair.

Interpersonal persuasion, the centerpiece of First Alliance's promotional campaign and subject of this chapter, offers a glimpse into a realm of persuasion that is somewhat different from those discussed so far in the book. Unlike purely psychological approaches, it focuses on the dyad, or two-person unit (persuader and persuadee). In contrast to attitude-based research, it centers on changing behavior—on inducing people to comply with the persuader's requests. Unlike message-oriented persuasion research, which focuses on modifying views about political or social issues, it explores techniques people employ to accomplish interpersonal objectives—for example, how they "sell themselves" to others.

Drawing on the fields of interpersonal communication and social psychology, interpersonal persuasion research examines the strategies people use to gain compliance. It looks at how individuals try to get their way with others (something we all want to do). It examines techniques businesses use to convince customers to sign on the dotted line, strategies charities employ to gain donations, and methods that health practitioners use to convince people to take better care of their health. To gain insight into these practical issues, interpersonal persuasion scholars develop theories and conduct empirical studies—both experiments and surveys. In some ways, this is the most practical, down-to-earth chapter in the book; in other ways, it is the most complicated because it calls on taxonomies and cognitive concepts applied to the dynamic dance of interpersonal communication. [...].

The first portion of the chapter looks at a variety of techniques that have amusing sales pitch names like foot-in-the-door and door-in-the-face. These persuasive tactics are known as **sequential influence techniques**, in which persuasive communications follow one another in a step-by-step fashion. Influence in such cases "often proceeds in stages, each of which establishes the foundation for further changes in beliefs or behavior. Individuals slowly come to embrace new opinions, and actors often induce others to gradually comply with target requests" (Seibold, Cantrill, & Meyers, 1994, p. 560). The second section of the chapter focuses more directly on the communication aspect of interpersonal persuasion. It looks at the strategies that people—you, me, our friends, and parents—use to gain compliance, how researchers study this, and the many factors that influence compliance-gaining.

Compliance-Gaining

You want to dine out with someone, but you disagree about which restaurant it is going to be; someone in the department must do an unpleasant job, but you want to make sure that in any case it will not be you; you want to make new work arrangements, but you are afraid your boss will not agree; you want to get your partner to come with you to that tedious family party, but you suspect that he or she does not want to come along.

(van Knippenberg et al., 1999, p. 806)

Add to these more serious requests for compliance: an effort to convince a close friend to return to school after having dropped out for a couple of years, a doctor's attempt to persuade a seriously overweight patient to pursue an exercise program, a husband's effort to persuade his wife to quit hitting the bottle. Such requests are pervasive in everyday life. They speak to the strong interest human beings have in getting their way—that is, in persuading others to comply with their requests and pleas. This section of the chapter moves from an exploration of how professional persuaders achieve their goals to an examination of us—how we try to gain compliance in everyday life. The area of research is appropriately called compliance-gaining.

Compliance-gaining is defined as "any interaction in which a message source attempts to induce a target individual to perform some desired behavior that the target otherwise might not perform" (Wilson, 2002, p. 4). Notice that the focus of compliance-gaining is on communication. It examines not only the psychology of the individual's request for compliance, but also the broader interaction, the dyadic (one-on-one) conversation between people, or among individuals. This is important because it calls attention to the dynamic interpersonal dance that characterizes so much of everyday persuasion. Interpersonal communication scholars, who have pioneered research in this area, have sought to understand how individuals try to get others to go along with their requests in social situations. They have probed the strategies people use, the impact of context on compliance-gaining strategies, and the goals individuals pursue to gain compliance from others.

How We Study Compliance-Gaining

One of the daunting issues researchers face is how to empirically study a broad area, like compliance-gaining. They could devise experiments of the sort conducted by psychologists researching FITD and DITF. Although these would allow researchers to test hypotheses, they would not tell them how compliance-gaining works in the real world that lies outside the experimenter's laboratory. Scholars could observe people trying to gain compliance—on the job, at school, or in social settings like bars (that might be fun!). However, this would provide an endless amount of data, too much to code meaningfully. Dissatisfied with these methodologies, scholars hit on the idea of conducting surveys that ask people how they would gain compliance, either in situations suggested by the researcher or in an open-ended manner, in the individuals' own words.

The first survey method is *closed-ended* in that it provides individuals with hypothetical situations and asks them to choose among various strategies for compliance. For example, researchers have asked participants to imagine that they have been carrying on a close relationship with a person of the opposite sex for 2 years. Unexpectedly, an old acquaintance happens to be in town one evening. Desirous of getting together with their old friend, but mindful that their current boyfriend or girlfriend is counting on getting together that night, respondents are asked to indicate how they would try to convince their current steady to let them visit their former acquaintance (Miller et al., 1977).

Subjects have also been asked to imagine that their neighbors, whom they do not know very well, own a dog that barks almost all night. This in turn incites the other local canines to do the same. Students are asked how they would attempt to convince the neighbors to curb their dog's nighttime antics (Cody, McLaughlin, & Jordan, 1980). Individuals are provided with a list of strategies, such as friendly appeals, moral arguments, manipulative tactics, and threats. They are asked to indicate on a Likert scale how likely they would be to use these techniques. (See Box 6.1 for a practical example of a closed-ended compliance-gaining measurement technique.)

Box 6.1 Compliance-Gaining At The Health Club

What techniques do salespersons at a health club use to induce customers to join? (See Figure 6.1.)

Some years back, one of my students, Karen Karp, visited a local health club and talked to salespeople in search of an answer to this question. Karp pretended she was interested in joining and listened as the salesperson made his spiel. She then categorized his responses using a classic scheme devised by Marwell and Schmitt (1967). Based on what the salesman had said and her extrapolations from the interview, she and I developed an example of each of the 16 Marwell and Schmitt tactics.

(Continued)

Figure 6.1 Thinking of joining a health club to shed some pounds? Be prepared for the health club's sales representative to employ some "friendly persuasion"! He or she will try to hook you by pitching a variety of classic compliance-gaining strategies—direct and indirect, rational and nonrational, and external and internal.

Image courtesy of iStock.

Tactic Example

1. Promise (If you comply, I will reward you)

   "If you begin your membership today, you'll receive a bonus of three free months."

2. Threat (If you do not comply I will punish you)

   "If you do not join today, you may find that people are kind of mean to you when you do join."

3. Expertise (If you comply, you will be rewarded because of "the nature of (positive) things")

   "Joining will guarantee that you'll maintain your health and that you'll get all the benefits of a healthy, totally in-shape body."

4. Expertise (If you do not comply, you will be punished because of "the nature of (negative) things")

   "If you do not join you'll end up looking fat."

5. Liking (Actor is friendly and helpful to get target in "good frame of mind" so that he will comply with request)

   "I think it's great that you've decided to begin an exercise program. The staff is here to help you reach your fitness goals."

6. Pre-giving (Actor rewards target before requesting compliance)

   "I'll give you a $50 bonus for coming in today; now, let's talk about how I can help you slim down."

7. Aversive stimulation (Actor continually punishes target, making cessation contingent upon compliance)

   "I won't let you leave this little room until you agree to join."

8. Debt (You owe me compliance because of past favors)

   "I've spent an hour showing you the club and demonstrating the machines; now I'm sure that you are ready to join."

9. Moral appeal (You are immoral if you do not comply)

   "Fitness is so important. I think it's almost immoral not to take good care of your health."

10. Self-feeling (You will feel better about yourself if you comply)

    (positive) "Why don't you sign up right now? You'll feel so good about yourself once you begin a workout program."

11. Self-feeling (You will feel worse about yourself if you do not comply)

    (negative) "You know how important regular exercise is. You'll feel bad about yourself if you do not take out a membership today."

12. Altercasting (A person with "good" qualities would comply)

    (positive) "I can tell that you're committed to looking and feeling healthy and fit. You're the kind of person who would really benefit from this club."

13. Altercasting (Only a person with "bad" qualities would not comply)

    (negative) "It's only laziness that keeps people from joining, but that's not you, is it?"

14. Altruism (I need your compliance very badly, so do it for me)

    (whispering) "I need to sign one more member this week."

15. Esteem (People you value will think better of you if you comply)

    (positive) "Begin a membership. Your family is going to be so proud of you when you start a fitness program."

16. Esteem (People you value will think worse of you if you do not comply)

    (negative) "Do not disappoint your family. Didn't you promise them that you would start taking better care of yourself?"

A second way to tap compliance-gaining is to use *open-ended* survey techniques. If a researcher wanted to employ an open-ended strategy, he or she might hand each respondent a sheet of paper. On the top of the page would appear the words:

On this page, write a paragraph about "How I Get My Way." Please be frank and honest (Falbo, 1977).

What would you say? How *do* you get your way? Are you rational, arguing incessantly like one of the nerds on the television program "The Big Bang Theory?" Are you a charmer, acting "sweety-sweet" until you get what you want? What *do* you do to get what you want? Researchers would classify the open-ended responses, placing them into a smaller number of categories that cut across different respondents' answers.

Closed- and open-ended techniques each have advantages and drawbacks. The closed-ended selection technique provides an efficient way to gather information. It also provides insights on how people try to gain compliance in representative life situations. Its drawback is that people frequently give socially desirable responses to closed-ended surveys. They are reluctant to admit that they sometimes use brutish, socially inappropriate tactics to get their way (Burleson et al., 1988).

The strength of the open-ended method is that it allows people to indicate, in their own words, how they get compliance. There is no speculation about hypothetical behavior in artificial situations. A drawback is that researchers must make sense of—and categorize—subjects' responses. This can be difficult and time consuming. Scholars may not fully capture or appreciate an individual's thought processes.

What We Know about Compliance-Gaining

Despite their limitations, when taken together, open- and closed-ended questionnaires have provided useful insights about compliance-gaining. Researchers, using both types of procedures, have devised a variety of typologies to map out the techniques people use to gain compliance. These typologies have yielded insights about the major strategies individuals (at least on American college campuses) use to influence others. Strategies can be classified according to whether they are:

1. *Direct versus indirect.* Direct techniques include assertion (voicing one's wishes loudly) and persistence (reiterating one's point). Indirect tactics include "emotion-target" (putting the other person in a good mood) and thought manipulation (trying to get your way by making the other person feel it is his idea) (Falbo, 1977; see also Dillard, Kinney, & Cruz, 1996).

2. *Rational versus nonrational.* Rational techniques include reason (arguing logically) and doing favors. Non-rational tactics include deceit (fast talking and lying) and threat (telling her I will never speak to her again if she doesn't do what I want) (Falbo, 1977).

3. *Hard-sell versus soft-sell.* Hard-sell tactics include yelling, demanding, and verbal aggression. Soft-sell techniques include kindness, flattery, and flirting (Kipnis & Schmidt, 1996).

4. *Dominance-based versus non-dominance-based.* Dominance-oriented strategies emphasize the power the communicator has over the target, while the latter employ a more egalitarian, conciliatory approach (Dillard et al., 1997).

5. *External versus internal.* Tactics can be externally focused, such as rewards or punishments. To motivate a child to study, a parent could use a carrot, like promise ("I'll raise your allowance if you study more"), or a stick, like aversive stimulation ("You're banned from driving until you hit the books"). Techniques can also be internally focused—that is, self-persuasion-type appeals designed to engage the recipient. These include positive self-feeling ("You'll feel good about yourself if you study a lot") and negative self-feeling ("You'll be disappointed with yourself in the long run if you don't study more"; see Marwell & Schmitt, 1967; Miller & Parks, 1982).

Notice that the same techniques can be categorized in several ways. Threat could be direct, nonrational, hard-ball, and external. Positive self-feeling could be indirect, rational, and soft-sell, as well as internal. This cross-categorization occurs because there is not one but a variety of compliance-gaining taxonomies, constructed by different scholars, for different purposes. Nonetheless, these five sets of labels provide a useful way of categorizing compliance-gaining behavior.

Contextual Influences

People are complex creatures. They use different techniques to gain compliance, depending on the situation. In one situation, a person may use reason; in another she may scream and yell, employing verbal aggression. We are all chameleons, to a degree. Which situations are the most critical determinants of compliance-gaining? Scholars have studied this issue, delineating a host of important contextual influences on strategy selection. The following factors are especially important.

Intimacy

Contexts differ in the degree to which they involve intimate associations between persuader and persuadee. As you move along the continuum from stranger to acquaintance to friend to lover or family member, you find that the same individual can behave very differently, depending on which of these "others" the person is trying to influence. In an old but still engaging study, Fitzpatrick and Winke (1979) reported that level of intimacy predicted use of conflict-reducing strategies. Focusing on people casually involved in romantic relationships, those in serious relationships, and married partners, the investigators found that married persons were especially likely to employ emotional appeals or personal rejections ("withholding affection and acting cold until he or she gives in") to resolve differences. "You always hurt the one you love," Fitzpatrick and Winke observed. They explained:

> Individuals in a more committed relationship generally have less concern about the strengths of the relational bonds. Consequently, they employ more spontaneous and emotionally toned strategies in their relational conflicts ... In the less committed relationships, the cohesiveness of the partners is still being negotiated ... Undoubtedly, it would be too risky for them to employ the more open conflict strategies of the firmly committed.
>
> (1979, p. 10)

This is not to say that everyone uses more emotional or highly manipulative tactics in intimate settings than in everyday interpersonal encounters. These findings emerged from one study, conducted at one point in time. However, research indicates that intimacy can exert an important impact on compliance-gaining behavior (Cody & McLaughlin, 1980).

Dependency

We use different strategies to gain compliance, depending on whether we are dependent on the person we are trying to influence. People are more reluctant to use hard-ball tactics when the other has control over important outcomes in their lives (van Knippenberg et al., 1999). Graduate teaching assistants who say they "dominate arguments" and "argue insistently" with disgruntled undergraduate students acknowledge that they prefer to use nonconfrontational techniques, even sidestepping disagreements, when discussing job-related conflicts with the professor (Putnam & Wilson, 1982). It is only natural to be more careful when trying to gain compliance from those who have control over important outcomes in your life. Thus, when people lack power, they are more likely to employ rational and indirect tactics "because no other power base is available to them" (Cody & McLaughlin, 1985).

Rights

People employ different tactics to get their way, depending on whether they believe they have the right to pursue a particular option. If they do not feel they have the moral right to make a request, they may use softer tactics. However, if they believe they have the right to make a request, or if they feel they have been treated unfairly, they are more apt to employ hard rather than soft techniques (van Knippenberg et al., 1999). Consider the marked change in tactics employed by people trying to convince smokers to quit smoking in public places. Decades ago, individuals who objected to smokers polluting public space said little, afraid they would offend smokers. Nowadays, nonsmokers, redefining the meaning of public space and feeling they have the right to insist that smokers not puff in public, frequently use uncompromising, even nonrational, tactics to induce smokers to put out a cigarette. This change in compliance-gaining strategies resulted from years of social protest against smoking. Protests against problematic social norms, and subsequent changes in the law, can empower ordinary people, encouraging them to use feistier techniques to get their way.

Cultural and Individual Differences

Individuals differ dramatically in how they go about trying to get their way. Some people are direct; others are shy. Some individuals worry a great deal about hurting others' feelings; other individuals care not a whit. Some people respect social conventions; other people disregard them.

If individuals differ in their compliance-gaining strategies, can research elucidate or specify the differences? You bet! Scholars have focused on two factors that influence compliance-gaining choices: the macro factor, culture, and a micro variable: the personality factor, self-monitoring.

One important aspect of culture is the degree to which the society emphasizes individualism or collectivism. Individualism stresses independence, self-determination, and pursuit of one's self-interest. Collectivism emphasizes concern with group harmony, maintaining positive interpersonal relationships, and a "we" rather than "I" identification. On a cultural level, Western nations like the United States are individualistic, while Asian societies, such as South Korea and Japan, tend to be more collectivist.

In intriguing studies, Min-Sun Kim and colleagues have found that culture influences choice of compliance-gaining strategies. When asked to identify the most important determinants of whether a request is effective, South Korean students emphasized the degree to which the request is sensitive to the other individual's feelings and does not create disapproval. By contrast, U.S. students maintained that a request is more effective when it is made as clearly and directly as possible. South Korean students regard an indirect strategy like hinting as relatively effective for gaining compliance, while American students put a higher premium on direct statements (Kim & Bresnahan, 1994; Kim & Wilson, 1994). Naturally, there are additional differences within Western and Asian cultures that complicate matters. Regardless of country of origin, students whose self-concepts revolve around independence place more emphasis on being direct. Students whose self-concepts center on group harmony put a higher premium on not hurting the other individual's feelings (Kim & Sharkey, 1995).

A second factor that influences compliance-gaining is the personality factor, self-monitoring. High self-monitors, attuned as they are to the requirements of the situation, tend to adapt their strategy to fit the person they are trying to influence (Caldwell & Burger, 1997). Low self-monitors are more apt to use the same technique with different people. High self-monitors are more likely to develop elaborate strategic plans prior to the actual influence attempt (Jordan & Roloff, 1997). In keeping with their concern with image management, high self-monitors are more apt than low self-monitors to include in their plans a consideration of how they could manipulate their personal impression so as to achieve their goals.

Do you use the same techniques with different people and across different situations? If so, you may be a low self-monitor. Do you vary your strategies to fit the constraints of the situation? In this case, you could be a high self-monitor. Research provides facts about compliance-gaining in everyday life and can also offer insights into our own behavior.

Application

Compliance-gaining richly explains people's choice of behavioral persuasion techniques in a variety of situations, ranging from the amusing—how individuals try to convince people not to give them traffic tickets (see Box 6.2)—to the serious: communication that occurs in medical settings. Compliance-gaining research has particularly enriching implications for health. It offers guidelines to doctors on how they can improve their style of communicating medical information, provides clues on how young adults can convince their partners to practice safe sex, and suggests ways that pre-teens can, say, turn down shady requests to experiment with drugs (Burgoon et al., 1989; Perloff, 2001).

To appreciate the ways this research can shed light on social problems, I invite you to consider another issue that has become so commonplace we have become desensitized to its serious effects. The problem is child abuse. Child abuse and neglect are important problems both in the United States and abroad. Parents can abuse their children through physical, sexual, and verbal aggression, as well as through outright neglect. Abusive parents employ a battery of cruel and aggressive strategies to induce their children to comply with their requests. Lynn Oldershaw and colleagues (1986) conducted an observational study to examine whether abusive mothers differed from non-abusive moms in their compliance-gaining strategies.

The researchers compared 10 physically abusive mothers and 10 non-abusive moms, watching them interact for 45 minutes with one of their children, a 2- to 4-year-old. They carefully classified the mothers' ways of seeking compliance from their toddlers, categorizing them into power-assertive techniques, such as threat, humiliation, and negative physical touch, and positive pro-social strategies like modeling, reasoning, and bargaining. There were stark and disturbing differences between abusive and comparison moms.

For abusive mothers, the interaction was all about their power over the child. They employed power-assertive strategies, like those used above, or were more likely than comparison mothers to command their children to engage in a particular behavior. They tended to issue their commands without offering any rationale and without conveying a favorable vocal tone. Not only were the abusive mothers' techniques cruel, they were ineffective. Abused children were less likely to comply with their mothers' requests for compliance than non-abused children. Even when their kids did comply, abusive mothers were as likely to respond with criticism, such as "It's about time you did that," as with compliments. Comparison mothers typically complimented their kids when they complied (see Wilson, 2010).

The study leaves a powerful imprint. One feels terrible for the kids: 2- to 4-year-old toddlers. But the implications are as important as the findings are heart-rending. If mothers could be taught to seek compliance in more humane ways, perhaps future abuse could be halted. We need to persuade moms to seek compliance in different ways. This is not an easy task. But, thanks to Oldershaw and his associates' study, we have some clues as to where to begin (see Figure 6.2).

Figure 6.2 Compliance-gaining research offers clues about how parents can gain compliance from their children without resorting to power-assertive techniques like threat or physical aggression.

Image courtesy of Shutterstock.

Box 6.2   Compliance and The Cops

You're driving home one evening, speeding a little because you've got to get ready for a party later that night. The radio's blaring and you're feeling good as you tap your fingers and sing the words of a song you've heard many times before. Out of the corner of your eye you see a couple of lights, but ignore them until you see them again—the telltale flashing light of a police car. Your heart skips a beat as you realize the police car is following you. The siren is sounding now and you get that terrible sinking feeling and agonizing fear that something bad is going to happen.

At this point, many of us faced with the impending possibility of a speeding ticket search our minds ferociously for an excuse, an extenuating reason, a white or black lie, a rhetorical rabbit we can pull out of the hat to convince the officer not to give us a ticket (see Figure 6.3). Of course, in an ideal world, if one ran afoul of the law, he or she would admit it and graciously take responsibility for the mistake. But this is not an ideal world, and many individuals are probably more willing to shade the truth a little than to come clean and suffer the indemnity of a fine and points on their record. Thus, many people try to persuade the police officer not to ticket them, relying on a variety of compliance-gaining techniques.

How do people try to secure compliance from a police officer when they are stopped for traffic violations? Jennifer Preisler and Todd Pinetti, students

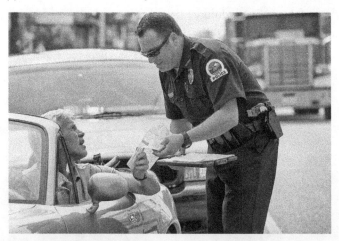

Figure 6.3 When a police officer turns on the flashing light and signals for a driver to pull over, people frequently dream up lots of reasons—some based in fact, others much less so—to persuade the officer not to give them a ticket. Individuals differ in the compliance-gaining techniques they employ (and their success in avoiding the ticket). Understandable as it is to try to persuade your way out of a ticket, the more prudent and safety-conscious approach is to acknowledge the error and try to be a better driver.
Image courtesy of Getty Images.

in a communication class some years back, explored this issue by talking with many young people who had found themselves in this predicament.

Their research, along with my own explorations, uncovered some interesting findings, including the following responses from young people regarding how they have tried to persuade a police officer not to ticket them:

- "I will be extra nice and respectful to the officer. I will apologize for my negligence and error. I tell them about the police officers I know."
- "I flirt my way out of it, smile a lot. [Or I say] 'My speedometer is broken. Honestly, it hasn't worked since August.'"
- "When I am stopped for speeding, I usually do not try to persuade the officer to not give me a ticket. He has the proof that I was speeding, so I don't try to insult his intelligence by making up some stupid excuse. I do try to look very pathetic and innocent, hoping maybe he will feel bad for me and not give me a ticket."
- "I turn on the dome light and turn off the ignition, roll down the window no matter how cold it is outside. I put my keys, driver's license, and proof of insurance on the dashboard, and put my hands at 10 and 2 on the wheel. I do all this before the officer gets to the window. I am honest and hope for the best. I have tried three times and all three were successful."
- "The officer said, 'I've been waiting for an idiot like you [who he could pull over for speeding] all night.' I told him, 'Yeah, I got here as fast as I could.' He laughed for about two minutes straight and let us go."
- "I gain compliance by smiling [big] and saying, 'Officer, what seems to be the problem?'"
- "I'm on my way to church."
- "The line that I have used to get out of a ticket is 'My wife's in labor.'"
- "My technique is when I am getting pulled over, I reach into my glove compartment and spray a dab of hair spray onto my finger. Then I put it in my eyes and I start to cry. I have gotten pulled over about 15 to 20 times and I have only gotten one ticket."

Many people suspect that gender intervenes—that is, male police officers are more forgiving of females than of males who violate a traffic law. Research bears this out. Male police officers issued a greater percentage of citations to male drivers than did female police officers. In a similar fashion, female police officers issued a greater percentage of their traffic citations to female drivers than did male officers (Koehler & Willis, 1994). Police officers may be more lenient with opposite-sex than same-sex offenders; they may find the arguments provided by opposite-sex individuals to be more persuasive because they are attracted sexually to the drivers. Or they may be less apt to believe excuses offered by members of their own gender.

Beyond Compliance-Gaining

Compliance-gaining research has richly informed our knowledge of inter-personal persuasion. Unfortunately, the area reached an impasse because of a series of procedural problems. For all the advantages that compliance-gaining typologies offer practitioners, they are filled with methodological problems. Strategies are frequently defined ambiguously, inconsistently, or so specifically that it is difficult to know what the strategies mean (Kellermann & Cole, 1994; see also Wilson, 2002). Critics have also noted that much of the research involves responses to hypothetical situations, rather than actual compliance-gaining behavior.

The good news is that the intuitive strength of the area—a down-to-earth explanation of how people go about gaining compliance—has generated new research perspectives. An important framework focuses on the persuasion objectives individuals seek to attain in interpersonal situations.

Interpersonal Persuasion Goals

The research begins with the insight that people do not approach compliance-gaining with a blank slate. Instead, they define a situation in a particular way, pursuing goals and enacting plans. People have primary and secondary goals (Dillard, Segrin, & Harden, 1989; Wilson, 2010). A primary goal structures the interaction, propelling individuals to seek a particular behavior from the target. Primary or key influence goals include:

- Asking a favor ("Can you drive me to the airport?")
- Giving advice ("I think you should quit drinking")
- Obtaining permission ("Professor, can I get an extension on my paper?")
- Sharing activity ("Let's see a movie"); and
- Enforcing obligations ("You promised to clean the kitchen. Come on, it's not fair if you don't do your part.")

(Dillard & Knobloch, 2011)

These are everyday, down-to-earth influence objectives. So too are secondary goals. Secondary goals determine how people approach their primary goal. Focusing on the interpersonal dynamics of the situation, secondary goals influence individuals as they pursue their primary objectives. Secondary goals include:

- maintaining a positive public impression, or face;
- avoiding behaviors that would tarnish another person's image or face;
- maintaining interpersonal relationships; and
- avoiding resource risks, such as wasting time or money.

It is a complex dance. People have multiple, sometimes conflicting, goals they want to accomplish in a particular situation (Dillard, 1990b). What's more, people are always balancing intrapersonal and interpersonal needs. They want to maintain their autonomy, yet need approval from others (Brown & Levinson, 1987). They want to get their way, but recognize that this can threaten another's image, autonomy, or "face" (Wilson, Aleman, & Leatham, 1998). They don't want to hurt the other's feelings, but recognize that if they are too nice they may kill the clarity of their request with politeness and ambiguity.

People frequently must balance their desire to achieve a *primary goal*—influencing the target's behavior—with an attempt to meet a *secondary goal* also, such as maintaining a good public impression, not damaging a friendship, or doing the morally right thing (Dillard, et al., 1989; Meyer, 2007; Wilson, 2002). There is a yin and yang between primary goals, which push the persuader toward action, and secondary goals, which pull or constrain the individual from going too far. We all have been in situations where we want to get our way, but realize that if we are too argumentative or dismissive of the other person's feelings, we will destroy a valued relationship.

Scholars have studied how people process these matters and go about balancing conflicting needs. Their models emphasize that people have elaborate cognitive structures regarding compliance-gaining and ways to achieve their goals (Wilson, 1999). This is fascinating because we all go about the business of trying to get our way, but rarely give any thought to how we think about trying to gain compliance or how we process, in our own minds, "all that stuff going on in the situation." Interpersonal communication models and research shed light on such issues.

Theoretical frameworks have focused on communicators' face or interpersonal presentation needs. People want to gain important others' approval of their inter-personal behavior (positive face), while not wanting to lose their autonomy or have their actions restricted without reason (negative face; see Brown & Levinson, 1987).

A core model that offers an integrative perspective to goals and interpersonal interaction is James P. Dillard's (1990b) goal-driven approach. According to a goals approach, when persuaders are more concerned with achieving primary than secondary goals, they will interpersonally engage the target, generating and editing plans to help implement the goal. When the primary and secondary goals are equally important, persuaders will choose an influence strategy that takes into account their concern about not thwarting secondary goals. In these cases, the dynamics of influence are more complex. Seeking a strategy that will not interfere with secondary goals, they may mentally consider or reformulate their plans before confronting the other person.

Application

To appreciate how all this works in real life, consider the following example:

Professors sometimes require group projects, in which students work together on a task and complete a group paper. While opinions are divided on group projects—some students find them unfair, others like group interaction—they have been a consistent part of university classes for a long time. The primary goal is successful completion of the project. A secondary goal arises when one student in the group fails to pull his weight and other students must decide how to communicate their dissatisfaction to the slacker in a way that preserves their reputation, does not unduly threaten the slacker's face, and does not destroy the relationship. If the primary goal is paramount, other students may tell the slacker off, demanding he put in his fair share of the work, with little concern about offending him. If primary and secondary goals are weighed equally—perhaps because the slacker is a friend—then the other students will tread more carefully, mentally mulling over strategies before they act, balancing bluntness with politeness, and perhaps avoiding a strategy that would totally embarrass their friend.

It is a dicey situation. Researchers find that when people possess incompatible goals—such as trying to convince a target to do something she most definitely does not want to do, while at the same time not hurting her feelings in the slightest—they pause more and don't communicate as effectively (Greene et al., 1993). The incongruity of goals puts stress on the mental system. Thus, the best advice in this situation may be not to beat around the bush. Persuaders may be most effective when they honestly and unambiguously share their objection to the slacker, in a way that respects their friend's autonomy, but also communicates the importance of the primary goal.

Of course, as any of us who have valiantly embarked on this strategy only to be ignored or criticized by our slacker friend will attest, this technique is not guaranteed to work. Much depends on the content of the request, the manner in which it is implemented, and the personality of the persuader and target. The nature of the relationship also matters. Strategies will vary, depending on so-called intimacy (how well you know the slacker and nature of the interpersonal relationship), dominance (whether one of you has power over the other), and the benefits that the paper and the relationship offer both parties.

If this strikes you as interesting, but vague, you are right! The strength of interpersonal persuasion research has been in articulating the cognitive and situational dynamics of interpersonal influence contexts. Its shortcoming has been in laying out predictions or hypotheses about optimum strategies to achieve persuasion goals. Nevertheless, the interpersonal goals approach helpfully advances knowledge by shedding light on the cognitive and interpersonal dynamics of everyday compliance-gaining situations. It underscores the emotional messiness of everyday persuasion. By articulating goals and the mental activities in which persuaders engage, it helps to clarify the nature of interpersonal persuasion.

Ethical Issues

"Communication is founded on a presumption of truth," two scholars aptly note (Buller & Burgoon, 1996, p. 203). Yet persuasion commonly involves some shading of truth, a tinting that is rationalized by persuaders and lamented by message receivers. Interpersonal persuasion—from the sequential influence techniques discussed earlier in the chapter to the endless variety of compliance-gaining tactics just described—sometimes seems to put a premium on distorting communication in the service of social influence. Distorting communication in the service of social influence? A blunter, more accurate way to describe this is "lying."

Lying is remarkably common in everyday life. In two diary studies, college students reported that they told two lies a day. They admitted they lied in one of every three of their social interactions (DePaulo et al., 1996). To be sure, some of these lies were told to protect other people from embarrassment, loss of face, or having their feelings hurt. However, other lies were told to enhance the psychological state of the liars—for example, to make the liars appear better than they were, to protect them from looking bad, or to protect their privacy. Many of these were white lies that we have told ourselves; others were darker distortions, outright falsehoods (DePaulo et al., 1996).

Persuasion—from sequential influence tactics to compliance gaining—is fraught with lies. Even flattery involves a certain amount of shading of truth, a convention that many people admittedly enjoy and cherish (Stengel, 2000). All this has stimulated considerable debate among philosophers over the years. As discussed in Chapter 2, utilitarians argue that a lie must be evaluated in terms of its consequences. Deontological thinkers tend to disapprove of lies in principle because they distort truth. Related approaches emphasize that what matters is the motivation of the liar—a lie told for a good, virtuous end may be permissible under some circumstances (Gass & Seiter, 2011).

We cannot resolve this debate. In my view, social discourse—and the warp and woof of social influence—contain much truth, shading of truth, and lies. They also contain certain corrective mechanisms. Those who lie habitually run the risk of earning others' disapproval, or finding that even their truthful statements are disbelieved. Social norms operate to discourage chronic lying. So too do psychodynamic mechanisms that have evolved over human history. Guilt and internalized ethical rules help regulate people's desire to regularly stretch the truth.

However, a certain amount of lying is inevitable, indeed permissible, in everyday interpersonal communication. Social influence—and persuasive communication— are human endeavors, part of the drama of everyday life, in which people are free to pursue their own ends, restrained by internalized moral values and social conventions (Scheibe, 2000). Democratic, civilized society enshrines people's freedom to pursue their own interests and celebrates those who can exert influence over others. The "downside" of this is that some people will abuse their freedom and seek to manipulate others, distorting truth and using deceitful tactics. Human evolution has not yet evolved to the point that ethics totally trumps (or at least restrains) self-interest, and perhaps it never will. The best hope is education: increased self-understanding, development of humane values, and (trite as it may sound) application of the time-honored, but always relevant, Golden Rule.

Conclusions

This chapter has examined interpersonal persuasion—the many techniques individuals use to influence one another in dyadic or one-on-one interactions. Social psychological research has documented that gambits like foot-in-the-door and door-in-the-face can be especially effective in securing compliance. Make no mistake: these tactics do not always work, and many consumers have learned to resist them. However, they are used regularly in sales and pro-social charity work; under certain conditions, for various psychological reasons, they can work handily. Other tactics employed by professional persuaders—pre-giving exchange, low-balling, "that's-not-all," fear-then-relief, pique, and disrupt-then-reframe—can also influence compliance.

In everyday life, we employ a variety of tactics to get our way. Interpersonal communication scholars have developed typologies to categorize these techniques. Strategies vary in their directness, rationality, and emphasis on self-persuasion. Different strategies are used in different situations, and the same person may use a direct approach in one setting and a cautious, indirect technique in another. Culture and personality factors like self-monitoring also place limits on compliance-gaining choices. Compliance-gaining research has illuminated knowledge of interpersonal persuasion. Its strength is its rich exploration of dyadic interactions. Its shortcomings include absence of theory and lack of precision in strategy measurement.

Other approaches have extended interpersonal persuasion research, notably, those that explore the nature of primary and secondary goals. A primary goal structures an interaction between people, while a secondary objective focuses on the interpersonal dynamics of the situation. In some instances, what began as a secondary goal—maintaining a positive public face or not hurting someone's feelings—can become the preeminent goal in the situation.

Everyday interpersonal persuasion is complex and dynamic. Persuaders are constantly editing and reformulating plans so that they can balance primary and secondary goals. Compliance choices vary as a function of whether a primary or secondary goal is paramount, the nature of the situation, and the feelings that the compliance-gaining elicits. Research, focusing on ever-more cognitive aspects of individuals' strategic choices, is shedding light on the dynamics of everyday interpersonal persuasion.

Given the central role that interpersonal persuasion plays in everyday life and in business transactions, it behooves us to understand and master it. A practical strategy that experts suggest is to look to the behavior of highly effective persuaders. Successful persuaders recognize that persuasion requires give and take, flexibility, and ability to see things from the other party's point of view (Cody & Seiter, 2001; Delia, Kline, & Burleson, 1979; Waldron & Applegate, 1998). "Effective persuaders have a strong and accurate sense of their audience's emotional state, and they adjust the tone of their arguments accordingly," observes Jay A. Conger (1998, p. 93). He notes that they plan arguments and self-presentational strategies in advance and "enter the persuasion process prepared to adjust their viewpoints and incorporate others' ideas. That approach to persuasion is, interestingly, highly persuasive in itself" (p. 87).

References

Brown, P., & Levinson, S. C. (1987). *Politeness: Some universals in language usage*. Cambridge, UK: Cambridge University Press.

Buller, D. B., & Burgoon, J. K. (1996). Interpersonal deception theory. *Communication Theory, 6*, 203–242.

Burgoon, M., Parrott, R., Burgoon, J., Birk, T., Pfau, M., & Coker, R. (1989). Primary care physicians' selection of verbal compliance-gaining strategies. *Health Communication, 2*, 13–27.

Burleson, B. R., Wilson, S. R., Waltman, M. S., Goering, E. M., Ely, T. K., & Whaley, B. B. (1988). Item desirability effects in compliance gaining research: Seven studies documenting artifacts in the strategy selection procedure. *Human Communication Research, 14*, 429–486.

Caldwell, D. F., & Burger, J. M. (1997). Personality and social influence strategies in the workplace. *Personality and Social Psychology Bulletin, 23*, 1003–1012.

Cody, M. J., & McLaughlin, M. L. (1980). Perceptions of compliance-gaining situations: A dimensional analysis. *Communication Monographs, 47,* 132–148.

Cody, M. J., & McLaughlin, M. L. (1985). The situation as a construct in interpersonal communication research. In M. L. Knapp & G. R. Miller (Eds.), *Handbook of interpersonal communication* (pp. 263–312). Beverly Hills, CA: Sage.

Cody, M. J., McLaughlin, M. L., & Jordan, W. J. (1980). A multidimensional scaling of three sets of compliance-gaining strategies. *Communication Quarterly, 28,* 34–46.

Cody, M. J., & Seiter, J. S. (2001). Compliance principles in retail sales in the United States. In W. Wosinska, R. B. Cialdini, D. W. Barrett, & J. Reykowski (Eds.), *The practice of social influence in multiple cultures* (pp. 325–341). Mahwah, NJ: Lawrence Erlbaum Associates.

Delia, J. G., Kline, S. L., & Burleson, B. R. (1979). The development of persuasive communication strategies in kindergartners through twelfth graders. *Communication Monographs, 46,* 241–256.

DePaulo, B. M., Kashy, D. A., Kirkendol, S. E., Wyer, M. M., & Epstein, J. A. (1996). Lying in everyday life. *Journal of Personality and Social Psychology, 70,* 979–995.

Dillard, J. P. (1990b). A goal-driven model of interpersonal influence. In J. P. Dillard (Ed.), *Seeking compliance: The production of interpersonal influence messages* (pp. 41–56). Scottsdale, AZ: Gorsuch-Scarisbrick.

Dillard, J. P., Kinney, T. A., & Cruz, M. G. (1996). Influence, appraisals, and emotions in close relationships. *Communication Monographs, 63,* 105–130.

Dillard, J. P., & Knobloch, L. K. (2011). Interpersonal influence. In M. L. Knapp & J. A. Daly (Eds.), *The Sage handbook of interpersonal communication* (4th ed., pp. 389–422). Thousand Oaks, CA: Sage.

Dillard, J. P., Segrin, C., & Harden, J. M. (1989). Primary and secondary goals in the production of interpersonal influence messages. *Communication Monographs, 56,* 19–38.

Dillard, J. P., Wilson, S. R., Tusing, K. J., & Kinney, T. A. (1997). Politeness judgments in personal relationships. *Journal of Language and Psychology, 16,* 297–325.

Falbo, T. (1977). Multidimensional scaling of power strategies. *Journal of Personality and Social Psychology, 35,* 537–547.

Fitzpatrick, M. A., & Winke, J. (1979). You always hurt the one you love: Strategies and tactics in interpersonal conflict. *Communication Quarterly, 27,* 1–11.

Gass, R. H., & Seiter, J. S. (2011). *Persuasion, social influence, and compliance gaining* (4th ed.). Boston: Allyn & Bacon.

Greene, J. O., McDaniel, T. L., Buksa, K., & Ravizza, S. M. (1993). Cognitive processes in the production of multiple-goal messages: Evidence from the temporal characteristics of speech. *Western Journal of Communication, 57,* 65–86.

Henriques, D. B., & Bergman, L. (2000, March 15). Profiting from fine print with Wall Street's help, *The New York Times,* A1, C12–C13.

Jordan, J. M., & Roloff, M. E. (1997). Planning skills and negotiator goal accomplishment: The relationship between self-monitoring and plan generation, plan enactment, and plan consequences. *Communication Research, 24,* 31–63.

Kellermann, K., & Cole, T. (1994). Classifying compliance gaining messages: Taxonomic disorder and strategic confusion. *Communication Theory, 4,* 3–60.

Kim, M. S., & Bresnahan, M. (1994). A process model of request tactic evaluation. *Discourse Processes, 18,* 317–344.

Kim, M. S., & Sharkey, W. F. (1995). Independent and interdependent construals of self: Explaining cultural patterns of interpersonal communication in multicultural organizational settings. *Communication Quarterly, 43,* 20–38.

Kim, M. S., & Wilson, S. R. (1994). A cross-cultural comparison of implicit theories of requesting. *Communication Monographs, 61,* 210–235.

Kipnis, D., & Schmidt, S. (1996). The language of persuasion. In E. J. Coats & R. S. Feldman (Eds.), *Classic and contemporary readings in social psychology* (pp. 184–188). Upper Saddle River, NJ: Prentice Hall.

Koehler, S. P., & Willis, F. N. (1994). Traffic citations in relation to gender. *Journal of Applied Social Psychology, 24,* 1919–1926.

Marwell, G., & Schmitt, D. R. (1967). Dimensions of compliance-gaining behavior: An empirical analysis. *Sociometry, 30,* 350–364.

Meyer, J. R. (2007). Compliance gaining. In D. R. Roskos-Ewoldsen & J. L. Monahan (Eds.), *Communication and social cognition: Theories and methods* (pp. 399–416). Mahwah, NJ: Erlbaum Associates.

Miller, G. R., Boster, F., Roloff, M., & Seibold, D. (1977). Compliance-gaining message strategies: A typology and some findings concerning effects of situational differences. *Communication Monographs, 44,* 37–51.

Miller, G. R., & Parks, M. R. (1982). Communication in dissolving relationships. In S. Duck (Ed.), *Personal relationships 4: Dissolving relationships* (pp. 127–154). Orlando, FL: Academic Press.

Oldershaw, L., Walters, G. C., & Hall, D. K. (1986). Control strategies and noncompliance in abusive mother-child dyads: An observational study. *Child Development, 57,* 722–732.

Perloff, R. M. (2001). *Persuading people to have safer sex: Applications of social science to the AIDS crisis.* Mahwah, NJ: Lawrence Erlbaum Associates.

Putnam, L. L., & Wilson, C. E. (1982). Communicative strategies in organizational conflicts: Reliability and validity of a measurement scale. In M. Burgoon (Ed.), *Communication yearbook 6* (pp. 629–652). Beverly Hills, CA: Sage.

Scheibe, K. E. (2000). *The drama of everyday life*. Cambridge, MA: Harvard University Press.

Seibold, D. R., Cantrill, J. G., & Meyers, R. A. (1994). Communication and interpersonal influence. In M. L. Knapp & G. R. Miller (Eds.), *Handbook of interpersonal communication* (2nd ed., pp. 542–588). Thousand Oaks, CA: Sage.

Stengel, R. (2000). *You're too kind: A brief history of flattery*. New York: Simon & Schuster.

van Knippenberg, B., van Knippenberg, D., Blaauw, E., & Vermunt, R. (1999). Relational considerations in the use of influence tactics. *Journal of Applied Social Psychology, 29,* 806–819.

Waldron, V. R., & Applegate, J. L. (1998). Person-centered tactics during verbal disagreements: Effects on student perceptions of persuasiveness and social attraction. *Communication Education, 47,* 53–66.

Wilson, S. R. (1999). Developing theories of persuasive message production: The next generation. In J. O. Greene (Ed.), *Message production* (pp. 15–44). Mahwah, NJ: Lawrence Erlbaum Associates.

Wilson, S. R. (2002). *Seeking and resisting compliance: Why people say what they do when trying to influence others*. Thousand Oaks, CA: Sage.

Wilson, S. R. (2010). Seeking and resisting compliance. In C. R. Berger, M. E. Roloff, & D. R. Roskos-Ewoldsen (Eds.), *The handbook of communication science* (2nd ed., pp. 219–235). Thousand Oaks, CA: Sage.

Wilson, S. R., Aleman, C. G., & Leatham, G. B. (1998). Identity implications of influence goals: A revised analysis of face-threatening acts and application to seeking compliance with same-sex friends. *Human Communication Research, 25,* 64–96.

Persuasion Real-World Lab

Name: _____

Date: _____

For this real-world lab, you will ask someone to do a favor for you. The favor should be relatively easy, but not something they would usually do. For example, I might ask my husband to take our dogs on a walk while I do something else in the house. We usually walk our dogs together or I take them out on my own, so my husband taking them out alone is relatively uncommon but not unheard of. You might ask a roommate to do your share of the chores or clean up your dishes or ask a coworker to help you out at work (if this is not part of their job description). Make sure it is something they *could* do but might take some convincing to do. Also make sure the favor is not something that will get you or the other person in trouble!

1. Before you ask for your favor, make a plan. Answer the following questions to create your plan:

   ○ What are you going to ask for?
   _____
   _____

   ○ Why might the person you are asking resist doing the favor for you?
   _____
   _____

   ○ Which compliance-gaining strategies are most appropriate for the favor you are asking?
   _____
   _____

   ○ Which compliance-gaining strategies will work best on the person you are asking?
   _____
   _____

   ○ How do you know? What do you know about them that helps you know which compliance-gaining strategies to use?
   _____
   _____

○ What, exactly, do you plan to say?

_____

_____

2. Go and ask for your favor. Then, report how it went.

○ Describe the interaction.

_____

_____

○ Did the conversation go according to plan? If yes, what worked well? If no, what went wrong?

_____

_____

○ Did the person agree to do the favor? Why do you think they agreed or disagreed?

_____

_____

3. Next, reflect on the last time someone asked you to do something you weren't already planning to do. Answer the questions about the interaction.

○ Who asked and what did they ask you to do? Briefly describe the situation.

_____

_____

○ How did they ask? Try to write down word for word what they said. If you have the conversation via text message or email, even better. Copy it.

_____

_____

○ Now, analyze their request for compliance-gaining strategies. What strategies did they use? Were they effective? Why or why not?

_____

_____

4. How can compliance-gaining strategies help us achieve our goals?

_____

_____

_____

CHAPTER 7

Attachment and Communication

Introduction to the Chapter

Attachment plays a role in how we relate to others and make sense of ourselves. This chapter details attachment theory and how attachment works across the lifespan. The chapter describes both infant and adult attachment, explains attachment theory, and describes how attachment figures change over time. You will learn about the "strange situation" and how attachment theory was developed. Perhaps most interesting is how our attachment bonds in childhood play a role in our relationships as adults. You will read about research that has identified how people with different attachment styles are unique from one another and whether people can change their attachment styles throughout their lives.

Selection from "Attachment Across the Lifespan"

By Cindy Hazan, Mary Campa, and Nurit Gur-Yaish

Attachment Theory and Research

Attachment theory grew out of an invitation in 1950 from the World Health Organization to the British psychiatrist John Bowlby to report on the mental health of the many London children who had been orphaned by the Second World War. His conclusion, that healthy adjustment required a "continuous and warm relationship" with at least one adult caregiver, had positive effects on policy but suffered from the lack of a specific mechanism to explain the association between "maternal deprivation" and poor developmental outcomes. The search for this mystery mechanism led Bowlby into scientific literatures far removed from his training as a psychoanalyst, including those on ethology, evolutionary biology, control systems theory, and cognitive science. The result was a comprehensive theory of attachment that eventually filled three volumes (Bowlby, 1969/1982, 1973, 1980).

The Attachment Behavior System

A basic assumption of the theory is that, because of their extreme immaturity at birth, human infants can survive only if an adult is available and willing to provide protection and care. Thus, as a result of natural selection, a behavioral system evolved to promote proximity to and the development of the kind of bond with a protector/caregiver needed to ensure survival.

The dynamics of the attachment system are readily observable in the behavior of all normal year-old infants in relation to their primary attachment figure—typically their mother. So, too, are the defining features of attachment relationships. The baby stays close and continuously monitors her whereabouts (*proximity maintenance*), retreats to her for comfort if needed (*safe haven*), resists and is distressed by separations from her (*separation distress*), and explores happily as long as she is present and attentive (*secure base*). The attachment system is activated by fear or anxiety, typically as a result of perceived threat or separation from attachment figures; otherwise the system is quiescent, which potentiates the activation of other behavior systems such as exploration or affiliation. In theory, the attachment system is active across the lifespan and the same four behavioral features define attachment at all ages. A subset of these behaviors may be observed in other types of close relationships (e.g., seeking proximity to friends or using them as a safe haven and source of comfort), but attachment relationships by definition are characterized by the presence of all four (see Parke et al., this volume). [...].

Attachment Hierarchies in Infancy and Childhood

In theory, infants and children form multiple attachments but attachment figures differ systematically in their importance. Specifically, attachment relationships are thought to be organized hierarchically such that individuals have one preferred or primary attachment figure on whom they principally rely for meeting attachment needs and then several secondary attachment figures. Our knowledge of infant and child attachment hierarchies has not advanced much since the early work by Ainsworth in Uganda and Schaffer and Emerson in Scotland (discussed in Bowlby, 1969/1982). The majority of infants that they studied had formed at least one secondary attachment by 18 months and several had established five or more. These secondary attachment figures included fathers, grandmothers, siblings, other adults, and older children.

In a recent study, Bennett (2003) investigated attachment formation in infants adopted by lesbian couples. She found that while all became attached to both mothers, within 18 months following adoption the majority had developed a primary attachment to one. Neither time spent with the child nor legal status vis-à-vis the child was related to the development of a primary bond. Rather it was the mother who provided the more sensitive care who became the primary attachment figure.

The Transition to Adulthood

Although his writings focused mainly on infancy and childhood, Bowlby (1979) was explicit in claiming that attachment is integral to human behavior across the entire lifespan, "from the cradle to the grave." Nevertheless, with development and maturation, predictable changes occur. Separations from attachment figures, in terms of both physical distance and duration, become more tolerable and less distressing and attachment behaviors assume new forms and targets.

In a study of children and adolescents aged 6 to 17, Hazan and Zeifman (1994) found that the four attachment-defining functions (proximity maintenance, safe haven, separation distress, and secure base) are gradually transferred from parents to peers. In their sample, even the youngest children sought proximity to friends over parents, whereas it was only in late childhood that they began to turn more often to friends than parents as sources of comfort and support. Less than one-third of those younger than 15 years reported experiencing separation distress in relation to their peers or using them as bases of security, compared to nearly one-half between the ages of 15 and 17. In this older group, the targets of separation distress and secure base behaviors were almost exclusively romantic partners.

Fraley and Davis (1997) extended this work with a sample of young adults and, like Hazan and Zeifman (1994) found that attachments are transferred from parents to peers in an ordered sequence. Fraley and Davis found that perceptions of peers also impacted the process. Those who perceived their peers as caring, supportive, and trustworthy were more likely to direct attachment behaviors to them. In a similar study Trinke and Bartholomew (1997) investigated the transfer of attachment behaviors within a network of figures. They found that adolescents who were in romantic relationships directed most attachment behaviors to their partners (indicating that the partners had become primary attachment figures), followed by mother, father, siblings, and best friends. Adolescents who were not in a romantic relationship at the time of the study had a similar ordering of the same attachment figures (minus partners, of course); however, their average use of each figure was higher than it was for those who had romantic partners.

Taken together, the results of these studies suggest the following: First, attachment behaviors are transferred from parents to peers sequentially, in a step-like function, beginning with proximity seeking and ending with secure base. Second, as new attachment figures are integrated, individuals' attachment hierarchies undergo reorganization (e.g., a former primary figure may become secondary). Third, those who assume the position of primary attachment figure are likely to be the ones perceived as most available and responsive.

As noted earlier, the two prototypes of attachment are relationships between offspring and parents and between adult romantic partners. There are, however, several important differences between these two types of attachment bonds. For one, attachments between infants and caregivers are complementary; infants seek protection and care from their attachment figures but do not provide protection or care in return. Parental behaviors are regulated by a different innate mechanism, i.e., the caregiving system. In contrast to the attachment system, the care-giving system is activated by another's distress as opposed to one's own. Adult romantic relationships are typically more reciprocal. That is, each partner serves alternately as both a provider and a recipient of care. An additional and obvious difference between parent–child and romantic relationships is that the latter are by definition sexual in nature. Thus, in the course of normal development, the network of attachment relationships expands beyond the family to includes mates, with these latter relationships involving the integration of the attachment, care-giving, and sexual mating systems (Hazan & Shaver, 1994; Shaver, Hazan, & Bradshaw, 1988).

The Ontogeny of Adult Attachment Bonds

Whether adult attachments develop in a manner that parallels attachment formation in infancy is an empirical question yet to be answered, but Zeifman and Hazan (1997) proposed that Bowlby and Ainsworth's four-phase model might serve as a useful provisional research guide. They likened the adult counterpart of the infant pre-attachment phase to what Eibl-Eibesfeldt (1989) called the "proceptive program," the rather indiscriminant flirting of males and females of reproductive age to signal their interest in potential mates. These playful, sexually charged exchanges continue when couples first get together and are more characteristic of their interactions than attachment behaviors per se. In contrast, the behavior of romantically involved couples show many resemblances to infant–caregiver interactions (Shaver & Hazan, 1988), including prolonged mutual gazing, cuddling, nuzzling, and "baby talk." Zeifman and Hazan suggested that these types of exchanges may be indicative of the second phase, attachment-in-the-making. This suggestion is consistent with Bowlby's view that, "In terms of subjective experience, the formation of a bond is described as falling in love" (1979, p. 69). In infancy, the onset of the third phase, clear-cut attachment, is indicated by the presence of all attachment behaviors. Zeifman and Hazan proposed that the selective orientation of these behaviors toward a partner might signal clear-cut attachment in adult couples as well. The childhood indicators of the fourth phase, goal-corrected partnership, include a marked decline in attachment behaviors. Zeifman and Hazan hypothesized that the normative reduction in these behaviors as romantic relationships progress may indicate a comparable phase in adult attachment formation. [...].

Attachment Hierarchies in Adolescence and Adulthood

A central premise of attachment theory is that parents remain attachment figures throughout life but eventually assume a secondary position relative to romantic partners. The studies described above on the transfer of attachment behaviors from parents to peers provide evidence consistent with this claim. However, many questions regarding adolescent and adult attachment hierarchies have yet to be answered, including such questions as how many attachment figures the average individual has across his or her life and by what processes attachment hierarchies are reorganized as new figures are added or old figures replaced.

In their study of attachment hierarchies in young adults, Trinke and Bartholomew (1997) found that the average number of attachment figures per individual was five, including parents, siblings, best friends, and in some cases romantic partners. It is unknown whether the number is unique to this sample or perhaps this age group. Ainsworth (1989) was of the mind that most if not all of an individual's attachment figures are permanent members of the attachment hierarchy. "These secondary or supplementary attachments may differ from primary attachments in their longevity ... to be sure ... [but their] influence may continue to be valued and the representational model of the relationship may persist. In that sense the attachment continues" (p. 711). This perspective is similar to the one that Bowlby eventually adopted. In 1980 he renamed the final phase of the separation reaction from detachment to "reorganization." (See Fraley and Shaver, 1999, for a contemporary discussion of these issues.)

On a related matter, what happens when a long-term partner dies or a long-term couple divorces? (see also Simpson and Tran, this volume). Divorce, not death, is currently the most common cause of partner loss (Pinsof, 2002), and it presumably has important implications for the attachment hierarchies of the partners as well as their children. So too may the increasing tendency of young adults to cohabit or engage in "serial" pair bonding (Pinsof, 2002). Whereas in the past many individuals had just one romantic attachment figure in their lifetimes, today's youth can expect to have several if not many. And given the current rates of divorce and remarriage, they can also expect to have more parental attachment figures than previous generations.

Buunk and Mutsaers (1999) explored the question of whether former romantic attachment figures remain in the hierarchy of attachments or not. They assessed three aspects of relationships between ex-spouses: attachment, friendship, and hostility. They found little evidence for continued attachment, and while friendship was more prevalent it was also relatively rare. More common were feelings of hostility. About 12 percent of their sample admitted hating their exes, and 64 percent agreed with the statement, "The less contact with my ex-partner, the better." Sadly, those with children expressed the highest levels of hostility. According to Ainsworth (1989), "It is clear that the attachment component is long lasting tending to persist long after the pair has been parted, even when the parting was much desired" (p. 713). What is less clear is how long attachments endure and under what circumstances. Much empirical work remains to be done.

Individual Differences in Infant Attachment

Bowlby believed that in order to fully understand individual variations it was first necessary to explain normal attachment functioning, which was the primary focus of his first volume (Bowlby, 1969/1982) and of most early attachment research (see Marvin & Britner, 1999). But the emphasis shifted quickly with the introduction of a new experimental paradigm and the discovery of different patterns of infant attachment (Ainsworth, Blehar, Waters, & Wall, 1978).

Ainsworth et al. (1978) developed their paradigm—the "strange situation"—for the purpose of empirically testing Bowlby's theory, and specifically the hypothesized dynamics of the attachment behavior system. Accordingly, it was designed for infants who were past the phase of clear-cut attachment, old enough to self-locomote, and of the age when separation distress typically peaks (i.e., 12 months). The paradigm included two brief separations from the primary caregiver, which in theory should elicit anxiety, activate the attachment system, and trigger proximity- and contact-seeking behaviors.

The results, reported in Ainsworth et al. (1978), are by now well known. The majority of infants tested behaved just as attachment theory would predict. They actively engaged in exploration when their mother was present, resisted and were distressed by her absences, sought contact with her upon reunion, and were sufficiently soothed to resume exploring. These infants were classified as "securely" attached. The label was necessitated by the unexpected discovery of two additional and very different patterns. A minority of the infants, classified as "avoidantly" attached, exhibited little if any overt distress during the separations and, more importantly, actively avoided contact with their mothers during reunions. An even smaller minority of infants, labeled "ambivalently" attached, engaged in relatively little active exploration in the mother's presence, were extremely upset by the separations, and yet when reunited both sought and actively resisted comfort (see also Parke et al., this volume).

In an attempt to understand and account for these different patterns, Ainsworth et al. turned to the data that they had collected during regular extended home visits in the preceding 12 months. The one variable that reliably predicted the pattern of behavior that infants showed in the laboratory was the way that their mothers had previously responded to their bids for contact comfort. Mothers of secure infants tended to respond promptly and warmly; mothers of avoidant infants were consistently rejecting; and mothers of ambivalent infants responded unpredictably and non-contingently, at times responsive and at other times rejecting or intrusive.

Ainsworth et al. (1978) explained the association between strange situation behavior and previous experiences in terms of what Bowlby called "working models." The idea is that while the attachment system is inborn, the quality of attachment bonds depends on the quality of interactions between infants and caregivers. Specifically, infants record in memory what happens when they seek contact comfort from various attachment figures, and these memories form the bases of expectations and mental representations that guide future behavior with these same figures. For example, an infant who has learned through experience that his mother is consistently available and responsive will seek contact with her when distressed, and be comforted by it. In contrast, an infant who has learned that seeking contact with his mother when he is distressed tends to result in painful rejection will actively avoid her, especially when he is upset. And an infant who has learned that bids for contact with his mother have unpredictable results will feel both angry and anxious and his behavior will reflect these mixed emotions.

It should be noted that a small percentage of infants in normative samples, and a larger proportion in high-risk (e.g., maltreated) samples, are difficult to classify using Ainsworth et al.'s three-category classification system because they fail to display a coherent pattern of behavior in relation to attachment figures. Main and Solomon (1986) developed a set of guidelines for a fourth classification, "disorganized" attachment. For a thorough review of the precursors and correlates of disorganized attachment see Lyons-Ruth & Jacobvitz (1999).

Ainsworth et al.'s claim that the quality of infant–caregiver bonds is shaped primarily by interpersonal experience, as opposed to being a simple byproduct of infant temperament, has been amply supported by research (see Vaughn & Bost, 1999). Whether the infant patterns represent only the quality of a specific relationship at a specific point in time or stable individual differences that could influence the quality of relationships with other people at subsequent points in time is an issue to which we return below.

Individual Differences in Adult Attachment

The subfield of adult attachment grew more out of Ainsworth et al.'s research than Bowlby's theory. It was founded on self-report and interview measures designed to capture adult versions of the infant patterns (Bartholomew & Horowitz, 1991; Brennan & Shaver, 1995; Collins & Read, 1990; Feeney & Noller, 1990; George, Kaplan, & Main, 1996; Hazan & Shaver, 1987; Levy & Davis, 1988; Simpson, 1990). Significant changes have occurred in the measurement and conceptualization of adult attachment patterns, including whether there are three primary patterns or four. But the current view is that attachment differences are better conceptualized in terms of continuous dimensions than discrete categories or typologies (Fraley & Waller, 1998). The two dimensions that appear to underlie all self-report and interview measures of adult attachment, as well as the three patterns of infant attachment identified by Ainsworth et al. (1978), are "avoidance" and "anxiety" (Brennan, Clark, & Shaver, 1998). The avoidance dimension represents the behavioral tendency to avoid interpersonal closeness, especially as a potential source of comfort when distressed. The anxiety dimension, which is more emotional, represents a strong desire for interpersonal closeness coupled with equally strong doubts about the reliability and responsiveness of others. From a dimensional perspective, "secure" attachment is defined by a combination of low avoidance and low anxiety (see Crowell, Fraley, & Shaver, 1999, for a detailed overview of adult attachment measurement issues).

Literally hundreds of studies have documented the correlates of individual differences in adult attachment. Here we provide a few representative examples from the romantic relationship literature. (A comprehensive review can be found in Feeney, 1999.) For the sake of clarity, we employ a single terminology to report results based on different approaches to measurement. For example, the term "avoidance" will be used whether avoidance was assessed by interview or self-report methods using discrete categories or continuous dimensions.

Attachment security is associated with a wide variety of positive intrapersonal and interpersonal variables. Individuals high in attachment security report experiencing positive emotions more often and negative emotions less often in romantic relationships than do their "insecure" counterparts (Simpson, 1990). They characterize their romantic relationships as being relatively high in trust and closeness and relatively low in jealousy or fears of intimacy (Hazan & Shaver, 1987). They are more likely to offer support to a distressed partner and seek support from a partner when distressed (Simpson, Rholes, & Nelligan, 1992). They are comparatively flexible and discriminating self-disclosers as well as good listeners (Mikulincer & Nachshon, 1991) and more sensitive caregivers to their partners (Feeney, 1995; Kunce & Shaver, 1994). They are less likely to be sexually unfaithful to their partners (Hazan, Zeifman, & Middleton, 1994) and show better marital adjustment, especially if their partner is also high in attachment security (Senchak & Leonard, 1992). Finally, they cope more constructively with separations from their partners (Feeney, 1998) and with romantic relationship break up (Feeney & Noller, 1992).

Attachment anxiety is associated with a wide variety of negative intrapersonal and interpersonal variables. Individuals high in attachment anxiety report experiencing more frequent and intense mood swings in romantic relationships, and also more jealousy, than do their less anxious counterparts (Hazan & Shaver, 1987). Their relationships are more likely to be characterized by "neurotic love" involving preoccupation, dependence, mania, and addictive reliance on romantic partners (Feeney & Noller, 1990), and they tend to be intrusive caregivers to their partners (Kunce & Shaver, 1994). They feel anxious even when imagining a relationship with a hypothetical partner (Carnelley & Pietromonaco, 1991). At their jobs, they are motivated more by a desire for affection from coworkers than successful performance (Hazan & Shaver, 1990). Finally, they have comparatively more interpersonal disagreements and conflicts (Tidwell, Shaver, Lin, & Reis, 1991) and tend to engage in destructive patterns of conflict with their partners (Feeney, Noller, & Callan, 1994; see also Pietromonaco, Greenwood, & Barrett, 2004).

Attachment avoidance is also associated with a host of negative intrapersonal and interpersonal variables, but the correlates are different from those of attachment anxiety. Individuals high in attachment avoidance tend to view others more negatively than their less avoidant counterparts and are more pessimistic about the prospect of lasting love (Hazan & Shaver, 1987). They are less likely to provide comfort and support to their partners and less likely to seek comfort and support when they are distressed (Simpson et al., 1992; see also Feeney & Collins, 2004). They tend to have more distant interpersonal interactions (Tidwell et al., 1991) and to be perceived by acquaintances as hostile (Kobak & Sceery, 1988). They have a higher rate of casual sex and alcohol consumption (Shaver & Brennan, 1991). Finally, in response to romantic relationship breakup they report comparatively less upset and more relief (Feeney & Noller, 1992).

Stability and Change

A common misconception is that attachment theory predicts perfect stability of attachment patterns across the lifespan (e.g., an individual who is high on avoidance during infancy will continue to be so during childhood, adolescence, and adulthood). In fact, Bowlby (1973) labeled the psychological structures that underlie different patterns of attachment *working* models precisely to emphasize that they are not immutable.

Bowlby (1973) specified three mechanisms that contribute to the stability of attachment patterns across time and relationships:

1. Although working models are constructed on the basis of social experience, they can also influence social experience. For example, an individual high in

attachment anxiety may behave in a manner that evokes model-confirming reactions from others.

2. The attachment system is especially sensitive to environmental influences during the early years of life, but this sensitivity declines with maturation.

3. On the basis of early experience individuals construct prototypes of attachment relationships that can influence the nature and course of subsequent attachment relationships.

Research has shown that patterns of attachment are moderately stable over time, and similarly stable across both short and long assessment intervals (Baldwin & Fehr, 1995; Fraley, 2002; Kirkpatrick & Hazan, 1994; Klohnen & Bera, 1998). It has also been shown that change in attachment patterns tends to correspond systematically to intrapersonal and interpersonal changes (e.g., Davila & Cobb, 2003). Change can occur as a result of new relationship experiences inconsistent with individuals' working models, increased understanding of early model-shaping experiences, and major life events that radically alter individuals' environments or relationships (see Feeney, 1999; Hesse, 1999).

In a dynamic systems approach to these issues, Fraley and Brumbaugh (2004) translated Bowlby's (1973) propositions regarding stability and change into testable mathematical models. According to the result of their analyses, "Bowlby's theory predicts that the degree of stability in attachment can fall anywhere between 0.00 and 1.00" (p. 127).

References

Ainsworth, M. D. S. (1972). Attachment and dependency: A comparison. In J. L. Gewirtz (Ed.), *Attachment and dependency* (pp. 97–137). Washington, DC: Winston.

Ainsworth, M. S. (1989). Attachment beyond infancy. *American Psychologist, 44,* 709–716.

Ainsworth, M. S., Blehar, M. C., Waters, E., & Wall, S. (1978). *Patterns of attachment: A psychological study of the strange situation.* Hillsdale, NJ: Lawrence Erlbaum Associates, Inc.

Bakermans-Kranenburg, M. J., Van Ijzendoorn, M., & Juffer, F. (2003). Less is more: Meta-analyses of sensitivity and attachment interventions in early childhood. *Psychological Bulletin, 129,* 195–215.

Baldwin, M. W., & Fehr, B. (1995). On the instability of attachment style ratings. *Personal Relationships, 2,* 247–261.

Bartholomew, K., & Horowitz, L. M. (1991). Attachment styles among young adults: A test of a four-category model. *Journal of Personality and Social Psychology, 61,* 226–244.

Bennett, S. (2003). Is there a primary mom? Parental perceptions of attachment bond hierarchies within lesbian adoptive families. *Child and Adolescent Social Work Journal*, *20*, 159–173.

Berscheid, E., & Peplau, L. A. (1983). The emerging science of relationships. In Kelley, H. H., Berscheid, E., Christensen, A., Harvey, J. H., Huston, T. L., Levinger, G., et al. (Eds.), *Close relationships* (pp. 1–19). New York, NY: Freeman.

Bowlby, J. (1973). *Attachment and loss* (Vol. 2). New York, NY: Basic Books.

Bowlby, J. (1979). *The making and breaking of affectional bonds*. London, UK: Tavistock.

Bowlby, J. (1980). *Attachment and loss* (Vol. 3). New York, NY: Basic Books.

Bowlby, J. (1982). *Attachment and loss* (Vol. 1). New York, NY: Basic Books. (Original work published 1969.)

Bowlby, J. (1988). *A secure base: Parent–child attachment and healthy human development*. London, UK: Basic Books.

Brennan, K. A., Clark, C. L., & Shaver, P. R. (1998). Self-report measurement of adult attachment: An integrative overview. In W. S. Rholes & J. A. Simpson (Eds.), *Attachment theory and close relationships* (pp. 46–76). New York, NY: Guilford Press.

Brennan, K. A., & Shaver, P. R. (1995). Dimensions of adult attachment, affect regulation, and romantic relationship functioning. *Personality and Social Psychology Bulletin*, *21*, 267–283.

Burlingham, D., & Freud, A. (1944). *Infants without families*. Oxford, UK: Allen & Unwin.

Buunk, B. P., & Mutsaers, W. (1999). The nature of the relationship between remarried individuals and former spouses and its impact on marital satisfaction. *Journal of Family Psychology*, *13*, 165–174.

Carnelley, K. B., & Pietromonaco, P. R. (1991). Thinking about a romantic relationship: Attachment style and gender influence emotional reactions and perceptions. Presented at the third annual meeting of the American Psychological Society, Washington, DC.

Carter, C. S. (1998). Neuroendocrine perspectives on social attachment and love. *Psychoneuroendocrinology*, *23*, 779–818.

Carter, C. S., Lederhendler, I. I., & Kirkpatrick, B. (Eds.). (1997). The integrative neurobiology of affiliation. *Annals of The New York Academy of Sciences*, *807*.

Cicchetti, D., & Toth, S. L. (1987). The application of a transactional risk model to intervention with multi-risk maltreating families. *Zero to Three*, *7*, 1–8.

Cicchetti, D., & Toth, S. L. (1995). Child maltreatment and attachment organization: Implications for intervention. In R. Muir & S. Goldberg (Eds.), *Attachment theory: Social, developmental, and clinical perspectives* (pp. 279–308). Hillsdale, NJ: Analytic Press, Inc.

Collins, N. L., & Read, S. J. (1990). Adult attachment, working models, and relationship quality in dating couples. *Journal of Personality and Social Psychology*, *58*, 644–663.

Crowell, J. A., Fraley, R., & Shaver, P. R. (1999). Measurement of individual differences in adolescent and adult attachment. In P. R. Shaver & J. Cassidy (Eds.), *Handbook of attachment: Theory, research, and clinical applications* (pp. 434–465). New York, NY: Guilford Press.

Davila, J., & Cobb, R. J. (2003). Predicting change in self-reported and interviewer-assessed adult attachment: Tests of the individual difference and life stress models of attachment change. *Personality and Social Psychology Bulletin, 29*, 859–870.

Dessaulles, A., Johnson, S., & Denton, W. H. (2003). Emotion-focused therapy for couples in the treatment of depression: A pilot study. *The American Journal of Family Therapy, 31*, 345–353.

Diamond, G., Siqueland, L., & Diamond, G. M. (2003). Attachment-based family therapy for depressed adolescents: Programmatic treatment development. *Clinical Child and Family Psychology Review, 60*, 107–126.

Dozier, M., Albus, K., Fisher, P., & Sepulveda, S. (2002). Interventions for foster parents: Implications for developmental theory. *Development and Psychopathology, 14*, 843–860.

Dozier, M., & Sepulveda, S. (2004). Foster mother state of mind and treatment use: Different challenges for different people. *Infant Mental Health Journal, 25*, 368–378.

Dozier, M., & Tyrrell, C. (1998). The role of attachment in therapeutic relationships. In S. Rholes & J. Simpson (Eds.), *Attachment theory and close relationships* (pp. 221–248). New York, NY: Guilford Press.

Eibl-Eibesfeldt, I. (1989). *Human ethology: Foundations of human behavior*. Hawthorne, NY: Aldine de Gruyter.

Feeney, J. A. (1995). Adult attachment, coping style and health locus of control as predictors of health behavior. *Australian Journal of Psychology, 47*, 171–177.

Feeney, J. A. (1998). Adult attachment and relationship-centered anxiety: Responses to physical and emotional distancing. In W. S. Rholes & J. A. Simpson (Eds.), *Attachment theory and close relationships* (pp. 46–76). New York, NY: Guilford Press.

Feeney, J. A. (1999). Adult romantic attachment and couple relationships. In J. Cassidy & P. R. Shaver (Eds.), *Handbook of attachment: Theory, research, and clinical applications* (pp. 355–377). New York, NY: Guilford Press.

Feeney, B. C., & Collins, N. L. (2004). Interpersonal safe haven and secure base caregiving processes in adulthood. In J. A. Simpson & S. W. Rholes (Eds.), *Adult attachment: Theory, research, and clinical implications* (pp. 267–299). New York, NY: Guilford Press.

Feeney, B. C., & Kirkpatrick, L. A. (1996). Effects of adult attachment and presence of romantic partners on physiological responses to stress. *Journal of Personality and Social Psychology, 70*, 255–270.

Feeney, J. A., & Noller, P. (1990). Attachment style as a predictor of adult romantic relationships. *Journal of Personality and Social Psychology, 58*, 281–291.

Feeney, J. A., & Noller, P. (1992). Attachment style and romantic love: Relationship dissolution. *Australian Journal of Psychology, 44*, 69–74.

Feeney, J. A., Noller, P., & Callan, V. J. (1994). Attachment style, communication and satisfaction in the early years of marriage. In D. Perlman & K. Bartholomew (Eds.), *Attachment processes in adulthood* (pp. 269–308). Philadelphia, PA: Jessica Kingsley Publishers.

Fonagy, P., Steele, H., & Steele, M. (1991). Maternal representations of attachment during pregnancy predict the organization of infant–mother attachment at one year of age. *Child Development, 62*, 891–905.

Fox, N. A., & Card, J. A. (1999). Psychophysiological measures in the study of attachment. In J. Cassidy & P. R. Shaver (Eds.), *Handbook of attachment: Theory, research, and clinical applications* (pp. 226–245). New York, NY: Guilford Press.

Fraley, R. (2002). Attachment stability from infancy to adulthood: Meta-analysis and dynamic modeling of developmental mechanisms. *Personality and Social Psychology Review, 6*, 123–151.

Fraley, R., & Brumbaugh, C. C. (2004). A dynamical systems approach to conceptualizing and studying stability and change in attachment security. In J. Simpson & S. Rholes (Eds.), *Adult attachment: Theory, research, and clinical implications* (pp. 86–132). New York, NY: Guilford Press.

Fraley, R., & Davis, K. E. (1997). Attachment formation and transfer in young adults' close friendships and romantic relationships. *Personal Relationships, 4*, 131–144.

Fraley, R., & Shaver, P. R. (1999). Loss and bereavement: Attachment theory and recent controversies concerning "grief work" and the nature of detachment. In P. Shaver & J. Cassidy (Eds.), *Handbook of attachment: Theory, research, and clinical applications* (pp. 735–759). New York, NY: Guilford Press.

Fraley, R.C., & Waller, N. G. (1998). Adult attachment patterns: A test of the typological model. In W. S. Rholes & J. A. Simpson (Eds.), *Attachment theory and close relationships* (pp. 77–114). New York, NY: Guilford Press.

George, C., Kaplan, N., & Main, M. (1996). The Adult Attachment Interview (3rd ed.). Unpublished manuscript, Department of Psychology, University of California, Berkeley, CA.

Greenberg, L. S., & Johnson, S. M. (1988). *Emotionally focused therapy for couples.* New York, NY: Guilford Press.

Gump, B. B., Polk, D. E., Kamarck, T. W., & Shiffman, S. M. (2001). Partner interactions are associated with reduced blood pressure in the natural environment: Ambulatory monitoring evidence from a healthy, multiethnic adult sample. *Psychosomatic Medicine*, *63*, 423–433.

Hazan, C., & Shaver, P. (1987). Romantic love conceptualized as an attachment process. *Journal of Personality and Social Psychology*, *52*, 511–524.

Hazan, C., & Shaver, P. R. (1990). Love and work: An attachment-theoretical perspective. *Journal of Personality and Social Psychology*, *59*, 270–280.

Hazan, C., & Shaver, P. R. (1994). Attachment as an organizational framework for research on close relationships. *Psychological Inquiry*, *5*, 1–22.

Hazan, C., & Zeifman, D. (1994). Sex and the psychological tether. *Advances in Personal Relationships*, *5*, 151–177.

Hazan, C., Zeifman, D., & Middleton, K. (1994, July). *Attachment and sexuality*. Paper presented at the 7th International Conference on Personal Relationships, Groningen, The Netherlands.

Hennessy, M. B. (1997). Hypothalamic–pituitary–adrenal responses to brief social separation. *Neuroscience and Biobehavioral Reviews*, *21*, 11–29.

Hesse, E. (1999). The adult attachment interview: Historical and current perspectives. In P. R. Shaver & J. Cassidy (Eds.), *Handbook of attachment: Theory, research, and clinical applications* (pp. 434–465). New York, NY: Guilford Press.

Hofer, M. A. (1973a). The role of nutrition in the physiological and behavioral effects of early maternal separation on infant rats. *Psychosomatic Medicine*, *35*, 350–359.

Hofer, M. A. (1973b). Maternal separation affects infant rats' behavior. *Behavioral Biology*, *9*, 629–633.

Hofer, M. A. (1975). Studies on how early maternal separation produces behavioral change in young rats. *Psychosomatic Medicine*, *37*, 245–264.

Hofer, M. A. (1976). The organization of sleep and wakefulness after maternal separation in young rats. *Developmental Psychobiology*, *9*, 189–205.

Hofer, M. A. (1984). Relationships as regulators: A psychobiologic perspective on bereavement. *Psychosomatic Medicine*, *46*, 183–197.

Hofer, M. A. (1987). Early social relationships: A psychobiologist's view. *Child Development*, *58*, 633–647.

Johnson, S., Maddeaux, C., & Blouin, J. (1998). Emotionally focused family therapy for bulimia: Changing attachment patterns. *Psychotherapy*, *35*, 238–247.

Johnson, S. M. (1996). *Creating connection: The practice of emotionally focused marital therapy*. New York, NY: Brunner/Mazel.

Johnson, S. M. (2003). The revolution in couple therapy: A practitioner–scientist perspective. *Journal of Marital and Family Therapy*, *29*, 365–384.

Johnson, S. M. (2004). Attachment theory: A guide for healing couple relationships. In J. Simpson & S. Rholes (Eds.), *Adult attachment: Theory, research, and clinical implications* (pp. 367–387). New York, NY: Guilford Publications.

Kelley, H. H., Berscheid, E., Christensen, A., Harvey, J. H., Huston, T. L., Levinger, G., et al. (1983). *Close relationships.* New York, NY: Freeman.

Kilmann, P. R., Laughlin, J. E., Carranza, L. V., Downer, J. T., Major, S., & Parnell, M. M. (1999). Effects of an attachment-focused group preventive intervention on insecure women. *Group Dynamics, 3,* 138–147.

Kirkpatrick, L. A., & Hazan, C. (1994). Attachment styles and close relationships: A four-year prospective study. *Personal Relationships, 1,* 123–142.

Klohnen, E. C., & Bera, S. (1998). Behavioral and experiential patterns of avoidantly and securely attached women across adulthood: A 31-year longitudinal perspective. *Journal of Personality and Social Psychology, 74,* 211–223.

Kobak, R., & Sceery, A. (1988). Attachment in late adolescence: Working models, affect regulation, and representations of self and others. *Child Development, 59,* 135–146.

Kunce, L. J., & Shaver, P. R. (1994). An attachment-theoretical approach to caregiving in romantic relationships. In D. Perlman & K. Bartholomew (Eds.), *Attachment processes in adulthood* (pp. 205–237). Philadelphia, PA: Jessica Kingsley.

Levy, M. B., & Davis, K. E. (1988). Love styles and attachment styles compared: Their relations to each other and to various relationship characteristics. *Journal of Social and Personal Relationships, 5,* 439–471.

Liddle, H. A., & Schwartz, S. J. (2002). Attachment and family therapy: The clinical utility of adolescent–family attachment research. *Family Process, 41,* 455–476.

Lieberman, A. F., Van Horn, P., Grandison, C. M., & Pekarsky, J. H. (1997). Mental health assessment of infants, toddlers, and preschoolers in a service program and a treatment outcome research program. *Infant Mental Health Journal, 18,* 158–170.

Lyons Ruth, K., & Jacobvitz, D. (1999). Attachment disorganization: Unresolved loss, relational violence, and lapses in behavioral and attentional strategies. In P. R. Shaver & J. Cassidy (Eds.), *Handbook of attachment: Theory, research, and clinical applications* (pp. 434–465). New York, NY: Guilford Press.

Main, M., & Solomon, J. (1986). Discovery of an insecure-disorganized/disoriented attachment pattern. In M. W. Yogman & T. B. Brazelton (Eds.), *Affective development in infancy* (pp. 95–124). Westport, CT: Ablex Publishing.

Marvin, R., Cooper, G., Hoffman, K., & Powell, B. (2002). The circle of security project: Attachment-based intervention with caregiver–pre-school child dyads. *Attachment and Human Development, 4,* 107–124.

Marvin, R. S., & Britner, P. A. (1999). Normative development: The ontogeny of attachment. In J. Cassidy & P. R. Shaver (Eds.), *Handbook of attachment: Theory, research, and clinical applications* (pp. 44–67). New York, NY: Guilford Press.

Mikulincer, M. (1998). Adult attachment style and individual differences in functional versus dysfunctional experiences of anger. *Journal of Personality and Social Psychology, 74*, 513–524.

Mikulincer, M., & Nachshon, O. (1991). Attachment styles and patterns of self-disclosure. *Journal of Personality and Social Psychology, 61*, 321–331.

Paivio, S. C., & Nieuwenhuis, J. A. (2005). Efficacy of emotion focused therapy for adult survivors of child abuse: A preliminary study. *Journal of Traumatic Stress, 14*, 115–133.

Pietromonaco, P. R., Greenwood, D., & Barrett, L. F. (2004). Conflict in adult close relationships: An attachment perspective. In J. A. Simpson & S. W. Rholes (Eds.), *Adult attachment: Theory, research, and clinical implications* (pp. 267–299). New York, NY: Guilford Press.

Pinsof, W. M. (2002). The death of "till death us do part": The transformation of pair-bonding in the 20th century. *Family Process, 41*, 135–157.

Robertson, J. (1953). Some responses of young children to loss of maternal care. *Nursing Times, 18*, 382–386.

Senchak, M., & Leonard, K. E. (1992). Attachment styles and marital adjustment among newlywed couples. *Journal of Social and Personal Relationships, 9*, 51–64.

Shaver, P., Hazan, C., & Bradshaw, D. (1988). Love as attachment. In R. J. Sternberg & M. L. Barnes (Eds.), *The psychology of love* (pp. 68–99). New Haven, CT: Yale University Press.

Shaver, P. R., & Brennan, K. A. (1991). Measures of depression and loneliness. In P. Shaver & J. P. Robinson (Eds.), *Measures of personality and social psychological attitudes* (pp. 195–289). San Diego, CA: Academic Press.

Shaver, P. R., & Hazan, C. (1988). A biased overview of the study of love. *Journal of Social and Personal Relationships, 5*, 473–501.

Simpson, J. A. (1990). Influence of attachment styles on romantic relationships. *Journal of Personality and Social Psychology, 59*, 971–980.

Simpson, J. A., Rholes, W. S., & Nelligan, J. S. (1992). Support seeking and support giving within couples in an anxiety-provoking situation: The role of attachment styles. *Journal of Personality and Social Psychology, 62*, 434–446.

Tidwell, M., Shaver, P. R., Lin, Y., & Reis, H. T. (1991). *Attachment, attractiveness and daily social interactions.* Paper presented at the 62nd meeting of the Eastern Psychological Association, New York.

Trinke, S. J., & Bartholomew, K. (1997). Hierarchies of attachment relationships in young adulthood. *Journal of Social and Personal Relationships, 14*, 603–625.

Uchino, B. N., Cacioppo, J. T., & Kiecolt-Glaser, J. K. (1996). The relationship between social support and physiological processes: A review with emphasis on underlying mechanisms and implications for health. *Psychological Bulletin, 119,* 488–531.

Uvnas-Moberg, K. (1994). Oxytocin and behaviour. *Annals of Medicine, 26,* 315–317.

Uvnas-Moberg, K. (1997). Physiological and endocrine effects of social contact. In I. Lederhendler & S. Carter (Eds.), *The integrative neurobiology of affiliation* (pp. 146–163). New York, NY: New York Academy of Sciences.

Uvnas-Moberg, K. (1998). Oxytocin may mediate the benefits of positive social interaction and emotions. *Psychoneuroendocrinology, 23,* 819–835.

van den Boom, D. C. (1995). Do first-year intervention effects endure? Follow-up during toddlerhood of a sample of Dutch irritable infants. *Child Development, 66,* 1798–1816.

Van Ijzendoorn, M. H. (1992). Intergenerational transmission of parenting: A review of studies in nonclinical populations. *Developmental Review, 12,* 76–99.

Vaughn, B. E., & Bost, K. K. (1999). Attachment and temperament: Redundant, independent, or interacting influences on interpersonal adaptation and personality development? In P. R. Shaver & J. Cassidy (Eds.), *Handbook of attachment: Theory, research, and clinical applications* (pp. 434–465). New York, NY: Guilford Press.

Ziefman, D., & Hazan, C. (1997). A process model of adult attachment formation. In S. Duck (Ed.), *Handbook of personal relationships: Theory, research and interventions* (2nd ed., pp. 179–195). New York, NY: Wiley.

Attachment Real-World Lab

Name: _____

Date: _____

For this real-world lab, you will find out your attachment style. Go to https://tinyurl.com/CommAttachment and select "Begin Option B." Complete the quiz.

1. Which of the four attachment styles represents you? Name the style and draw the grid with the dot that represents your style (this grid is populated for you at the end of the survey).

_____

_____

_____

_____

_____

_____

2. In your own words, define your attachment style (definitions can be found in the reading and at the end of the quiz).

_____

_____

_____

_____

3. Does the definition of your attachment style fit how you see yourself? If not, what would you change? If it does fit, what about the definition strikes you as especially accurate?

_____

_____

_____

_____

_____

_____

_____

_____

4. Do some research online about your attachment style and what it means for how you interact with others. Be sure to find credible sources. Psychology Today (https://www.psychologytoday.com/us/basics/attachment) has many articles about attachment. You can also use Google Scholar (www.scholar.google.com) to search for academic articles or look for videos on Youtube. One place to start is this *New York Times* article that describes how the four attachment styles interact with others in the workplace: https://nyti.ms/2R7ij8V. Be aware that some articles use different names for the three insecure attachment styles, but if you pay close attention you can figure out how the names match up. In a couple of paragraphs, describe the article or video you found (including where you found it) and what you learned about your attachment style.

_____

_____

_____

_____

_____

_____

_____

_____

_____

_____

_____

_____

_____

_____

_____

_____

_____

_____

_____

_____

_____

_____

_____

_____

CHAPTER 8

Secrets, Self-Disclosure, and Privacy

Introduction to the Chapter

Have you ever kept something a secret from someone you love? Did you do it to protect yourself, to protect them, or to protect your relationship? Maybe keeping the secret was protecting you both. This chapter describes the ideology of openness that is prevalent in U.S. culture and presents an alternative to openness: secrets and avoidance. The chapter will reveal how secrets and avoidance can be both "good" and "bad" for interpersonal relationships. You will learn about deception and when it can be beneficial to all parties to keep information from others. You will also learn about communication privacy management theory, which explains how and why people develop rules for managing private information.

Selection from "The Dark Side (and Light Side) of Avoidance and Secrets"

By Tamara Afifi, John Coughlin, and Walid Afifi

The Smith Family

Mom's secret: "I haven't told the kids that their father has a drinking problem. I'm afraid of what it will do to their relationship if they found out."

Dad's secret: "A long time ago I had an affair. My wife doesn't know about it."

Daughter's secret: "My mom thinks that I don't know about my dad's drinking, but I do. I've had to take the keys from him many times when he was driving drunk."

Son's secret: "I've experimented with drugs."

The Johnson Family

Mom's secret: "My husband has told the children many times about his days in Vietnam. But he was never in Vietnam. The stories have gone on for so long that I don't know what to do. I wish he would tell them the truth."

Dad's secret: "I told the kids that I served in Vietnam when I didn't."

Son's secret: "I've had sex with my girlfriend and I haven't told my parents."

These examples are from a recent study that asked family members to identify secrets that they were keeping from others in their family (T. D. Afifi, Olson, & Armstrong, 2005). Such secrets exemplify the dark side of secrets that is prominently depicted in the media and in research literature. Secrets are often overtly deceptive (e.g., when a father lies about being in Vietnam), they can indicate problems in relationships (e.g., when the secret involves an extramarital affair), and they can even threaten individuals' personal health (e.g., when a family colludes to hide the father's alcoholism). Given the potential for extremely negative outcomes associated with keeping secrets, it is not surprising that popular culture and scholarly writing typically focus on the benefits of open communication and the dangers of avoiding such openness (Parks, 1982). In fact, the popular culture and much scholarly writing are influenced by an ideology of openness, in which intimate disclosures are seen as the core of good communication (Parks, 1982).

Despite the general ideology of intimacy, one can point to instances when guarding secrets is anything but dark. The identities of people who were quoted at the beginning of this chapter, for example, have been kept confidential through the use of pseudonyms. Moreover, several scholars have suggested that focusing on the benefits of open communication is incomplete without recognizing that there can also be benefits to avoiding topics or keeping secrets. Dialectical theorists (e.g., Baxter, 1990; Baxter & Montgomery, 1996), for instance, suggest that people experience drives for both openness and closeness in relationships, and Petronio's (1991, 2000, 2002) communication privacy management theory highlights the risks (and benefits) involved with revealing private information.

In short, there are two divergent positions regarding topic avoidance and secrets. Most prominently, an ideology of openness pervades popular culture and much scholarly writing. Accepting this ideology implies a clear place for phenomena like topic avoidance and secret keeping—they would be squarely in the dark side of relationships. In contrast, several scholars have questioned the depiction of topic avoidance and keeping secrets as dark, instead focusing on how they may have both good and bad consequences.

In this chapter we review the evidence for these divergent positions. We begin with a discussion of the key terms, focusing on distinctions among the concepts of topic avoidance, secrets, and deception. Next, we elucidate the notion of the ideology of openness and provide examples from popular media and scholarly research on relationships. Then, we review the abundant evidence that openness is typically helpful in relationships and avoiding communication is generally harmful. Finally, we discuss why topic avoidance and keeping secrets may be useful despite the ample evidence that it usually is harmful, and we discuss specific conditions when avoiding and keeping secrets are likely to be beneficial.

Distinguishing Among Avoidance, Secrets, and Related Concepts

The focus of this chapter is on two constructs, topic avoidance and secret keeping. Both concepts involve not discussing information, which is similar to other constructs like privacy, nondisclosure, and deception. However, topic avoidance and secret keeping are conceptually distinguishable from such constructs. Although space concerns preclude a thorough discussion of how topic avoidance and secret keeping correspond to related constructs, three points are particularly important for understanding the scope of this chapter.

First, it is important to discuss how topic avoidance and secrecy are related to the notion of privacy and the management of private information. In the case of secrecy, several scholars (e.g., Bellman, 1981; Kelly, 2002) have suggested that secrecy involves keeping information from people who have a legitimate claim to the information (e.g., the information affects them directly), whereas privacy involves information that the others have no right to know. Although this distinction would provide a mutually exclusive distinction between privacy and secrecy, it does not seem applicable to much of the literature on secrets in close relationships. One commonly reported secret that families keep from outsiders, for example, is when a daughter experiences premarital pregnancy (Karpel, 1980, Vangelisti, 1994). With the exception of the father of the unborn child, it is difficult to argue that this information directly affects outsiders, but family members nevertheless often consider such information to be secret from everyone outside the family (Vangelisti, 1994; Vangelisti & Caughlin, 1997). Thus, direct pertinence does not seem to provide a tenable basis for distinguishing privacy from secrecy. Instead, we base our conceptualization of secrecy on that of Bok (1983) and Petronio (2002). Rather than being completely separate from privacy, secrecy is the special case of managing private information that involves intentional concealment of the information (Caughlin & Petronio, 2004). This intentional concealment is important. As Petronio (2002) argued, revealing any private information involves some level of risk, but the effort inherent in purposefully concealing secret information suggests that such information typically is viewed as particularly risky to reveal. In short, secret information is a subset of the larger category of private information; it is the type of private information that is viewed as risky enough that it is worth intentionally concealing.

For similar reasons, topic avoidance is also more specific from the general notion of privacy management. Topic avoidance differs from secret keeping in that there is not necessarily a presumption that the topic is something unknown to the other person. Partners in a romantic relationship, for instance, can collaborate implicitly or explicitly to avoid discussing a topic about which they disagree (Roloff & Ifert, 1998). Still, regardless of whether a person avoiding a topic believes that the other person already knows the information, the notion of topic avoidance implies that one intentionally avoids discussing the topic (W. A. Afifi & Guerrero, 2000; Golish & Caughlin, 2002). That is, topic avoidance does not refer to private information that is not discussed because it simply does not "come up." Topic avoidance implies that one takes active steps to avoid a topic or is at least willing to do so if the topic is likely to be introduced.

A second point that is crucial to understand the scope of this chapter is a recognition that avoidance and secrecy are not merely the opposite of disclosure. People often think of information regulation along a continuum from secret keeping, in which information is purposefully withheld from others, to self-disclosure, where individuals verbally share personal information about themselves that is not readily available to others (Derlega, Metts, Petronio, & Margulis, 1993; Rosenfeld, 1979). This position is intuitively viable given that disclosing a secret, by definition, means that it is no longer being kept. Nevertheless, there are both theoretical and empirical reasons to conceptualize secrecy as something other than the opposite of self-disclosure. Theoretically, the opposite of self-disclosure would be the absence of self-disclosures, which could occur even if a person is not engaging in the intentional act of keeping a secret. That is, secret keeping involves a degree of intentionality that makes it qualitatively different than nondisclosure (Kelly & McKillop, 1996). Empirically, there is evidence that disclosure and secrecy are separable constructs. Finkenauer and Hazam (2000), for instance, reported that both disclosure and the concealment of secrecy accounted for unique variation in married partners' satisfaction. Also, in a study of people's standards for what counts as good family communication, Caughlin (2003) found that preferences regarding open disclosures and preferences for avoiding some issues were distinct factors, implying that some people prefer high levels of both open communication and avoidance. Clearly, such results are incongruent with the notion that secret keeping and avoidance are merely the opposite of disclosure. These findings also align somewhat with the assumptions of dialectical theory (Baxter, 1990; Baxter & Montgomery, 1996) and communication privacy management theory (Petronio, 1991, 2000, 2002) that people need both openness and closedness to maintain satisfactory relationships.

Third, it is important to distinguish between the concepts of secrecy and deception, which is defined as "the ways in which people send messages that are designed to foster beliefs contrary to what the message sender believes is the true state of affairs" (Burgoon & Hoobler, 2002, p. 271). Some scholars view keeping secrets as inherently deceptive (e.g., Lane & Wegner, 1995). This view is based on the fact that secret keeping involves an intentional effort to hide true information from a target. Certainly, there are cases in which keeping a secret involves various types of deception (e.g., Frijns, 2005). Sometimes people engage in outright lies to keep a secret; for example, one participant in a recent study about secrets reported that she had told her boyfriend that she had only had sex with two other men but had, in fact, slept with more than that (Caughlin, Afifi, Carpenter-Theune, & Miller, 2005). Secrets can also involve information that constitutes lies of omission; for instance, one of the most common secrets reported by college students involves not mentioning to one's dating partner that one has been having romantic encounters with somebody outside the dyad (Caughlin et al., 2005). Such secrets presumably involve deception because the secret keeper likely is attempting to foster the false belief in the dating partner that the relationship is monogamous.

Although many secrets are kept through deception, there are also many instances of secret keeping that are not necessarily targeted at fostering false beliefs. In many families, for example, information about finances is kept secret from outsiders (Vangelisti, 1994). Rather than being motivated to create a false impression, such secrets are typically kept because the information is seen as private or nobody else's business (Vangelisti & Caughlin, 1997). Instead of being instances of trying to create a false impression in others, secrets like withholding financial information appear to be more of an attempt to avoid making any particular impression at all regarding finances.

Granted, some scholars would suggest that attempts to manage one's impression (including trying to avoid making any particular impression) are inherently deceptive. Goffman (1959) certainly suggested that self-presentation involves being at least somewhat duplicitous. From this perspective, any information that is withheld (including secrets or avoided topics) would be viewed as deceptive. However, such a conceptualization of deception would be so broad that it would mean that practically all interpersonal communication is deceptive because impression management is such a ubiquitous goal in interpersonal communication (e.g., Dillard, 1990). Unless one has such an overly broad conceptualization of deception, there are numerous instances of secret keeping that are not deceptive, per se.

In sum, secrets and avoidance are related to concepts like privacy, nondisclosure, and deception, but they are distinguishable from such concepts. Understanding the distinctiveness of secrecy and avoidance from these other concepts, like rumination, is important for establishing the boundaries of this chapter and are elaborated further in the following sections. Next, we discuss the ideology of openness that pervades both the popular culture and much scholarly literature.

Ideology of Openness

One only has to look at the cover of popular magazines to be inundated with messages about the impact of avoidance and secrets on relational quality. Indeed, the notion of a secret often conjures up images of behavior that is deviant or socially unacceptable (Frijns, 2005). As Frijns (2005) noted, "Keeping secrets means you have something to hide, something censurable and shameful. Like a self-inflicted disease, secrecy is assumed to compromise mind and body, ultimately causing great harm to the keeper's physical and psychological well-being" (p. 24). Conversely, it is commonly assumed that if people can be completely open with one another it will produce satisfying, long-lasting relationships. For instance, one popular slogan in women's magazines often reads, "Ten ways to get your man to open up to you," as if openness is the key to relational bliss.

Moreover, the value placed on openness permeates discussions beyond those related to relational satisfaction. There are numerous examples in the media of the value of absolute openness for family health, like organ donation, sexual behaviors, and drug use. Various popular outlets routinely suggest that it is "time to talk" about financial issues related to health care (e.g., Price, 1999; Roberts, 2003). One article recommended that baby boomers have conversations with their parents about end-of-life decisions, even if the parent was not sick at the time (Weston, 2005). Along with the article came a letter that people were encouraged to send to their parents. The letter had 24 sets of questions designed to create an open dialogue about these issues. A few of the questions included the following:

- Do you have adequate health insurance? Are you familiar with what is and what is not covered? Would you be willing to have a professional … review your coverage to be sure it's sufficient?

- Have you purchased or considered a "medigap" policy to help cover expenses not covered by Medicare? (Medicare is the government-provided health care program for the elderly.) (Weston, 2005)

The scholarly literature also frequently assumes that open communication is inherently good. As Parks (1982) pointed out more than two decades ago, relational researchers tend to promote an "ideology of intimacy" or an "ideology of openness" by equating openness with healthy relationships. Part of his argument was that researchers often assume that relationships are good or high in quality only to the extent that they exhibit openness, intimacy, and disclosure. Several communication scholars have challenged the benefits of complete openness (e.g., Baxter & Wilmot, 1985; Bochner, 1982; Petronio, 2002; Rawlins, 1982), but even with these critiques of the ideology of openness, researchers still generally equate avoidance and secrets with the dark side and complete openness as the bright side of personal and relational health. Consider, for example, the two most widely used measures of marital satisfaction, the Dyadic Adjustment Scale

(Spanier, 1976) and the Marital Adjustment Test (Locke & Wallace, 1959). Both of these scales include an item asking spouses how often "do you confide in your mate?" (Locke & Wallace, 1959, p. 252; Spanier, 1976, p. 27). Including an item about openness on satisfaction indexes suggests that disclosure is not just related to satisfaction—disclosure partly constitutes satisfaction. That is, confiding in one's partner is always part of the bright side of relationships and nothing dark can come of confiding in one's spouse.

The flip side of the ideology of openness is that avoidance and secrets are inherently dark. One illustration comes from a recent article entitled "Silence and Cancer: Why Do Families and Patients Fail to Communicate?" (Zhang & Siminoff, 2003). Such a title (and the overall tenor of the article) implies that topic avoidance is inherently a failure. Although there are certainly some negative outcomes associated with avoiding topics, depicting avoidance as a failure (rather than a choice or a strategy, for instance) focuses the attention on the dark aspects of avoidance, implicitly dismissing any potential benefits of avoidance (e.g., family members' perceptions that they can protect each other through avoidance). Rather than treating the risks and potential benefits of avoidance as an empirical issue to be examined, much research (e.g., Jourard, 1971; Pennebaker, 1995) simply assumes that avoidance is inherently bad.

The Dark Side of Avoidance and Secrets: The Negative Consequences of Withholding Information

Most of the research on secrets and avoidance has focused on the negative consequences of withholding information. Much of this work has emphasized the adverse psychological and physiological effects of concealing information and the benefits of revealing information (Belloch, Morillo, & Gimenez, 2004). Although the primary focus of this chapter is on avoidance, it is important to recognize that one cost of avoidance can be the opportunity cost associated with not disclosing. Thus, before reviewing the literature specifically addressing the costs of avoiding and keeping secrets, it is important to consider the potential rewards of disclosure.

Benefits of Disclosure

Much of the research on the benefits of disclosing information has its roots in clinical psychology. Early work by Jourard (1971) and others (for review, see Pennebaker, 1995) illustrated the importance of openness for individuals' physical and mental health. As Pennebaker, Kiecolt-Glaser, and Glaser (1988) noted, the disclosure that occurs during psychotherapy can reduce distress and produce positive behavioral and psychological outcomes for people. Also, the research on stress and coping suggests that active, problem-solving coping tends to be more effective than prolonged uses of avoidant coping (Lazarus & Folkman, 1984). That is, confronting and discussing stressful or traumatic life events typically leads to less anxiety and stress than does avoiding discussions of such events. Studies also show that social support can buffer some of the adverse effects of stress (Albrecht, Burleson, & Goldsmith, 1994). Because one function of disclosure is to elicit social support (Derlega et al., 1993), talking about adverse events can help individuals secure comfort from others.

Even if others are unwilling or unable to provide useful support, there is strong evidence that disclosure can be helpful anyway. Numerous studies have found that the act of sharing secrets, either orally or through writing, is beneficial to people's physical and mental health (for a review, see Smyth & Pennebaker, 2001). Victims of traumatic life events who talk or write about these experiences show fewer physical ailments than victims who fail to disclose them (Deters & Range, 2003; Francis & Pennebaker, 1992; Pennebaker & Hoover, 1986; Pennebaker et al., 1988; Smyth, 1998). For instance, Pennebaker et al. (1988) assigned 50 healthy undergraduates to either write about a painful traumatic experience or a superficial topic for 4 consecutive days. Their results showed that writing about traumatic experiences led to improved immune system functioning. Such improvements in psychological and physiological health are particularly strong when writing or talking about the secrets leads to greater insights about them (Kelly & Carter, 2001; Kelly, Klusas, von Weiss, & Kenny, 2001; Pennebaker, 1995).

The importance of disclosure for individuals' well-being has resulted in questions about the extent to which the tendency to conceal information could represent a clinically diagnosed personality trait (Kahn, Lamb, Champion, Eberle, & Schoen, 2002). Certain personality characteristics may make it so that some individuals are more likely to conceal information than others, and this tendency to conceal may be detrimental to their health. For instance, Kahn and Hessling (2001) found that people who were considered high disclosers evidenced higher scores on self-esteem, life satisfaction, and positive affect than people who were considered concealers.

The Costs of Concealment

In addition to the lost opportunity of revealing, there appear to be direct costs of concealing. These costs are incurred at both the individual and relational levels.

Individual Costs of Concealment

There is considerable literature that points to the costs of concealment. Much of this research has focused on the link between secrecy and attempts to suppress thoughts about the secret. The basic argument is that people keeping a secret attempt to avoid thinking about that secret (Lane & Wegner, 1995). Curiously, attempts to suppress a thought can actually produce an increase in the frequency or intrusiveness of the thought (Abramowitz, Tolin, & Street, 2001; Major & Gramzow, 1999). A classic example of thought suppression is Wegner, Schneider, Carter, and White's (1987) "white bear" experiment. The overall finding was that people who were deliberately told to not to think of a particular phrase ("white bear") actually had more frequent thoughts of the phrase. The attempt to suppress one's thoughts produced a preoccupation with the very thing that was to be suppressed. Bouman (2003) also discovered that directing people to avoid talking about a certain topic leads them to experience intrusive thoughts about the topic.

Such attempts to suppress thoughts and the intrusive thoughts that follow are more than a mere annoyance to secret keepers. Indeed, mounting evidence shows that thought suppression has deleterious effects (Abramowitz et al., 2001; Belloch et al., 2004; Purdon & Clark, 2001). Secret keeping and the thought suppression that accompanies it are often associated with psychological distress (e.g., Petrie, Booth, & Pennebaker, 1998), various other aspects of psychopathology like obsessive–compulsive disorder and dysfunctional attachment styles (Bouman, 2003; Kahn et al., 2002; Vrij, Paterson, Nunkoosing, Soukara, & Oosterwegel, 2002), and even diminished physical health, including greater susceptibility to stress-related diseases (Pennebaker, 1989; Petrie et al., 1998).

Two theoretical models that have been used to explain the role of suppression in avoidance and secrecy are the preoccupation model of secrecy (Lane & Wegner, 1995) and the fever model (Stiles, 1987). The first assumption of the preoccupation model of secrecy is that secrecy creates thought suppression (Lane & Wegner, 1995). People attempt to repress the secret from their memory to prevent inadvertent disclosures of it. They are continually reminded of the need to suppress the secret because they are surrounded by people from whom they are keeping the secret. The second assumption is that this thought suppression, in turn, produces intrusive thoughts. Finally, such intrusive thoughts foster even greater efforts at thought suppression. Thus, the cycle of attempted thought suppression and intrusive thoughts can become self-sustaining, and even lead to frequent rumination or preoccupation with the secret.

Lane and Wegner's (1995) model provides important insight into the theoretical foundation of the dark side of secret keeping. This model does not address, however, the extent to which thought suppression and the preoccupation with a secret encourages or inhibits people's revelations of their secrets. A partial answer to this question may rest with the assumptions of the fever model (Stiles, 1987). According to this model, withholding information can make people distressed and they are likely to disclose information to others to relieve the distress (Stiles, Shuster, & Harrigan, 1992). The link between disclosure and distress is analogous to a fever and a physical infection. When people conceal information it can produce intrusive, unwanted thoughts and preoccupation with the topic of concealment. This accumulation of worry and stress can produce distress, like a fever that slowly builds with a physical ailment. The fever model suggests that people typically attempt to relieve such distress by disclosing. In the fever metaphor, disclosure allows the body to restore to health and rid itself of the distress that plagues it. It serves a cathartic function by directly or indirectly relieving the psychological distress (Stiles et al., 1992). Thus, the fever model suggests that the more people ruminate about their secret, the more likely they are to reveal the secret to others to reduce their distress.

Of course, if the processes implied by the fever model were the only ones operating, secret keeping would not be particularly problematic: People who became overly distressed would feel compelled to reveal their secret. Other factors must be operating so that people sometimes do not reveal despite distress. The association between rumination and concealment, for instance, probably depends on the impression management concerns of the secret keeper. Consistent with the fever model, W. A. Afifi and Caughlin (in press) found that rumination, after controlling for identity and impression management concerns, encouraged the revelation of secrets. However, when controlling for rumination, identity and impression management concerns discouraged the revelation of secrets. As these authors explained, rumination works in concert with identity and impression management issues to determine the circumstances under which people will be likely to reveal a secret. The degree to which the secret is an important part of one's identity is associated with the tendency to ruminate. Nevertheless, "if individuals can overcome the rumination-induced pressures to reveal, then identity-driven motivations will inhibit revelation" (W. A. Afifi & Caughlin, in press, p. 22). W. A. Afifi and Caughlin (in press) also found that individuals with lower self-esteem were more likely to disclose their secret. People with low self-esteem also tended to ruminate about the secret and the combination of the low self-esteem and rumination may have produced a desire to disclose the secret to confirm their own negative beliefs about the self. Such findings indicate that the consequences of secret keeping and any associated rumination are likely to be more complex than usually thought. We return to this point in greater detail later when we discuss conditions when avoiding communication may be beneficial.

Interpersonal Consequences of Withholding Information

Because so much research assumes that complete openness is essential to relational quality, there is surprisingly little research that examines the exact nature of the association between avoidance or secret keeping and relational well-being (Caughlin & Golish, 2002). As Caughlin and Golish (2002) contended, there seems to be an inconsistency between the current theories of information regulation and most of the empirical work in this area. Researchers using a dialectical perspective (e.g., Baxter, 1990; Baxter & Montgomery, 1996) point out repeatedly that a balance between openness and closedness is necessary for maintaining healthy relationships. Petronio's (1991, 2000, 2002) work with her communication privacy management theory also suggests that people often have good reasons to withhold information. On the surface, these theories seem to contradict much of the empirical work on avoidance and secrets, which suggests that these phenomena typically are associated with dissatisfaction in romantic relationships and families (Caughlin & Golish, 2002; Caughlin et al., 2000; Golish, 2000; Vangelisti, 1994).

One group of studies pertinent to this issue is the investigations examining whether there might be a curvilinear association between self-disclosure in marriage and marital satisfaction (e.g., Burke, Weir, & Harrison, 1976; Jorgensen & Gaudy, 1980). Some scholars have suggested that too much self-disclosure may be as harmful as too little (Gilbert, 1976). The actual findings from such studies, however, tend to support a positive linear correlation between disclosure and satisfaction (Burke et al., 1976; Jorgensen & Gaudy, 1980). Several studies on avoidance have produced similar findings (e.g., Caughlin & Golish, 2002; Finkenauer & Hazam, 2000; Frijns, 2005; Golish, 2000). For example, Golish (2000) tested for curvilinear associations between young adults' topic avoidance and their satisfaction with the members of their stepfamily and found that these associations were inverse and linear.

There is also strong evidence for an inverse association between secret keeping and relational satisfaction (e.g., Caughlin et al., 2000; Vangelisti, 1994; Vangelisti & Caughlin, 1997). Moreover, there seems to be a social comparison component that influences the process. For example, Vangelisti (1994) found that people who thought that their family had more secrets than other families were more likely to be dissatisfied than people whose impression was that their family was comparatively free of secrets. She also found that satisfaction was inversely associated with the perception that family members were keeping taboo secrets, or secrets that involve topics that are socially inappropriate or stigmatized, from one another.

Family members can also become dissatisfied when they believe that certain members of the family are privy to information from which other members, including themselves, are being excluded (e.g., Braithwaite, Olson, Golish, Soukup, & Turman 2001; Caughlin et al., 2000). For instance, stepchildren can avoid topics or keep them secret from their new stepparent as a way to communicate that their stepparent is not yet a part of their family (T. D. Afifi, 2003; Braithwaite et al., 2001; Golish & Caughlin, 2002). Consistent with this notion, Caughlin et al. (2000) found that college students in stepfamilies reported that their original parents and siblings were more likely to know their secrets than were their stepparents and stepsiblings. Consequently, restricting privacy boundaries through avoidance and secrets can be one way that family members signal who is "in" and "out" of their family. Nevertheless, the negative consequences of such management strategies may also be high. Individuals' perceptions of their counterparts' secrecy often produce relational dissatisfaction, feelings of rejection, and reciprocal avoidance behaviors (Caughlin & Golish, 2002; Finkenauer & Hazam, 2000; Frijns, 2005).

Another consequence of avoidance and secrecy is that they can prevent people from building and sustaining equitable and fulfilling connections with one another. As research on the chilling effect suggests (e.g., Cloven & Roloff, 1993; Roloff & Cloven, 1990), people may refrain from introducing certain topics or raising relational complaints for fear of how their counterpart will respond (see Cupach, chap. 6, this volume). The power of the other person can suppress an individual's opinions and ideas (Solomon & Samp, 1998). Over time, this can foster a negative cycle of power imbalances and avoidance (T. D. Afifi & Olson, 2005). For instance, individuals may withhold secrets from family members because they have responded with aggressiveness to past secrets (T. D. Afifi et al., 2005).

Existing power imbalances and expectations for conformity within a family may also reinforce the desire to continue to conceal secrets from family members (T. D. Afifi & Olson, 2005). Because of the negative reactions that individuals expect from their family members, they may simply refrain from revealing sensitive information to them. Unfortunately, however, such avoidance tendencies have been linked to depression and stress in families (Koerner & Fitzpatrick, 1997). People who become habitual avoiders can also become invisible to their family members about the things they avoid. For example, a daughter may avoid talking about her career with her parents and siblings because she thinks that they perceive it as distracting from her responsibilities as a parent. As a result, the family members never ask her about her work and do not often recognize it as an important part of her life.

Although the primary focus in this chapter is on the impact of individuals avoiding topics or keeping secrets, it is also important to recognize that avoidance can occur as part of a pattern in which both people play a role. Roloff and Ifert (1998), for instance, noted that relational partners can agree to declare a topic taboo. Other times, the extent of avoidance may become part of a dyad's conflict, as in the demand–withdraw pattern, where one person demands to talk about an issue and the partner avoids or refuses to talk about the matter (Christensen & Heavey, 1990; Heavey, Layne, & Christensen, 1993). Avoidance that occurs as part of this pattern appears to be quite harmful in most cases. Demand–withdraw is associated with dissatisfaction in marriages (Caughlin & Huston, 2002; Heavey, Christensen, & Malamuth, 1995), and it predicts divorce (Gottman & Levenson, 2000). Demand–withdraw patterns between divorced parents also predict negative outcomes for the children, such as feelings of being caught or being put in the middle of their parents' disputes (T. D. Afifi & Schrodt, 2003a).

Moreover, demand–withdraw between parents and adolescents is associated with low self-esteem and high drug usage by the adolescents (Caughlin & Malis, 2004). Caughlin and Malis (2004) found that one form of avoidance between parents and adolescents was associated with the teenager's use of alcohol and drugs. There are probably multiple reasons for such associations, but one partial explanation involves the evidence that children's perceptions that their parent is unapproachable or avoidant are related to the likelihood that they will engage in risky behavior like drugs, alcohol, and sexual activity (Booth-Butterfield & Sidelinger, 1998).

As has been illustrated, there is ample evidence that avoiding communication in various guises is part of the dark side of interpersonal communication. The vast majority of the research literature seems, at first glance, to be consistent with the ideology of openness. Yet a closer examination of this literature suggests that there are limits to the ideology of openness and that avoidance and secret keeping have bright aspects that accompany their dark ones.

Reasons to Question the Ideology of Openness

Toward the beginning of this chapter, we quoted from an article urging adult children to ask their parents detailed questions about their finances and health. The intent of such discussions is good, and a frank conversation about topics like the size of the parents' estate can have benefits (e.g., helping the parents better prepare for financial changes). However, articles such as the one cited here typically focus on such benefits without giving much credence to the risks often involved in frank discussions. Asking one's parents if they have adequate health insurance and if they understand what Medicare is, for example, involves potential threats to the parents' identity because such questions imply that the child believes the parents may be unprepared or incompetent. Moreover, asking questions about retirement spending or the size of the family estate can come across as greedy. Unfortunately, when risks like these are recognized in the popular press, they typically are portrayed as excuses for not doing "the right thing"—talking about these topics in a completely open and frank manner.

A more balanced viewpoint is that there are benefits and costs involved when one discloses and there are other benefits and costs involved when one avoids or keeps secrets (T. D. Afifi & Schrodt, 2003b; W. A. Afifi & Burgoon, 1998; W. A. Afifi & Guerrero, 1998; Baxter, 1990; Petronio, 2002). Although the popular press and much scholarship downplay the benefits of avoiding communication, there is clear evidence that such benefits exist in at least some circumstances (see Raush, Barry, Hertel, & Swain, 1974). For example, Vangelisti (1994) found that secrets can increase cohesion if the secret is something that certain family members (or the family as a whole) share. Additionally, Finkenauer, Engels, and Meeus (2002) discovered that secrets serve important developmental functions for adolescents by helping them build emotional autonomy from their parents.

In our view, greater attention should be paid to the relative balance of pros and cons of avoiding communication. Keeping a secret or avoiding communication often involves trade-offs between certain costs and other benefits, as in cases when a family member copes with the additional stress of keeping a secret to benefit other family members (Caughlin & Petronio, 2004). Indeed, Petronio (2002) argued that people already do make such calculations when deciding whether to conceal private information.

In addition to the arguments that there can be benefits to keeping secrets and avoiding topics, there is strong evidence that people in even the most healthy relationships withhold some information. Several separate studies have shown, for instance, that almost everyone reports that their family has at least one secret (Vangelisti & Caughlin, 1997; Vangelisti, Caughlin, & Timmerman, 2001). Similarly, T. D. Afifi et al. (2005) discovered that the majority of mothers, fathers, and children in families reported being quite close and satisfied with their family despite keeping secrets from each other. If secrets are kept in most happy families, it is difficult to argue that eliminating such secrets would make the families even happier. A more plausible explanation is that withholding information is sometimes benign or even useful. Thus, rather than focusing exclusively on the overall dark effects of topic avoidance and secrecy, it is equally important to consider the conditions and contexts in which avoiding or keeping secrets are more or less harmful or beneficial.

References

Abramowitz, J. S., Tolin, D. F., & Street, G. P. (2001). Paradoxical effects of thought suppression: A meta-analysis of controlled studies. *Clinical Psychology Review, 21,* 683–703.

Afifi, T. D. (2003). "Feeling caught" in stepfamilies: Managing boundary turbulence through appropriate privacy coordination rules. *Journal of Social and Personal Relationships, 20,* 729–756.

Afifi, T. D., & Olson, L. (2005). The chilling effect and the pressure to conceal secrets in families. *Communication Monographs, 72,* 192–216.

Afifi, T. D., Olson, L., & Armstrong, C. (2005). The chilling effect and family secrets: Examining the role of self protection, other protection, and communication efficacy. *Human Communication Research, 31,* 64–598.

Afifi, T. D., & Schrodt, P. (2003a). "Feeling caught" as a mediator of adolescents' and young adults' avoidance and satisfaction with their parents in divorced and non-divorced households. *Communication Monographs, 70,* 142–173.

Afifi, T. D., & Schrodt, P. (2003b). Uncertainty and the avoidance of the state of one's family/relationships in stepfamilies, post-divorce single parent families, and first marriage families. *Human Communication Research, 29,* 516–533.

Afifi, W. A., & Burgoon, J. K. (1998). "We never talk about that": A comparison of cross-sex friendships and dating relationships on uncertainty and topic avoidance. *Personal Relationships, 5,* 255–272.

Afifi, W. A., & Caughlin, J. P. (in press). A close look at revealing secrets and some consequences that follow. *Communication Research.*

Afifi, W. A., & Guerrero, L. K. (1998). Some things are better left unsaid II: Topic avoidance in friendships. *Communication Quarterly, 46,* 231–250.

Afifi, W. A., & Guerrero, L. K. (2000). Motivations underlying topic avoidance in close relationships. In S. Petronio (Ed.), *Balancing the secrets of private disclosures* (pp. 165–180). Mahwah, NJ: Lawrence Erlbaum Associates.

Albrecht, T. L., Burleson, B. R., & Goldsmith, D. (1994). Supportive communication. In M. L. Knapp & G. R. Miller (Eds.), *Handbook of interpersonal communication* (2nd ed., pp. 419–449). Thousand Oaks, CA: Sage.

Argyle, M., & Henderson, M. (1984). The rules of friendship. *Journal of Social and Personal Relationships, 1,* 211–237.

Argyle, M., Henderson, M., & Furnham, A. (1985). The rules of social relationships. *British Journal of Social Psychology, 24,* 125–139.

Baxter, L. A. (1990). Dialectical contradictions in relationship development. *Journal of Social and Personal Relationships, 7,* 69–88.

Baxter, L. A., Dun, T., & Sahlstein, E. (2001). Rules for relating communicated among social network members. *Journal of Social and Personal Relationships, 18,* 173–199.

Baxter, L. A., & Montgomery, B. M. (1996). *Relating: Dialogues & dialectics.* New York: Guilford.

Baxter, L. A., & Wilmot, W. W. (1985). Taboo topics in close relationships. *Journal of Social and Personal Relationships, 2,* 253–269.

Beach, W. (1996). *Conversations about illness.* Mahwah, NJ: Lawrence Erlbaum Associates.

Bellman, B. L. (1981). The paradox of secrecy. *Human Studies, 4,* 1–24.

Belloch, A., Morillo, C., & Gimenez, A. (2004). Effects of suppressing neutral and obsession-like thoughts in normal subjects: Beyond frequency. *Behaviour Research and Therapy, 42,* 841–857.

Bochner, A. P. (1982). On the efficacy of openness in close relationships. In M. Burgoon (Ed.), *Communication yearbook 6* (pp. 109–123). Beverly Hills, CA: Sage.

Bok, S. (1983). *Secrets: On the ethics of concealment and revelation.* New York: Vintage Books.

Booth-Butterfield, M., & Sidelinger, R. (1998). The influence of family communication on the college-aged child: Openness, attitudes and actions about sex and alcohol. *Communication Quarterly, 46,* 295–308.

Bouman, T. K. (2003). Intra-and interpersonal consequences of experimentally induced concealment. *Behaviour Research and Therapy, 41,* 959–968.

Braithwaite, D. O., Olson, L., Golish, T. D., Soukup, C., & Turman, P. (2001). "Becoming a family": Developmental processes represented in blended family discourse. *Journal of Applied Communication Research, 29,* 221–247.

Burgoon, J. K., & Hoobler, G. D. (2002). Nonverbal signals. In M. L. Knapp & J. A. Daly (Eds.), *Handbook of interpersonal communication* (3rd ed., pp. 240–299). Thousand Oaks, CA: Sage.

Burke, R. J., Weir, T., & Harrison, D. (1976). Disclosure problems and tensions experienced by marital partners. *Psychological Reports, 38,* 531–542.

Canary, D., Cupach, B., & Spitzberg, B. (1995). *Relationship conflict.* Thousand Oaks, CA: Sage.

Caughlin, J. P. (2002). The demand/withdraw pattern of communication as a predictor of marital satisfaction over time: Unresolved issues and future directions. *Human Communication Research, 28,* 49–85.

Caughlin, J. P. (2003). Family communication standards: What counts as excellent family communication and how are such standards associated with family satisfaction? *Human Communication Research, 29,* 5–41.

Caughlin, J., & Afifi, T. D. (2004). When is topic avoidance unsatisfying?: A more complete investigation into the underlying links between avoidance and dissatisfaction in parent-child and dating relationships. *Human Communication Research, 30,* 479–513.

Caughlin, J. P., Afifi, W. A., Carpenter-Theune, K. E., & Miller, L. E. (2005). Reasons for, and consequences of, revealing personal secrets in close relationships: A longitudinal study. *Personal Relationships, 12,* 43–59.

Caughlin, J., & Golish, T. (2002). An analysis of the association between topic avoidance and dissatisfaction: Comparing perceptual and interpersonal explanations. *Communication Monographs, 69,* 275–296.

Caughlin, J. P., Golish, T. D., Olson, L. N., Sargent, J. E., Cook, J. S., & Petronio, S. (2000). Intrafamily secrets in various family configurations: A communication boundary management perspective. *Communication Studies, 51,* 116–134.

Caughlin, J. P., & Huston, T. L. (2002). A contextual analysis of the association between demand/withdraw and marital satisfaction. *Personal Relationships, 9,* 95–119.

Caughlin, J. P., & Malis, R. S. (2004). Demand/withdraw communication between parents and adolescents: Connections with self-esteem and substance use. *Journal of Social and Personal Relationships, 21,* 125–148.

Caughlin, J. P., & Petronio, S. (2004). Privacy in families. In A. L. Vangelisti (Ed.), *Handbook of family communication* (pp. 379–412). Mahwah, NJ: Lawrence Erlbaum Associates.

Caughlin, J. P., & Ramey, M. E. (2005). The demand/withdraw pattern of communication in parent–adolescent dyads. *Personal Relationships, 12,* 337–357.

Christensen, A., & Heavey, C. L. (1990). Gender and social structure in the de-mand/withdraw pattern of marital conflict. *Journal of Personality and Social Psychology, 59,* 73–81.

Cline, R. J. W. (1989). Communication and death and dying: Implications for coping with AIDS. *AIDS and Public Policy, 4,* 40–50.

Cloven, D. H., & Roloff, M. E. (1993). The chilling effect of aggressive potential on the expression of complaints in intimate relationships. *Communication Monographs, 60,* 198–219.

Coyne, J. C., & Smith, D. A. F. (1994). Couples coping with a myocardial infarction: Contextual perspective on patient self-efficacy. *Journal of Family Psychology, 8,* 43–54.

Dailey, R. M., & Palomares, N. A. (2004). Strategic topic avoidance: An investigation of topic avoidance frequency, strategies used, and relational correlates. *Communication Monographs, 71,* 471–496.

Derlega, V. J., Metts, S., Petronio, S., & Margulis, S. T. (1993). *Self-disclosure.* Newbury Park, CA: Sage.

Derlega, V. J., Winstead, B. A., & Folk-Barron, L. (2000). Reasons for and against disclosing HIV-sero-positive test results to an intimate partner: A functional perspective. In S. Petronio (Ed.), *Balancing the secrets of private disclosures* (pp. 53–71). Mahwah, NJ: Lawrence Erlbaum Associates.

Derlega, V. J., Winstead, B. A., Oldfield, E. C., & Barbee, A. P. (2003). Close relationships and social support in coping with HIV: A test of sensitive interaction systems theory. *AIDS and Behavior, 7,* 119–129.

Deters, P. B., & Range, L. M. (2003). Does writing reduce posttraumatic stress disorder symptoms? *Violence and Victims, 18,* 569–580.

Dillard, J. P. (1990). A goal-driven model of interpersonal influence. In J. P. Dillard (Ed.), *Seeking compliance: The production of interpersonal influence messages* (pp. 41–56). Scottsdale, AZ: Gorsuch Scarisbrick.

Ennett, S. T., Bauman, K. E., Foshee, V. A., Pemberton, M., & Hicks, K. A. (2001). Parent–child communication about adolescent tobacco and alcohol use: What do parents say and does it affect youth behavior? *Journal of Marriage and Family, 63,* 48–62.

Finkenauer, C., Engels, R. C. M. E., & Meeus, W. (2002). Keeping secrets from parents: Advantages and disadvantages of secrecy in adolescence. *Journal of Youth and Adolescence, 31,* 124–136.

Finkenauer, C., & Hazam, H. (2000). Disclosure and secrecy in marriage: Do both contribute to marital satisfaction? *Journal of Social and Personal Relationships, 17,* 245–263.

Francis, M. E., & Pennebaker, J. W. (1992). Putting stress into words: The impact of writing on physiological, absentee, and self-reported emotional well-being measures. *American Journal of Health Promotion, 6,* 280–287.

Frijns, T. (2005). *Keeping secrets: Quantity, quality and consequences.* Amsterdam: Free University of Amsterdam.

Fuligni, A. J., & Eccles, J. (1993). Perceived parent–child relationships and early adolescents' orientations toward peers. *Developmental Psychology, 29,* 622–632.

Gilani, N. P. (1999). Conflict management of mothers and daughters belonging to individualistic and collectivistic cultural backgrounds: A comparative study. *Journal of Adolescence, 22,* 853–865.

Gilbert, S. J. (1976). Self-disclosure, intimacy and communication in families. *The Family Coordinator, 25,* 221–231.

Goffman, E. (1959). *The presentation of self in everyday life.* Garden City, NY: Doubleday.

Goldsmith, D. J. (2004). *Communicating social support.* New York: Cambridge University Press.

Golish, T. D. (2000). Is openness always better?: Exploring the role of topic avoidance, satisfaction, and parenting styles of stepparents. *Communication Quarterly, 48,* 137–158.

Golish, T. D. (2003). Stepfamily communication strengths: Understanding the ties that bind. *Human Communication Research, 29,* 41–80.

Golish, T. D., & Caughlin, J. (2002). "I'd rather not talk about it": Adolescents' and young adults' use of topic avoidance in stepfamilies. *Journal of Applied Communication Research, 30,* 78–106.

Gottman, J. M. (1994). *What predicts divorce? The relationship between marital processes and marital outcomes.* Hillsdale, NJ: Lawrence Erlbaum Associates.

Gottman, J. M., & Levenson, R. W. (2000). The timing of divorce: Predicting when a couple will divorce over a 14-year period. *Journal of Marriage and the Family, 62,* 737–745.

Greene, K., & Faulkner, S. L. (2002). Expected versus actual responses to disclosure in relationships of HIV-positive African American adolescent females. *Communication Studies, 53,* 297–317.

Guerrero, L. K., & Afifi, W. A. (1995a). Some things are better left unsaid: Topic avoidance in family relationships. *Communication Quarterly, 43,* 276–296.

Guerrero, L. K., & Afifi, W. A. (1995b). What parents don't know: Topic avoidance in parent–child relationships. In T. Socha & G. Stamp (Eds.), *Parents, children, and communication: Frontiers of theory and research* (pp. 219–247). Mahwah, NJ: Lawrence Erlbaum Associates.

Heavey, C. L., Christensen, A., & Malamuth, N. M. (1995). The longitudinal impact of demand and withdrawal during marital conflict. *Journal of Consulting and Clinical Psychology, 63,* 797–801.

Heavey, C. L., Layne, C., & Christensen, A. (1993). Gender and conflict structure in marital interaction: A replication and extension. *Journal of Consulting and Clinical Psychology, 61,* 16–27.

Jorgensen, S. R., & Gaudy, J. C. (1980). Self-disclosure and satisfaction in marriage: The relation examined. *Family Relations, 29,* 281–287.

Jourard, S. M. (1971). *Self-disclosure: An experimental analysis of the transparent self.* New York: Wiley-Interscience.

Kahn, J. H., & Hessling, R. M. (2001). Measuring the tendency to conceal versus disclose psychological distress. *Journal of Social and Clinical Psychology, 20,* 41–65.

Kahn, J. H., Lamb, D. H., Champion, C. D., Eberle, J. A., & Schoen, K. A. (2002). Disclosing versus concealing distressing information: Linking self-reported tendencies to situational behavior. *Journal of Research in Personality, 36,* 531–538.

Karpel, M. A. (1980). Family secrets: Implications for research and therapy. *Family Process, 19,* 295–306.

Kelly, A. E. (2002). *The psychology of secrets.* New York: Kluwer Academic/Plenum.

Kelly, A. E., & Carter, J. E. (2001). Dealing with secrets. In C. R. Snyder (Ed.), *Coping with stress: Effective people and processes* (pp. 196–221). New York: Oxford University Press.

Kelly, A. E., Klusas, J. A., von Weiss, R. T., & Kenny, C. (2001). What is it about revealing secrets that is beneficial? *Personality and Social Psychology Bulletin, 27,* 651–665.

Kelly, A. E., & McKillop, K. J. (1996). Consequences of revealing personal secrets. *Psychological Bulletin, 120,* 450–465.

Klinetob, N. A., & Smith, D. A. (1996). Demand–withdraw communication in marital interaction: Tests of interspousal contingency and gender role hypotheses. *Journal of Marriage and the Family, 58,* 945–958.

Koerner, A. F., & Fitzpatrick, M. A. (1997). Family type and conflict: The impact of conversation orientation and conformity orientation on conflict in the family. *Communication Studies, 48,* 59–76.

Lane, J. D., & Wegner, D. M. (1995). The cognitive consequences of secrecy. *Journal of Personality and Social Psychology, 69,* 237–253.

Lazarus, R. S., & Folkman, S. (1984). *Stress, appraisal, and coping.* New York: Springer.

Locke, H. J., & Wallace, K. M. (1959). Short marital adjustment and prediction tests: Their reliability and validity. *Journal of Marriage and Family Living, 21,* 251–255.

Major, B., & Gramzow, R. H. (1999). Abortion as stigma: Cognitive and emotional implications of concealment. *Journal of Personality and Social Psychology, 77,* 735–745.

Makoul, G., & Roloff, M. (1998). The role of efficacy and outcome expectations in the decision to withhold relational complaints. *Communication Research, 25,* 5–29.

O'Keefe, B. J. (1988). The logic of message design: Individual differences in reasoning about communication. *Communication Monographs, 55,* 80–103.

Parks, M. R. (1982). Ideology in interpersonal communication: Off the couch and into the world. In M. Burgoon (Ed.), *Communication yearbook 6* (pp. 79–107). Beverly Hills, CA: Sage.

Pennebaker, J. W. (1989). Confession, inhibition, and disease. *Advances in Experimental Social Psychology, 22,* 211–244.

Pennebaker, J. W. (Ed.) (1995). *Emotion, disclosure, and health.* Washington, DC: American Psychological Association.

Pennebaker, J. W., & Hoover, C. W. (1986). Inhibition and cognition: Towards an understanding of trauma and disease. In R. J. Davidson, G. E. Schwartz, & D. Shapiro (Eds.), *Consciousness and self-regulation* (Vol. 4, pp. 107–136). New York: Plenum.

Pennebaker, J. W., Kiecolt-Glaser, J., & Glaser, R. (1988). Disclosure of traumas and immune function: Health implications for psychotherapy. *Journal of Consulting and Clinical Psychology, 56,* 239–245.

Petrie, K. J., Booth, R. J., & Pennebaker, J. W. (1998). The immunological effects of thought suppression. *Journal of Personality and Social Psychology, 75,* 1264–1272.

Petronio, S. (1991). Communication boundary management: A theoretical model of managing disclosure of private information between marital couples. *Communication Theory, 1,* 311–335.

Petronio, S. (2000). The boundaries of privacy: Praxis of everyday life. In S. Petronio (Ed.), *Balancing the secrets of private disclosures* (pp. 37–49). Mahwah, NJ: Lawrence Erlbaum Associates.

Petronio, S. (2002). *Boundaries of privacy: Dialectics of disclosure*. Albany: State University of New York Press.

Petronio, S., Reeder, H. M., Hecht, M. L., & Mon't Ros-Mendoza, T. (1996). Disclosure of sexual abuse by children and adolescents. *Journal of Applied Communication Research, 24*, 181–199.

Price, G. (1999). How are your finances, Dad? *Personal Investment, 17*, 72–73.

Purdon, C., & Clark, D. A. (2001). Suppression of obsessive-like thoughts in nonclinical individuals: Impact on thought frequency, appraisal and mood state. *Behaviour Research and Therapy, 39*, 1163–1181.

Raush, H. L., Barry, W. A., Hertel, R. K., & Swain, M. A. (1974). *Communication conflict and marriage*. San Francisco: Jossey-Bass.

Rawlins, W. (1983). Openness as problematic in ongoing friendships: Two conversational dilemmas. *Communication Monographs, 50*, 1–14.

Roberts, S. S. (2003). Money & marriage: It's time to talk. *Diabetes Forecast, 56*(12), 70–73.

Roloff, M. E., & Cloven, D. H. (1990). The chilling effect in interpersonal relationships: The reluctance to speak one's mind. In D. D. Cahn (Ed.), *Intimates in conflict: A communication perspective* (pp. 49–76). Hillsdale, NJ: Lawrence Erlbaum Associates.

Roloff, M. E., & Ifert, D. E. (1998). Antecedents and consequences of explicit agreements declaring a taboo topic in dating relationships. *Personal Relationships, 5*, 191–205.

Roloff, M. E., & Ifert, D. E. (2000). Conflict management through avoidance: Withholding complaints, suppressing arguments, and declaring topics taboo. In S. Petronio (Ed.), *Balancing the secrets of private disclosures* (pp. 151–179). Mahwah, NJ: Lawrence Erlbaum Associates.

Rosenfeld, L. B. (1979). Self-disclosure avoidance: Why I am afraid to tell you who I am. *Communication Monographs, 46*, 63–74.

Sillars, A. L. (1998). (Mis)understanding. In B. H. Spitzberg & W. R. Cupach (Eds.), *The dark side of close relationships* (pp. 73–102). Mahwah, NJ: Lawrence Erlbaum Associates.

Sillars, A. L., Pike, G. R., Jones, T. S., & Redmon, K. (1983). Communication and conflict in marriage. In R. N. Bostrom (Ed.), *Communication yearbook 7* (pp. 414–429). Beverly Hills, CA: Sage.

Sillars, A. L., Roberts, L. J., Leonard, K. E., & Dun, T. (2000). Cognition during marital conflict: The relationship of thought and talk. *Journal of Social and Personal Relationships, 17*, 479–502.

Smyth, J. M. (1998). Written emotional expression: Effect sizes, outcome types, and moderating variables. *Journal of Consulting and Clinical Psychology, 66*, 174–184.

Smyth, J. M., & Pennebaker, J. W. (2001). What are the health effects of disclosure? In A. Baum, T. A. Revenson, & J. E. Singer (Eds.), *Handbook of health psychology* (pp. 339–348). Mahwah, NJ: Lawrence Erlbaum Associates.

Solomon, D. H., & Samp, J. A. (1998). Power and problem appraisal: Perceptual foundations of the chilling effect in dating relationships. *Journal of Social and Personal Relationships, 15,* 191–209.

Spanier, G. B. (1976). Measuring dyadic adjustment: New scales for assessing the quality of marriage and similar dyads. *Journal of Marriage and the Family, 38,* 15–28.

Stiles, W. B. (1987). Verbal response modes as intersubjective categories. In R. L. Russell (Ed.), *Language in psychotherapy: Strategies of discovery* (pp. 131–170). New York: Plenum.

Stiles, W. B., Shuster, P. L., & Harrigan, J. A. (1992). Disclosure and anxiety: A test of the fever model. *Journal of Personality and Social Psychology, 63,* 980–988.

Ting-Toomey, S., & Kurogi, A. (1998). Facework competence in intercultural conflict: An updated face-negotiation theory. *International Journal of Intercultural Relations, 22,* 187–225.

Tiplet, R. G., & Sugarman, D. B. (1987). Reactions to AIDS victims: Ambiguity breeds contempt. *Personality and Social Psychology Bulletin, 13,* 265–274.

Ullrich, P. M., Lutgendorf, S. K., & Stapleton, J. T. (2003). Concealment of homosexual identity, social support and CD4 cell count among HIV-seropositive gay men. *Journal of Psychosomatic Research, 54,* 205–212.

Vangelisti, A. L. (1994). Family secrets: Forms, functions and correlates. *Journal of Social and Personal Relationships, 11,* 113–135.

Vangelisti, A. L., & Caughlin, J. P. (1997). Revealing family secrets: The influence of topic, function, and relationships. *Journal of Social and Personal Relationships, 14,* 679–705.

Vangelisti, A. L., Caughlin, J. P., & Timmerman, L. (2001). Criteria for revealing family secrets. *Communication Monographs, 68,* 1–17.

Vrij, A., Paterson, B., Nunkoosing, K., Soukara, S., & Oosterwegel, A. (2003). Perceived advantages and disadvantages of secrets disclosure. *Personality and Individual Differences, 35,* 593–602.

Wegner, D. M., Schneider, D. J., Carter, S. R., & White, T. L. (1987). Paradoxical effects of thought suppression. *Journal of Personality and Social Psychology, 53,* 5–13.

Weston, L. P. (2005). Time to talk. Retrieved June 15, 2005, from http:// www.latimes.com/ business/investing/la-famtalk-story1a,1,4069419.story

Wheeless, L. R., & Grotz, J. (1976). Conceptualizing and measurement of reported self-disclosure. *Human Communication Research, 2,* 338–346.

Zhang, A. Y., & Siminoff, L. A. (2003). Silence and cancer: Why do families and patients fail to communicate? *Health Communication, 15,* 415–429.

Self-Disclosure Real-World Lab

Name: _____

Date: _____

A major part of understanding privacy and secrets is engaging in disclosure. Mutual vulnerability and disclosure fosters closeness in interpersonal relationships. For this real-world lab, you will disclose personal information to someone you want to get to know better to observe how disclosure can help you build a relationship with them.

First, go to https://nyti.ms/1BWQijj and read through the list of questions. The questions listed on that website are designed to accelerate intimacy between strangers (or acquaintances). To do this activity correctly, it will take some time. Plan to spend some quality face-to-face time with someone you know who you would like to get to know better. This should not be your best friend or someone you know extremely well already. Go through the list of questions together, giving each person a chance to answer. If you'd rather see the questions one at a time, you can use this website: http://36questionsinlove.com/. After the conversation, answer the reflection questions.

1. Do you feel closer to the person you spoke with after completing this activity? Why or why not?

   _____
   _____
   _____
   _____
   _____

2. Which question was the hardest for you to answer? Why?

   _____
   _____
   _____
   _____

3. Which question was the easiest for you to answer? Why?

_____

_____

_____

_____

4. What surprised you about this activity?

_____

_____

_____

_____

5. What nonverbal behaviors did you notice your partner doing?

_____

_____

_____

_____

6. Why do you think mutual vulnerability and shared disclosure accelerate relationship building?

_____

_____

_____

_____

7. Would this exercise have the same effect if it was done via technology (for example, the questions were asked and answered online via messaging or email?)

_____

_____

_____

_____

CHAPTER 9

Maintaining Long-Distance Relationships

Introduction to the Chapter

Have you ever been part of a long-distance dating relationship? Chances are, you or someone you know in college has. The research shows that long-distance romantic relationships (LDRR) might be just as common as geographically close relationships on college campuses. LDRRs come with a unique set of challenges and stressors that people in proximal relationships do not have to face. That said, LDRRs can thrive if treated with care. In this chapter, you will read about relationship maintenance strategies including how people in long-distance dating relationships maintain their relationships. This chapter covers concepts unique to LDRRs like idealization of one's partner and dives deep into how maintenance strategies are used in a specific context.

Long-Distance Dating Relationships

By Laura Stafford

....

Long-distance dating relationships (LDDRs) among college students have garnered more research attention from scholars of interpersonal communication than any other single type of LDR (Aylor, 2003). Estimates indicate that anywhere from 25% to 50% of college students are involved in a long-distance dating relationship at any given time and 75% of college students have at some time been involved in at least one LDDR (Dellmann-Jenkins, Bernard-Paolucci, & Rushing, 1994; Guldner & Swensen, 1995). LDDRs may be as prevalent on college campuses as geographically close dating relationships (Stafford, Merolia, & Castle, 2004). Given the epidemic proportion of college students involved in LDDRs, attention is not unwarranted, although it is unfortunate that our knowledge of LDDRs comes solely from couples wherein at least one of the partners is a college student.

The exact definition of a long-distance dating relationship varies from report to report and even from individual to individual. Physical parameters such as mileage or living in different cites are sometimes used (e.g., Carpenter & Knox, 1986; Helgeson, 1994). Others have defined LDDRs as those that participants consider long-distance (Dellmann-Jenkins et al., 1994). Such a definition likely captures each individual's relational reality better than researcher-imposed constructions as even two members of the same couple have been found to disagree as to whether or not their relationship is, or ever has been, a long-distance one (Stafford et al., 2004).

Success

What people want to know most about romantic long-distance relationships is "Do they work?" Guldner considers long-distance romantic relationships as working if the couple remains intact. Apparently so do most scholars, counselors, and romantic partners. However, it is safe to assume that the desire is not only to remain intact, but also, consistent with the definition of maintenance [...] long-distance dating partners also want their relationships to be characterized by relational qualities such as satisfaction, liking, commitment, trust, and so on. In addition, LDDRs are generally presumed to be stressful and depressing for the individuals involved. Seemingly then, successful LDDRs are those that remain intact for an unspecified period of time, are characterized by positive relational features such as satisfaction, and the individuals involved in the relationship have an absence of stress or depression. These alleged markers of success are discussed next, first turning to distress and dysfunction.

Distress, Dysfunction, and Coping

Alarm over anguish ridden, forlorn college students wandering the halls of academia appears unwarranted, or at least unverified. The assumption that LDDRs are depressing or stressful might be traced to Wendel (1975). He was interested in the feelings of high school sweethearts when one or both went away to college. He concluded that students felt a sense of "separateness and distance" (p. 45).

The legacy of dysfunction, distress, and depression among individuals in LDDRs became entrenched with the findings of Westefeld and Liddell (1982). As college counselors, they reported being confronted by students in "angst" over their long-distance romances. Based on discussion forums with students who were having difficulty coping with their LDDRs, they enumerated several problematic areas including economic difficulty from telephone and travel expenses, ambiguity in defining the parameters of other geographically close relationships, determining the best use of their time when they were physically together, coping with roller-coaster like emotions, and assessing whether they should continue their relationships. The most often cited aspect of their work is the reported angst and emotional stress. Most overlooked is their insight that individuals in LDDRs have difficulty "evaluating the relationship while at a distance" (Westefeld & Liddell, 1982, p. 550). This oversight is addressed later in this chapter.

In response to the concerns raised by long-distance dating partners, Westefeld and Liddell (1982) conducted workshops as a forum for students to exchange advice and they summarized the students' recommendations. Suggestions included simply recognizing and accepting that the situation is stressful; developing support networks in their present community; developing "creative ways of communicating while at a distance" (p. 550); setting rules for the separation in advance while being aware these might need to be flexible; using their limited time together wisely; and being honest and open with each other. Focusing on the positive aspects of the separation and attempting to be optimistic about the relationship were also advised. Although often repeated as coping strategies (e.g., Aylor, 2003; Rohfling, 1995), these suggestions are yet to be confirmed as actually beneficial.

Insightfully, Westefeld and Liddell (1982) felt that the primary benefit of the workshops was simply the venue itself. The forums allowed students to form connections with and receive support from proximal individuals with similar circumstances. Research supporting the importance of developing proximal community ties for the provision of companionship, support, and the like remains consistent (e.g., Carpenter & Knox, 1986; Holt & Stone, 1988; Schwebel, Dunn, Moss, & Renner, 1992; Wilmot & Carbaugh, 1986). Thus, it is possible that these connections eased the separation for some individuals.

Westefeld and Liddell (1982) drew their conclusions about LDDRs based only on individuals who sought counseling. Holt and Stone (1988) found that the less satisfied students were with their long-distance relationships, the more likely they were to seek counseling. Thus, Westefeld and Liddell's conclusions (1982) may not be representative of most students in LDDRs.

Still, the proclamation that distance and distress go hand in hand continues to be propagated. Guldner (1996) based in an attachment paradigm (see chap. 2, this volume) claimed that separation from a romantic partner inherently results in distress. Although, he did find that students involved in LDRs reported "feeling blue" more often than students in proximal relationships, he reported major depression to be no more frequent among individuals in LDDRs than among those in geographically proximal relationships. Nor did he find any differences in distress or psychological functioning between individuals in LDDRs and geographically close ones. Similarly, although Le and Agnew (2001) found geographically close dating partners were better able to meet needs for companionship, sexual activity, security, and emotional involvement than long distance partners, this was not associated with negative emotions.

LDDRs simply do not seem to be as inherently or uniformly problematic as some have claimed (e.g. Guldner, 1996). For example, Knox, Zusman, Daniels, and Brantley (2002) reported that by 5 months of separation approximately 20% of LDDRs had ended and another 20% reported their relationships were worse. Alternatively, nearly 20% also indicated the separation made their relationship better and just more than 30% gave mixed responses. In addition, students in LDDRs perform better academically than those in geographically close relationships; they also are better rested (Guldner, 1992, 1996; Guldner & Swensen, 1995).

Other work has also found both benefits and drawbacks to LDDRs (Sahlstein, 2004; Stafford et al., 2004). Individuals appear to appreciate the separation in order to focus on school or career when apart and then focus on their relationships when together (Stafford et al., 2004). This type of segmentation also occurs in long-distance dual career couples (see chap. 5, this volume). Many individuals also like the freedom and autonomy of a LDDR and concurrently miss their partners and wish they could spend more time together (Stafford et al., 2004). Sahlstein (2004), working from a dialectical perspective (see chap. 2, this volume) revealed paradoxical contradictions in LDDRs. When the long-distance partners see each other in person, they report a sense of rejuvenation, a reduction in uncertainty about their relationships, and form memories to help sustain them when apart. They also report pressure to make sure their time spent together is high quality and avoid disagreements. When separated again, many express feeling let down or sad on returning to their everyday lives without their partners. Yet they simultaneously enjoy the anticipation of seeing each other when they are apart. Although the sample size is relatively small (20 couples), Sahlstein's (2004) in-depth interviews provide a picture of the complexities of LDDRs. Moreover, the themes she identified reiterate those revealed in research long-distance marriages (see Gerstel & Gross, 1984; Winfield, 1985).

Maintenance as Success

Research has often focused on success as stability of dating partners (Cate, Levin, & Richmond, 2002). Remaining a couple is unequivocally viewed as successful and desirable. For example, Schwebel et al. (1992) stated a goal of their study of LDDRs was to understand the factors "involved in preserving the relationships" (1992, p. 22) in order to aid college counselors in advising students.

By the criteria of remaining a couple, LDDRs are as successful if not more so than proximal couples. Stephen (1986) found that LDDRs were more stable across time than geographically close couples. Reske and Stafford (1989) found that, after 6 months, 30% of geographically close relationships had dissolved, but none of the LDDRs in their sample had. Stafford and Reske (1990) also found a pattern of greater stability among LDRRs. The same pattern was not replicated by VanHorn et al. (1997). However, the timeframe for the Van Horn et al. (1997) study was 11 to 12 weeks compared to 6 months, 9 months, and 2 years for the studies of Reske and Stafford (1989), Stafford and Reske (1990), and Stephen (1986), respectively, which may account for the differences in relational termination rates.

If we go beyond stability and include other relational features as success, LDDRs appear to fare quite well. Most studies have found equal or even higher levels of satisfaction, commitment, and trust in LDDRs compared to geographically close ones (Guldner & Swensen, 1995; Lydon, Pierce, & O'Regan, 1997; Schwebel, Dunn, Moss, & Renner, 1992; Stafford & Reske, 1990; Stephen, 1986; VanHorn, et al., 1997).

Maintaining LDDRs

Approval of one's romantic involvements by one's friendship network repeatedly has been found to play a role in the stability of dating relationships in general (Cate, Levin, & Richmond, 2002; Felmlee, 2001; Sprecher & Felmlee, 2000). Given that LDDRs violate norms of proximity, individuals are not always validated by nearby friends or families. Sahlstein (2004) reported that long-distance dating partners find that their immediate social networks play both a positive and a negative role in the maintenance of their long-distance relationships. College students in LDDRs are surrounded by others in similar situations with whom to commiserate. "Perhaps the unique college environment inoculates these relationships against the impact of deficits in time spent together" (Guldner & Swensen, 1995, p. 319).

Some research has found an association between frequency of face-to-face (FtF) interaction and relational success. Holt and Stone (1988) reported that college partners who physically saw each other less than once a month and lived under 250 miles apart were less satisfied than dating partners who saw each other more frequently. Similarly, Dainton and Aylor (2002) asked how often college LDDR individuals saw each other and found that those who answered "never" were less satisfied and less committed than individuals with "periodic face to face contact" (p. 127). They found FtF contact to be positively associated with satisfaction, trust, commitment, and lowered jealousy. However, their findings were not longitudinal.

In addition to FtF communication, LDDRs use a variety of mediated means. Couples who exchange letters are more likely to stay together than those who do not (Guldner, 1992, as cited in Guldner, 1996). Similarly, Stafford and Reske (1990) found letters to be more highly associated with feelings of satisfaction, love, satisfaction with communication, and idealization in the relationship than FtF or telephone contact. Dainton and Aylor (2002) found that telephone time and Internet use among dating partners were positively associated with relational success as defined by increased satisfaction, trust, commitment, and lowered jealousy. They did not find the same associations for letters. This may be a function of expectations and availability. Access to e-mail was greater on college campuses at the time of the Dainton and Aylor study than when the Stafford and Reske study was conducted. In fact, Stafford and Reske did not even ask about e-mail usage. (See chap 5, this volume, on the use of letters and e-mail among deployed military personal and their families, and chap 9, this volume, for more on the role of the Internet in LDRs).

Yet even with these mediated means, some FtF contact is still thought to be important. Dainton and Aylor (2002) found that long-distance partners with no FtF contact were less certain of their relationships and less trusting of their partners than those with some FtT contact.

If some level of FtF interaction is important, then how long is too long to go without physically being in each other's presence? Too long is perceived as just slightly longer than the partners usually go without seeing each other. Individuals who reported seeing each other every week felt that more than a week was too long. If seeing each other once a month was normative for a couple, then anything over once a month was felt to be too long (Stafford, 2004).

Idealization as Relational Maintenance

In contrast to U.S. cultural expectations about frequent FtF interaction as the cornerstone for close relationships, Guldner and Swensen (1995) concluded that the amount of time long-distance couples spent together played little role in the maintenance of the relationship. Moreover, Stafford and Reske (1990) found that the greater the proportion of interaction spent FtF compared to frequency of other modes, the less satisfied with the relationship, the less satisfied with the communication, and the more likely the demise of the dating relationship.

This seeming paradox of limited FtF interaction contributing to stability was noted by Stephen (1986). He surmised that geographically close couples have the luxury of virtually unlimited conversation about a vast array of topics; LDR participants, on the other hand, talk about a much more limited range of topics, such as issues "related to love and intimacy" (Stephen, 1986, p. 206). He proposes that individuals minimize the importance of talk for the maintenance of their relationships as well as depend more on the talk they do have to construct relational realities. Likewise, Guldner and Swenson (1995) concluded that talk or quantity of time together simply are "not central to relationship satisfaction, intimacy, trust, or commitment" but rather, "some other factor associated with even small amounts of time spent together" (p. 320) must sustain these relationships.

Idealization [...] is proposed to be this mechanism. Restricted communication facilitates idealized images (Schulman, 1974; Stafford & Reske, 1990) and by default, LDDRs have restricted FtF communication. Stafford and Reske (1990) proposed that such positive illusions accounted for the longevity of geographically separated dating relationship; a lack of communication preempts couples from discovering undesirable attributes. Dainton and Aylor (2002) repeated this concern with idealization. They speculated that perhaps even long-distance couples with frequent, short, face-to-face visits may be acting on their "best behavior" allowing idealization to continue instead of actually becoming better acquainted. Other reports also suggest that LDDRs partners tend to present overly positive images of themselves to their partners when FtF (Sahlstein, 2004, Stafford et al., 2004). Long-distance partners avoid negative interactions when together to avoid ruining this precious time (Sahlstein, 2004; Stafford et al., 2004). When apart, they focus on plans for when together, ruminate about positive relational memories (Sahlstein, 2004), and day-dream about their partners (Allen, 1990, as cited in Honeycutt, 2003; Holt & Stone, 1988).

Although relational satisfaction and commitment have been proposed as the force holding LDDRs together, both satisfaction and commitment LDDRs co-occur with idealization. Schwebel et al. (1992) found that relational satisfaction among college students prior to separation in the fall was strongly related to the survival of the relationship throughout the school term. Individuals in long-distance dating relationships report a greater belief that their relationships will work out in the long run (Van Horn et al., 1997) or that they will marry at some point in the future (Stafford, 2004; Stafford & Reske, 1990) than their geographically close counterparts. Individuals in LDDRs also report a greater "moral burden" to continue the relationship than proximal partners and moral commitment has been found to be correlated with relationship stability (Lydon, Pierce, & O'Regan, 1997). However, increased investments and commitment has been found to lead to increased positive relational distortion (Rusbult et al., 2001), thus idealization may still be the mechanism maintaining these relationships.

In short, constrained communication appears to promote positive illusions, and positive illusions have been found to promote premarital stability (Murray & Holmes, 1996). However, there is little debate that interaction is necessary to acquire knowledge about one's partner, and "depth of acquaintance" has remained a consistent predictor of later marital quality and stability (Larson & Holman, 1994). "People need to spend sufficient time before marriage developing essential processes that will enhance their marriage" (Cate et al., 2002, p. 262). Couples who avoid conflict in premarital stages of relationships are subsequently at risk (Gottman & Krokoff, 1989). Everyday casual interaction can provide a safe context within which more specific discussions can occur and partners can learn about one another (Duck, 1990). Everyday casual interaction is sorely lacking in LDDRs. Though an often repeated finding is that the length of dating prior to marriage is associated with marital stability (Cate et al., 2002; Larson & Holman, 1994), it is undoubtedly not the passage of time per se that is important, but rather the interaction which takes place during this time. LDDRs survive and even thrive without this interaction raising concerns about future stability and satisfaction.

Becoming Geographically Close

Although individuals fear that separation may result in relational termination (Van Horn et al., 1997), minimal consideration has been given to the possibility of termination when long-distance couples become geographically close. To the extent that idealization held the couple together, the couple may be at risk for termination as overly idealized images may be difficult to maintain when day-to-day reality ensues.

Little is known about what happens when LDDRs become proximal. Preliminary results from a sample of approximately 100 long-distance dating individuals who subsequently moved to the same geographic location reveals that many individuals espouse desirable aspects of their long-distance status that they missed when moving to the same location (Stafford et al., 2004). Some individuals reported missing the freedom and autonomy to spend time with friends, on homework or jobs, or other activities, and the novelty or excitement of a LDDR. Of course, the expense or hassle of traveling was not missed, although some individuals actually reported increased expense; they now had to spend more money on dates. Spending FtF time appears to increase; so does conflict. Ironically, some report missing the feeling of missing each other or of anticipation of seeing each other; now permanently together the relationship was no longer interesting or exciting. In fact, LDDRs are likely to terminate on reunion as during separation (Stafford et al.).

Stafford et al., (2004) also found that some individuals indicated adjusting to each other and becoming aware of previously unknown aspects of their partner or relationship. Issues in adjusting or learning about each other were sometimes positive, other times negative, and sometimes were simple statements of fact. For example, some reported that they had not truly appreciated how wonderful their partner was until they came together full time, that they become emotionally closer, and enjoyed their increased FtF time. Others reported discovering personality flaws that had remained hidden while apart, or realizing they did not truly know the other person when they were apart. Some now felt smothered. Also prevalent were statements that the relationship was just as they expected it to be.

Stafford et al. also found a few couples terminated the relationship within a few days of permanently moving to the same location, and several relationships lasted only 1 or 2 months on uniting, even after a much longer time of being a couple in separate locations. Others were still together well over a year after uniting.

In short, moving to the same location invoked a wide range or responses, including relational termination for some and escalation for others. Moreover, the various factors that might be influential in transitioning to proximal couples, such as length of time dating prior to separation and length of separation were not predictive of relational demise when becoming proximal (Stafford et al., 2004).

Relational Demise as Success

A criterion of relational stability as success is simplistic at best. Adding other relational features generally considered positive, such as commitment or satisfaction, is not much better. Much ado is made of communication as necessary for relational development, with minimal accord granted to the possibility that increased interaction may result in increased knowledge and subsequent relational demise. Due to the restricted interaction, romanticized images of each other prevail in conjunction with overly positive self-presentations cyclically feeding into each other's romanticized images. Thus, long-distance partners "may have little idea of how idealized and inaccurate their images are" (Stafford & Reske, 1990, p. 278).

Stafford and Reske (1990) expressed misgivings over young adults making decisions regarding long-term commitments such as marriage in this idealized and unknowingly uninformed state. Concern is not with general positive perceptions of one's partner, but rather with potential critical inaccuracies derived by completing visions of one's partner or relationship from one's own mental prototype rather than based on information about the specific partner. In addition, previously masked areas of irreconcilable differences will inevitably surface when together on a daily basis. Given their limited interactions, long-distance couples may not be truly gaining knowledge about their partner in order to make informed decisions about marriage (Stafford et al., 2004).

Certainly some dating, in U.S. culture, is purely recreational. However, when dating is operating as mate selection, it may be likened to an extended interview process to determine if the two individuals are indeed suited. Long-distance dating partners should be urged to develop deeper relational knowledge and in doing so "couples will either address areas in which they differ or terminate the relationship"

(Stafford & Reske, 1990, p. 278). Either outcome is seen as a success, although it is unlikely the relational partners will see the latter as success, at least not immediately. However, it has been said, "the best divorce is one you get before you get married" (Hill, Rubin, & Peplau, 1976).

Conclusions

Individuals in LDDRs may be especially prone to idealized, inaccurate views of their partners. Romanticized visions and over-projections of similarity have generally been thought to occur in early stages of relationships and then dissipate with increased interaction. Distance may not allow for this dissipation.

No argument is made that idealized images should be avoided or abandoned, nor are they unique to LDDRs. On the contrary, "benevolent misconceptions" (Ickes & Simpson, 1997) protect even geographically close relationships. A certain amount of misunderstanding or optimistic adoration may well be necessary for the preservation of relationships in general (Sillars, 1998). Of course all of us want our relationships to be superior to others' relationships (Rusbult et al., 2000).

Positive illusions in and of themselves are not problematic. They have long been thought to be an important element of courtship (Waller, 1937). Furthermore, some idealization may be necessary to enter into long-term commitments and to sustain our relationships (Sabetelli, 1988). A conundrum exists in finding a balance between functional idealistic distortion and problematic perceptual inaccuracies. Seeing our romantic partners through rose colored glasses has many benefits (Hendrick & Hendrick, 1988). However, "it hardly seems pragmatic to gloss over the faults of a *potential* romantic partner" (Goodwin, Fiske, Rosen, & Rosenthal, 2002, p. 232, italics in original).

References

Aylor, D. (2003). Maintaining long-distance relationships. In D. J. Canary & M. Dainton (Eds.), *Maintaining relationships through communication: Relational, contextual, and cultural variations* (pp. 127–140). Mahwah, NJ: Lawrence Erlbaum Associates.

Carpenter, D., & Knox, D. (1986). Relationship maintenance of college students separated during courtship. *College Student Journal, 20,* 86–88.

Cate, R. M., Levin, L. A., & Richmond, L. S. (2002). Premarital relationship stability: A review of recent research. *Journal of Social and Personal Relationships, 19,* 261–284.

Dainton, M., & Aylor, B. (2002). Patterns of communication channel use in the maintenance of long-distance relationships. *Communication Research Reports, 19,* 118–129.

Dellmann-Jenkins, M., Bernard-Paolucci, T. S., & Rushing, B. (1994). Does distance make the heart grow fonder? A comparison of college students in long-distance and geographically-close dating relationships. *College Student Journal, 28,* 212–219.

Duck, S. W. (1990). Where do all the kisses go? Rapport, positivity and relational level of analysis of interpersonal enmeshment. *Psychological Inquiry, 1,* 47–53.

Felmlee, D. H. (2001). No couple is an island: A social network perspective on dyadic stability. *Social Forces, 79,* 1259–1287.

Gerstel, N., & Gross, H. (1984). *Commuter marriage: A study of work and family.* New York: Guilford.

Goodwin, S. A., Fiske, S. T., Rosen, L. D., & Rosenthal, A. M. (2002). The eye of the beholder: Romantic goals and impression biases. *Journal of Experimental Social Psychology, 38,* 232–241.

Gottman, J. M., & Krokoff, L. J. (1989). Marital interaction and satisfaction: A longitudinal view. *Journal of Consulting and Clinical Psychology, 57,* 47–52.

Guldner, G. T. (1992). *Propinquity and dating relationships: Toward a theory of long-distance romantic relationships including an exploratory study of college students' relationships-at-a-distance.* Unpublished manuscript, West Lafayette, IN.

Guldner, G. T. (1996). Long-distance romantic relationships: Prevalence and separation-related symptoms in college students. *Journal of College Student Development, 37,* 289–296.

Guldner, G. T., & Swensen, C. H. (1995). Time spent together and relationship quality: Long-distance relationships as a test case. *Journal of Social and Personal Relationships, 12,* 313–320.

Helgeson, V. S. (1994). Long-distance romantic relationships: Sex differences in adjustment and breakup. *Personality and Social Psychology Bulletin, 20,* 245–256.

Hendrick, C., & Hendrick, S. S. (1988). Lovers wear rose colored glasses. *Journal of Social and Personal Relationships, 5,* 161–183.

Hill, C. T., Rubin, Z., & Peplau, L. (1976). Breakups before marriage: The end of 103 affairs. *Journal of Social Issues, 32,* 147–168.

Holt, P A., & Stone, G. L. (1988). Heeds, coping strategies, and coping outcomes associated with long-distance relationships. *Journal of College Student Development, 29,* 136–141.

Honeycutt, J. M. (2003). *Imagined interactions: Daydreaming about communication.* Cresskill, NJ: Hampton Press.

Ickes, W., & Simpson, J. A. (1997). Managing empathic accuracy in close relationships. In W. Ickes (Ed.), *Empathetic accuracy* (pp. 218–250). New York: Guilford.

Knox, D., Zusman, M. E., Daniels, V., & Brantley, A. (2002). Absence makes the heart grow fonder? Long distance dating relationships among college students. *College Student Journal, 36,* 364–367.

Larson, J. H., & Holman, T. B. (1994). Premarital predictors of marital quality and stability. *Family Relations, 43,* 228–237.

Le, B., & Agnew, C. R. (2001). Need fulfillment and emotional experience in interdependent romantic relationships. *Journal of Social and Personal Relationships, 18,* 423–440.

Lydon, J., Pierce, T., & O'Regan, S. (1997). Coping with moral commitment to long-distance dating relationships. *Journal of Personality and Social Psychology, 73,* 104–113.

Murray, S. L., & Holmes, J. G. (1996). The construction of relationship realities. In G. J. O. Fletcher & J. Fitness (Eds.), *Knowledge structures in close relationships: A social psychological approach* (pp. 91–120). Mahwah, NJ: Lawrence Erlbaum Associates.

Reske, J., & Stafford, L. (1989, May). *Idealization and communication in long-distance and geographically close premarital relationships.* Paper presented at the Annual Conference of the International Communication Association, San Francisco.

Rohfling, M. (1995). "Doesn't anybody stay in one place anymore?" An exploration of the under-studied phenomenon of long-distance relationships. In J. Wood & S. W Duck (Eds.), *Under-studied relationships: Off the beaten track* (pp. 173–196). Thousand Oaks, CA: Sage.

Rusbult, C. E., Olsen, N., Davis, J. L., & Hannon, R A. (2001). Commitment and relationship maintenance mechanisms. In J. Harvey & A. Wenzel (Eds.), *Close romantic relationships.* Mahwah, NJ: Lawrence Erlbaum Associates.

Rusbult, C. E., Van Lange, P. A. M., Wildschut, T., Yovetich, A., & Verette, J. (2000). Perceived superiority in close relationships: Why it exists and persists. *Journal of Personality and Social Psychology, 79,* 521–545.

Sahlstein, E. (2004). Relating at a distance: Negotiating being together and being apart in long-distance relationships. *Journal of Social and Personal Relationships, 21,* 698–201

Schulman, M. L. (1974). Idealization in engaged couples. *Journal of Marriage and Family, 36,* 139–147.

Schwebel, A. I., Dunn, R. L., Moss, B. F., & Renner, M. A. (1992). Factors associated with relational stability in geographically separated couples. *Journal of College Student Development, 33,* 222–230.

Sillars, A. L. (1998). (Mis)understanding. In B. H. Spitzberg & W. R. Cupach (Eds.), *The dark side of close relationships* (pp. 73–102). Mahwah, NJ: Lawrence Erlbaum Associates.

Sprecher, S., & Felmlee, D. (2000). Romantic partners' perceptions of social network attributes with the passage of time and relationship transitions. *Personal Relationships, 7,* 325–340.

Stafford, L., Merolla, A. J., & Castle, J. D. (2004). *When long-distance dating relationships become geographically close relationships*. Manuscript submitted for publication.

Stafford, L., & Reske, J. R. (1990). Idealization and communication in long-distance premarital relationships. *Family Relations, 39*, 274–279.

Stephen, T (1986). Communication and interdependence in geographically separated relationships. *Human Communication Research, 13*, 191–210.

VanHorn, K. R., Arnone, A., Nesbitt, K., Desilets, L., Sears, T., Griffin, M., & Brudi, R. (1997). Physical distance and interpersonal characteristics in college students' romantic relationships. *Personal Relationships, 4*, 25–34.

Waller, W. (1938). *The family*. New York: Holt.

Wendel, W. C. (1975). High school sweethearts: A study in separation and commitment. *Journal of Clinical Child Psychology, 4*, 45–46.

Westefeld, J. S., & Liddell, D. (1982). Coping with long-distance relationships. *Journal of College Student Development, 23*, 550–551.

Wilmot, W. W., & Carbaugh, D. (1986). Long-distance lovers: Predicting the dissolution of relationships. *Journal of Northwest Communication Association, 14*, 43–59.

Winfield, F. E. (1985). *Commuter marriage: Living together, apart*. New York: Columbia University Press.

Long-Distance Romantic Relationship Real-World Lab

Name: _____

Date: _____

For this real-world lab, you will learn about LDRRs from someone who has experienced one. Identify a friend, parent, or other family member who has been part of a LDRR at some point in their life. Even if you have been in a LDRR yourself, find someone else to interview. There is always something to be learned by talking to someone else about their relationship.

Once you have identified who you will interview, describe your relationship to them here (e.g., "I interviewed my father.").

Ask your friend/parent/other family member the following questions and write down their answers:

1. How long were you in a long-distance romantic relationship? Or, if currently in a LDRR, how long have you been in a LDRR?

_____
_____
_____
_____
_____
_____
_____

2. What was it like being part of a LDRR?

_____
_____
_____
_____
_____

3. How did you maintain your relationship at a distance? (Ask them about how they communicated and other behaviors they used to maintain the relationship.)

_____

_____

_____

_____

_____

_____

4. What was it like when you were in the same place again? Was it ever awkward or uncomfortable after being apart for so long?

_____

_____

_____

_____

_____

_____

_____

CHAPTER 10

Social Support and Technology

Introduction to the Chapter

People use technology to develop, maintain, and dissolve their interpersonal relationships. This chapter focuses on how computer-mediated communication can be used for support seeking and support giving in interpersonal relationships with people you know and anonymous strangers. You will learn why the internet is an ideal place to seek support (e.g., interactions are asynchronous, writing is cathartic, you can reach a much larger social network) and about the various types of support. The chapter also includes information on social networks, including weak- and strong-tie networks, and explains how networks form to connect similar people online.

What Makes the Internet a Place to Seek Social Support?

By Martin Tanis

> Thank you so much! I can't begin to express how I feel with so much encouragement, love and support that everyone is giving me. Already I feel so much better knowing I have friends to help me get through this. I feel very blessed to have found you all. Thank you so much for your support and friendship, you'll never know what it means to me!
>
> Judith

This message was posted on an online social support group (OSSG) and clearly illustrates that people can find support and encouragement in times when they need it. (This and the other examples in this chapter serve merely as illustrations; for reasons of privacy names are fictional.) This chapter will focus on why people seek support in f OSSGs by looking at characteristics of computer-mediated communication (CMC) in general and online *communities* in particular, and examining how these characteristics may facilitate people who seek social support. More specifically, this chapter will address how the relative anonymity that CMC affords, the text-based character, and the possibilities for extending social networks may be reasons that people go online to seek support. These characteristics can influence not only *with whom* one interacts (due to the possibilities for extending one's network), but also have an impact on *how* one interacts (due to the impact of the text-based, anonymous character that can influence interpersonal communication).

Social support plays an important role in everyday life and it may contribute to mental as well as physical wellbeing (Albrecht & Goldsmith, 2003; Burleson *et al.*, 1994; Heany & Israel, 1995; Uchino *et al.*, 1996). Social support is found to be beneficial for people who go through a period of uncertainty or anxiety caused by a traumatic experience (Leffler & Dembert, 1998; Pennebaker & Harber, 1993), feel lonely or isolated because of a stigmatized personal characteristic (such as a deviant sexual preference, an extreme political or religious opinion, a history of imprisonment, etc., see: Davison *et al.*, 2000; McKenna & Bargh, 1998) and may help people who suffer from disorders such as depression, anxiety, obesity, cancer, HIV, etc (see: Cohen & Syme, 1985). Social support, consisting of a range of assistances that people can provide to one another in order to improve the quality of life, is found to be important because it can reduce feelings of stress, loneliness, or isolation; can provide people with useful knowledge and information; and may teach people strategies that help them to cope with the situation they are facing (Albrecht & Adelman, 1987; Buunk & Hoorens, 1992; Cohen & Wills, 1985; Colvin *et al.*, 2004; House & Kahn, 1985; Thoits, 1995).

Traditionally, social support was primarily provided by family, friends or colleagues; professionals such as family doctors, psychologists, or other healthcare professionals; or locally organized groups that meet on a regular basis to talk about a shared topic (with probably Alcoholics Anonymous the most well known). However, following the large increase in those who have access to the internet, people are able to interact with others who would otherwise be less easy or even impossible to reach, and in a manner that can be quite different from the more "traditional" face-to-face (FtF) forms of support, as will be elaborated on in this chapter. This may explain the exponential growth of social support groups online in the last decade (Burleson *et al.*, 1994; McKenna & Bargh, 1998; Rice, 2006; Wright & Bell, 2003).

OSSGs can take many forms, but the most common form in which people meet each other to exchange support online is via so-called *bulletin boards* or *discussion forums*. In these usenet or web-based discussion forums members can contribute by posting messages that others can read and respond to messages posted by others. The discussions have the form of *threads* that consist of reactions to previous postings, and members are free to start a new thread whenever they wish. Contributions are retained for a period of time and most forums offer the possibility of searching through the list for a specific topic of interest.

On these forums, active participation is not required and people can visit the forums without contributing to the discussion. People who do not contribute but only read postings are called *lurkers* (on some forums newcomers are even advised not to contribute if they have nothing to say, but first get acquainted with the mode of conduct of the group). By lurking, people can follow discussions by others and pick up information that is relevant to them. Web forums are generally not under supervision of health-care professionals and are accessible to all visitors (even though registration is sometimes required). Some forums are not moderated at all, and others have members (or administrators) that monitor the contributions and take action when inappropriate or irrelevant messages are posted.

Web forums are thereby easily accessible locations where people can give and receive support and where people who are interested can browse through the postings in an attempt to find the information they need. This makes them a good place not only for people who suffer from some kind of condition themselves, but also for their close relatives or caregivers: They can very easily visit web forums in order to increase their level of understanding and knowledge about the specific situation another is facing. Before going into more detail about how characteristics of these online groups may facilitate support seekers, I will first discuss what social support entails, and how different types of social support can be distinguished.

Online Social Support

Social support is a very broad concept that comprises many supportive functions such as instrumental, informational, or emotional assistance (House & Kahn, 1985). For the purpose of this chapter social support is defined as the "communication between recipients and providers that reduces uncertainty about the situation, the self, the other or the relationship and functions to enhance a perception of personal control in one's life experience" (Albrecht & Adelman, 1987: 19). Thus, next to *instrumental support*, consisting of providing goods or services and giving practical assistance with daily living, social support can be seen as a communication process through which people can exchange *informational* and *emotional* support (House & Kahn, 1985)—forms of support that are found to be most common in online health-related communities (Braithwaite *et al.*, 1999; Finn, 1999; Preece & Ghozati, 2001).

Informational support concerns the exchange of practical information such as tips on new types of medication, relevant addresses of institutes, knowledge about medical or psychological treatments, legal issues, but also stories of firsthand experiences of members. So, the primary function of this type of support is to expand the knowledge a person has (Reeves, 2000). This type of support is important because it gives people more control over the situation and can reduce uncertainty about the self in such a way that better decisions can be made (Albrecht & Adelman, 1987; Wright, 2002). The next fragment illustrates how firsthand experiences can be used for informational support:

Hi. Just wondering ... if any other restrictors have experienced dimmed eyesight. Definitely NOT "blacking out" (I've had that too, and this is completely different). This just feels like I can't quite see right, like the lights (indoors or out) need to be turned up a couple of notches. This could be nothing—or a touch of the flu, or maybe need a new eyeglass prescription, but I thought I'd check in with you and see if this sounded familiar to anyone. Thanks, Mike

Reaction: Mike, I don't know if this would count as dimmed eyesight but I have on occasion experienced visual disturbances somewhat akin to a sunspot before the eyes and all I get is peripheral vision. In my case I can always connect it to dehydration. I think the first move might be to get your eyes checked out. Perhaps it is just a matter of a prescription adjustment. It's just whenever I hear anyone describing vision problems I always think DRINK, DRINK, and DRINK some more but that is just the particular problem that I experience (and my doctor always "harps" at me to make sure that some of the fluid at least be something containing isotonic salts). [...]

Andy

Emotional support on the other hand, refers to the display of understanding what the other person goes through and involves showing compassion and commitment (Albrecht & Adelman, 1987; Albrecht & Goldsmith, 2003). The next fragment from a forum devoted to cancer is an example of this emotional support:

Hospice has told us that my father in law has at the longest 48 hours. Andrew and I are heartbroken. I think the hardest part is seeing him deteriorate. I know you guys care so much about us and my father in law so I wanted to write and let everyone know. I think in some way, death will be merciful for him. I want him to stay, but that is selfish of me. His entire backside is covered in open sores on top of all his other sufferings. I will let you guys know when the end comes, I can't write any more through all the tears. Sadly, Kirsty

Reaction: Sending you lots of hugs Kirsty, and to your family also. You will be in my prayers over the coming days. Hugs, Emily

So, in emotional support, empathy plays a vital role: Knowing what the other feels, feeling what the other feels, and responding to these feelings in an appropriate manner is a very important form of supporting someone (Levenson & Ruef, 1992: 234). This more affective type of support is characterized by comforting and encouraging and can be highly important for people's self-esteem (Reeves, 2000). Emotional support is found to be especially relevant in situations where people feel they cannot change the situation they are in, but have to adapt to it (Albrecht & Adelman, 1987; Wright, 2000a). Providing emotional support can also imply giving people the opportunity to tell their story. Talking about painful or traumatic experiences, or disclosing personal information can have a therapeutic effect (Pennebaker, 1997), and being there to listen can be a relatively passive but relevant form of social support. In particular in times of stress or misery, it can be comforting to be accompanied by others who are in the same or a similar situation (Davison *et al.*, 2000), because part of the social and emotional problems that people endure stem from feelings of being misunderstood or cut off from society. These feelings may very well result in depression, loneliness, and alienation (Braithwaite *et al.*, 1999) as is illustrated by the following fragment from a forum on dissociative disorder.

> hi there, feeling lonely. dunno what to say. just feeling lonely. not fitting anywhere. like shit. wanna hide, wanna run, maybe would even rather wanna have somebody hold me but that's totally impossible cuz it means I'd have to ask and I wouldnt do that, no way, never. So what am I whinin abot here? Dunno. Prolly it's simply my f*cking fault. better shut up, XX

And the reaction was:

> hiya there, just wanting to say i hear you and i see you, i know how it feels so much about not fitting anywhere ... shut up is maybe something that has been done too long and too often, i think more and more that it is ok and even good to not shut up anymore, it's not wrong or bad to speak or be visible imho even if it is often so hard.. you can email if you like or find

me on msn under the name of [name removed] i am here for
a while this evening

Thus, social support is important for people who find themselves confronted with distress, (inter)personal problems or unwanted life situations (House *et al,*. 1988; Pennebaker & Harber, 1993; Taylor *et al.*, 1986; Thoits, 1995; Wills, 1985; Wright & Bell, 2003) and a lot of this support can be provided by people who have similar experiences or at least feel empathic with the situation someone is facing. In the next part, I will elaborate on why online social support groups can be beneficial in providing this support. This is done by discussing a number of characteristics of CMC in general, and OSSGs in particular, that may prove to have an impact on social support seeking. First, I will discuss how the anonymity that online communication can provide may affect interactions, then I will focus on the possible consequences of the text-based and a-synchronous character of conversation, and, finally, the consequence of expanding one's social network will be discussed.

Anonymous Interactions

An important characteristic of OSSGs is that it can provide a sense of anonymity (Bordia, 1997; Rice & Gattiker, 2001; Sproull & Kiesler, 1991). In most forums or chat rooms, people do not have to reveal their name or other personal information, and visitors are free to make use of pseudonyms or nicknames (Finn, 1999). Not only do people not have to disclose their names, the absence of cues that reveal information about one's identity (such as first name, gender, age, appearance) is also believed to enhance feelings of anonymity (Sproull & Kiesler, 1986; Tanis & Postmes, 2003; Wallace, 1999). This (perception of) anonymity can result in strong feelings of shared identity and higher degrees of self-disclosure, as will be elaborated on in the next part.

Social Identification

Being more or less anonymous to one another may result in strong feelings of "groupiness" or cohesion (Lea *et al.*, 2001; Postmes *et al.*, 1998; Postmes *et al.*, 2001): Based on the Social Identity model of Deindividuation Effects, or SIDE model (Reicher *et al.*, 1995; Spears & Lea, 1992), it can be argued that in online support groups where people recognize themselves and others as sharing similarities on the basis of the situation they are facing, the absence of cues that might draw the attention to potential differences (such as differences in age, gender, appearance, cultural background, etc.) may even increase perceptions of similarity and a shared social identity (cf. Sassenberg & Postmes, 2002, and Utz, this volume). These feelings of shared identity may result in more interpersonal trust (Tanis & Postmes, 2005) and a stronger focus on the social norms of the group (Postmes *et al.*, 2001).

Self-Disclosure

Anonymity (or at least the perception of being anonymous) can also have consequences for the way people express themselves, and could partly explain why online groups are characterized by such high levels of self-disclosure (Joinson, 2001; Parks & Floyd, 1996; Rheingold, 1993; Swickert *et al.*, 2002; Wallace, 1999; Wright, 2000b): "Under the protective cloak of anonymity users can express the way they truly feel and think" (McKenna & Bargh, 2000: 62) as is illustrated in the following fragment of someone planning to leave her abusive husband:

> Hi, I don't know where to start. I guess I just want to say that I'm glad there is a place to talk and watch anonymously. Right now I'm having such a difficult time. [...] I just feel so guilty about leaving because he's trying so hard right now and he's being so nice. But I've had this planned for a month. [...] I just wanted to talk ... I needed to get this out in a place that felt safe. Thank you ...

Joinson (2001) found that people disclose more information about themselves in CMC compared to FtF interactions. A possible explanation for this is that the anonymity causes a reduction of public self-awareness and lowered feelings of accountability (Joinson, 2001). The anonymity can provide the freedom to express oneself with less shame and without the feeling that one's privacy is violated, and allows people to ask intimate or potentially embarrassing questions that they would not ask as easily in an *offline* context (Braithwaite *et al.*, 1999; Wallace, 1999). In this way OSSGs may open up possibilities for people to discuss topics that they feel embarrassed or ashamed to talk about face-to-face.

Text-Based Conversations

CMC differs from FtF interactions in that it is primarily text-based and a-synchronous. Even though the visual and auditory options of the internet increase (a number of forums offer possibilities for web cams and audio), the lion's share of the online interactions are in written form. Much of the early theorizing on mediated communication has predicted that this form of communication would be relatively cold, impersonal, and primarily task-focused because it is not capable of conveying nonverbal, social cues. This would make all forms of mediated communication inherently less suited for intimate interactions when compared to FtF communication (Connolly, *et al.*, 1990; Hiltz *et al.*, 1986; Kiesler *et al.*, 1984). However, this does not sit comfortably with the high number of individuals who voluntarily choose to open their heart, or engage in highly personal interactions by means of written text (from old-fashioned correspondence by letter to personal disclosures on the internet, or even via the technically limited form of text messaging).

In OSSGs, the text-based character has a number of benefits that may be highly relevant for exchanging informational or emotional support. There are cognitive benefits in writing, it is a-synchronous, there is an emphasis on the contribution, and it allows for selective self-presentation.

Cognitive Benefits of Writing

Research by Pennebaker and colleagues has shown that writing about personal or emotional issues can positively affect mental and physical health (Pennebaker, 1997; Pennebaker & Harber, 1993; Pennebaker *et al.*, 1997). Their findings suggest that the act of writing about emotional feelings or experiences causes cognitive changes which can work therapeutically: When disclosing personal feelings or traumatic experiences to others, individuals must narrate an understandable account of the situation. By doing so, they must formulate a coherent and insightful explanation of what they go through which provides them with more understanding of the situation they are in (Pennebaker *et al.*, 1997). Translating emotional experiences (such as traumas) into language seems more effective for the healing process than to express them in a different manner (Miller & Gergen, 1998; Pennebaker, 1997; Pennebaker & Harber, 1993; Pennebaker *et al.*, 1997).

A-Synchronous Interactions

A-synchronous interactions afford people the opportunity to carefully compose and formulate their messages without having to worry about interruptions or immediate responses by others. This gives people the chance to reflect upon messages before sending them to the group. Taking your time can be especially valuable when the topic of discussion is one that concerns sensitive or emotional issues (Braithwaite *et al.*, 1999; Walther, 1996; Weinberg *et al.*, 1995).

A more practical advantage of the way interactions are organized in online forums is that they are automatically stored on the website. This enables people to catch up with the discussion when unable to visit the forum on a regular basis, but also allows people to search for information in discussion threads that are no longer active but are still archived on the site. In this way, OSSGs have an important role in informational support, and can provide people with relevant information and knowledge.

Emphasis on Contribution

Another potential advantage of the text-based contribution is that people are valued for their contribution instead of on the basis of their physical appearance (Weinberg *et al.*, 1995). This can be liberating, especially for people who see themselves confronted with prejudices based on age, sex or ethnicity in their offline life, but also for people who suffer from stigmatized physical characteristics such as obesity, mutilation, skin problems, etc. (Erwin *et al.*, 2004; Wallace, 1999). Also for people whose ability to speak or hear is affected, or who have cognitive disabilities or other handicaps that cause them to take more time to express themselves, text-based interactions can be highly constructive: The problems these people face in FtF interactions can lead to a restriction in their opportunities to engage in social interaction. Text-based online interaction enables them to participate in the same manner as the other members, and it provides them with equal opportunities to partake in the discussion (Braithwaite *et al.*, 1999; Nelson, 1995).

Selective Self-Presentation

A different though related reason why people may choose to participate in OSSGs is that it provides them with the opportunity for selective self-presentation. According to the Social Information Processing perspective (SIP: Walther, 1992, 1996), people will adapt their linguistic and textual behaviors when using CMC. They do this in an attempt to overcome the nonverbal limitations of CMC in such a way that the presentation of socially revealing and relational signals that would normally be conveyed through a variety of channels will now be communicated via text only. This factor, however, also allows people to present themselves in a more friendly, knowledgeable, empathic way, because it gives them the opportunity to carefully shape their appearance, and enables selective self-presentation—often called *hyperpersonal* interaction (for detailed discussion of hyperpersonal interaction, see: Walther, 1996; Walther & Boyd, 2002). Selective self-presentation is believed to be very common in online communities, dating sites, online games, etc., and some research on hyperpersonality and social support exists (Walther & Boyd, 2002; Wright & Bell, 2003; Whitty, this volume). However, more research is needed as to how this might affect the process of social support and the perceptions that are formed of support seekers and providers.

Expanding Social Networks

Probably the most important reason why people seek social support on the internet is because it provides them with easy access to others who face a similar situation. Sitting in front of the computer, individuals can engage in social interactions with others all over the world who potentially have an understanding of their specific situation (Braithwaite *et al.*, 1999; Finn & Lavitt, 1994; Rice & Katz, 2001). The only restriction is that people need to have access to the internet, and must not feel too uncomfortable in reading and writing in the common language of the group. Online forums are not troubled by geographical barriers and the a-synchronicity of the interaction provides the members with flexibility in when they want to interact. Members can post and read messages at times that suit them best, which can be beneficial for people that have conflicting time schedules caused by work, different time zones, or other obligations. This might be why these groups are more easily found, chosen, or started online (Madara, 1997: 23).

So, these online groups can be a valuable extension to one's *offline* social network and increase the possibilities for finding support. This might be especially beneficial for people who live in isolated parts of the world, have disabilities that restrict their mobility, or have anxieties that cause them not to dare to leave their homes, but also for people who feel lonely, unique, or misunderstood and live in a social environment in which social support is not easily found (for example homosexuality in an orthodox religious community). However, OSSGs may provide people who just want to tell their story, seek information, or are looking for social interaction with a social network. Not only do they provide a network of others who are, at least to a certain degree, similar, but the online network may contain more diverse information and the type of relationship with people who provide support may vary to a greater extent than often found offline.

Networks of Perceived Similarity

The ease of access to a large number of people, unrestricted by time or place barriers, can provide a sense of universality and communality in online groups (Braithwaite *et al.*, 1999; Madara, 1997; Preece & Ghozati, 2001; Wright & Bell, 2003). Despite the fact that members of online communities can (and probably will) differ on a lot of dimensions, they may all find themselves in a similar situation, may be faced with the same mental or physical condition, or have gone through a similar traumatic experience. Contrary to one's offline environment, people voluntarily choose to participate in the online community because of an interest in the topic of concern. It is therefore not surprising that members perceive the others on the forum as more similar as compared to others in their offline networks (Wright, 2000b). This perceived similarity can even be increased by the absence of cues that may signal individual differences: As mentioned earlier when discussing the anonymity that OSSGs afford, the anonymity may result in increased attention to what all members in the group share, and thereby contribute to feelings of belonging and social identification (Lea *et al.*, 2001; Postmes *et al.*, 1998; Postmes *et al.*, 2001).

The Need to Belong

Finding similar others can be an important motivation for joining an online community because perceived similarity and the feeling that one is part of a larger group is part of the basic *need to belong* (Brewer, 1991; Deaux, 1993; McKenna & Bargh, 1998). For people who feel isolated or cut off in their offline environment because they feel unique, being surrounded by similar others can be especially important. The following fragment from a discussion forum about mood swings illustrates the need for being among others who recognize what someone is going through:

> This has been an interesting week—I feel like I'm on the verge
> of a crying jag, but ready to snap at any given second. I can
> feel tears in the back of my throat, but it doesn't stop me
> from saying or thinking really mean things about people. My
> patience has gotten to be virtually nill and I'm not sure where
> I'm at emotionally. Does anyone else feel like this?

Research has shown that in online support groups where people are surrounded by others who understand, very little suspicion exists, and interactions are characterized by low levels of negative emotional remarks and high levels of empathic communication (Finn, 1999; Preece & Ghozati, 2001; Wallace, 1999). People who find themselves in a similar situation tend to be more empathic and show more understanding: "the more similar we are the less we have to go outside of ourselves to gather cues and the more we can respond as we ourselves would naturally to the circumstances" (Hodge & Wegner, 1997, in Preece & Ghozati, 2001).

Being among similar others might be especially important for people who suffer from a stigmatized physical or mental condition (such as obesity, stuttering, schizophrenia, or manic depression), or who feel that an important part of their identity is not accepted by society (such as a deviant sexual preferences, or extreme religious or political beliefs). People who perceive themselves outsiders or outliers because they differ from others in an important part of their identity—i.e. that have a *marginalized identity* (Frable, 1993)—can have difficulties because they feel being unique or deviant from the people in their social circle.

Frable (1993) distinguishes between two forms of marginal identities: those that are conspicuous, and those that are concealable. OSSGs may prove beneficial for both of these groups. People with visible or *conspicuous marginal identities* (for example people who suffer from obesity, skin conditions, mutilation, or physical disabilities) can have a feeling that the first thing that others note about them is the part that is deviant. As a result, people can realize that those in their social environment act uncertainly and awkwardly when they are present, which can ultimately lead to feelings of isolation and social exclusion (see: Braithwaite *et al.*, 1999). In online interaction (i.e. in the absence of visual cues) people can feel liberated from this burden, and feel valued on the basis of their written contributions and not on the basis of their more or less unique physical appearance (Weinberg *et al.*, 1995).

The sense of being unique can even feel of greater importance to people who have *concealable marginal identities* (Frable, 1993; McKenna & Bargh, 1998) because for people with concealable marginal identity (such as a venereal disease, multiple personality syndrome, or a deviant sexual preference) the chance of recognizing someone with a similar condition is very small: "those with hidden conditions are not able to see similar others in their environment, so there is no visible sign of others who share the stigmatized feature"(McKenna & Bargh, 1998: 682). Especially when it concerns a stigmatized identity, it can be difficult to find support or understanding: It is not easy to take the first step in revealing stigmatized information about an important part of your identity, without knowing whether you can count on recognition or understanding. Therefore, members of this group run the risk of social exclusion and loneliness without the possibility of finding people to interact with on the internet (McKenna & Bargh, 1998).

Through participation in online social support communities, people can attain more self-esteem and confidence. According to McKenna and Bargh (1998), this can reduce the inner conflict between the marginalized part of the identity and the socially accepted standards, and result in more openness to discuss this aspect of identity with significant others such as friends and family.

Source for Social Comparison

As mentioned in the beginning of this chapter, informational support not only consists of *hard* information such as advice about medication, addresses of health-related institutes, etc. but also of stories about experiences and accounts of how others cope with a specific situation. People can use these accounts for social comparison (Davison *et al.*, 2000). Social comparison theory (Festinger, 1954) posits that people will compare themselves with others in times of uncertainty or anxiety. Therefore, the need for social comparison is inherent to a physical or mental healthcare setting, because of its high level of ambiguity and anxiety (Davison *et al.*, 2000). However, people can only compare themselves with others who are relatively similar to each other, which makes online support groups a good place for social comparison purposes.

There is, however, another reason why OSSGs may benefit social comparison. Research has shown that when the situation is humiliating or embarrassing, people do not want to be in the presence of others out of shame or loss of self-esteem (Sarnoff & Zimbardo, in Davison *et al.*, 2000). However, Davison *et al.* (2000) show that people who have illnesses that are perceived embarrassing, socially stigmatized, or disfiguring, seek support from similar others but prefer to do this online. Attentative conclusion would therefore be that because of the anonymity and the perception of privacy that online communities afford, partaking in online communities can be helpful for social comparison, even when the situation is embarrassing or socially stigmatized.

Weak-Tie Networks

The accessibility of the OSSGs, unrestricted by time and place barriers may result in users who differ a lot in their backgrounds, and have a large diversity in their relations to one another (from complete strangers to close friends). So, as a side-effect of looking for others who are similar—to the extent that an interest in the topic of discussion is shared—the people in these online networks may vary more compared to one's offline network, potentially making these groups more heterogeneous. Individuals become a member of an OSSG of their own accord, and often visit the community on a regular basis. But the only thing that binds the individuals together is the topic of interest of the group. When the personal situation (and the reason for attending the group) changes, the online community can become irrelevant, and people will most likely stop attending the group. As a result, at least some of the relationships will be of relatively short duration and be based on the shared interest only. Unlike one's offline social network, that largely consists of family, friends and colleagues with whom strong and usually long-lasting relationships exist, relations in online support communities often take the form of *weak ties* (Adelman *et al.*, 1987; Wright & Bell, 2003). *Weak ties* are relations between people who communicate on a regular basis, but who are not necessarily close to one another (Granovetter, 1973).

Even though strong social ties with relevant others are very important for social support (Cummings *et al.*, 2002; House *et al.*, 1988; Thoits, 1995; Wills, 1985), weak ties can play an important part in the wellbeing of people who seek support as well (Adelman *et al.*, 1987; Granovetter, 1973; Wright & Bell, 2003). Research has shown that an extended network may offer a large diversity of information (Granovetter, 1973; Rice & Katz, 2001; Wellman, 1997), and weak ties may be able to provide support that strong ties can not (Albrecht & Adelman, 1987; Thoits, 1995). These potential benefits will be discussed in the next section.

Networks of Varied Information

One of the characteristics of weak-tie networks is that they consist of people who vary in background, and come from different groups, communities, or cultures. Because members in a weak-tie network are themselves embedded in other social communities, they can open up totally different sources of knowledge and information, and thereby offer more variety than offline networks often do (Wellman, 1997). Therefore, one of the potential advantages of these online groups is that through these relations, information can be gathered that would otherwise be inaccessible. Members in online groups may especially benefit from this variety of information because of the layout of most web forums. In most forums, postings are archived for a period of time, which allows members to search for information about the topic of their interest, by which OSSGs have the potential to make a large amount of diverse information available for a large number of individuals.

Networks with Various Strengths of Relations

Weak-tie networks might also be beneficial in that they provide an opportunity for members to seek support and to talk about their situation without the risks that sometimes accompany talking to people who are close by (Thoits, 1995; Wright & Bell, 2003). In an offline situation support is most often provided by significant others that are close to the individual, such as parents, partners, family, friends, and colleagues (Wills, 1985). Even though these people have an important function in supporting (House & Kahn, 1985; Thoits, 1995), these more or less obligatory relations can have negative consequences in that they may lead to expectations and demands that can cause stress by themselves (Thoits, 1995).

People who are close by can push too hard, or anticipate seeing too swift improvements in the situation. Strong-tied others can also be so overprotective, causing the individual to suffer under the perception of complete dependency. Another potential downside of receiving support from significant others may be that they can be inclined to rule a verdict about the behavior that is responsible for causing the situation: Even though friends and family are close and bonds are strong, and despite the good intentions, they can sometimes be the first to judge (Wright & Bell, 2003), especially when people find themselves in a situation they can be held responsible for (for example HIV in relation to unsafe sex or intravenous use of drugs, cardiac disease in relation to not being able to give up smoking or drinking, financial problems in relation to a gambling addiction, etc.). Additionally, friends and family can have stronger role obligations that can result in listening to the problems not because they want to, but because they feel it is their duty to do so, which can be felt as a burden by the support seeker (Albrecht & Adelman, 1987).

So, it can be a relief to tell one's story to a relative stranger on the internet where relations tend to be looser, chosen voluntarily and have no reciprocal expectations (Thoits, 1995), just as it can be comforting to spill one's heart to a stranger on the train (Bargh & McKenna, 2004). Another advantage of asking support from weak ties has to do with the low risk in asking potentially embarrassing questions. According to Adelman *et al.* (1987) weak ties "allow people to seek information and support without having to deal with the uncertainty of how those in primary [strong-tie] relationships might respond" (p. 131), thereby facilitating "low-risk discussions about high-risk topics" (p. 133).

Conclusion

Online social support groups may form a valuable supplement to one's social network, and may be beneficial in providing people with social support. The anonymity can enhance feelings of cohesion and social identification (Lea *et al.*, 2001; Postmes *et al.*, 1998; Postmes *et al.*, 2001), and may stimulate self-disclosure (Joinson, 2001; Parks & Floyd, 1996) which enables people to talk more easily about sensitive topics (Braithwaite *et al.*, 1999; Wallace, 1999). The text-based character may have a therapeutic effect in itself because it forces individuals to formulate a coherent story that can improve their understanding of the situation (Miller & Gergen, 1998; Pennebaker *et al.*, 1997). The a-synchronous form allows people to carefully reflect on messages and compose reactions without having to worry about interruptions, and enables people to browse through interactions looking for relevant postings. Because of the written form, there can be more attention for the actual message instead of how one looks, which might be liberating for people that see themselves confronted with prejudices or who suffer from stigmatized physical characteristics (Erwin *et al.*, 2004; Wallace, 1999), and may provide opportunities for selective self-presentation (Walther, 1996; Walther & Boyd, 2002). Finally, online interactions are not restricted by geographical or time constraints and thereby enable people to get into contact with others that would otherwise never have been reached (Braithwaite *et al.*, 1999; Finn & Lavitt, 1994; Rice & Katz, 2001). This might make these weak-tie networks a good source of diverse information (Granovetter, 1973; Wellman, 1997), and the other users can offer support in a freer and less obligatory manner than often found offline (Albrecht & Adelman, 1987; Thoits, 1995).

So in general, online social support groups have a number of features that can make them a fruitful supplement for people who seek social support. However, there are also potential downsides to online support: Whereas close ties can provide assistance with adhering to health regimes, weak ties have less obligatory norms (Albrecht & Goldsmith, 2003). This makes online relations probably less suited for "forcing" people to take their medication, do their daily exercises, or restraining people from taking drugs or alcohol. The anonymity that online support groups offer to their members can also have some downsides. In these anonymous groups, people can be confronted with disinhibited behavior (Kiesler *et al.*, 1984; Sproull & Kiesler, 1986), people run the risk of being harassed or stalked online (Finn & Banach, 2000), and the information or advice people provide may be inaccurate or even harmful. However, these negative outcomes are only rarely reported in empirical studies (even though these potential dangers are almost always addressed in introductions or discussions), and more research is necessary that specifically focuses on these potentially negative consequences of online social support groups.

Future research should also address who it is that makes use of these groups, and how personal characteristics determine whether or not participation in OSSGs has positive effects on mental as well as physical well-being. Do OSSGs have a different effect on users that are socially isolated or introvert, which see the OSSG as their main platform for social interaction because of the safety they may provide, or extravert people that use the internet as an extension of their online network? Is there a difference between people that primarily use the groups to gather information, or people that mainly come to the groups to get emotional support? These and other questions would be interesting to answer for they would provide us with more understanding of how computer-mediated communication in general has become an integrated part of everyday life, and how online social support groups in particular may benefit the wellbeing of people that seek support.

References

Adelman, M. B., Parks, M. R., & Albrecht, T. L. (1987) "Beyond close relationships: Support in weak ties." In T. L. Albrecht & M. B. Adelman (eds.), *Communicating Social Support*. Newbury Park: Sage, pp. 126–147.

Albrecht, T. L., & Adelman, M. B. (1987) "Communicating social support: A theoretical perspective." In T. L. Albrecht & M. B. Adelman (eds.), *Communicating Social Support*. Newbury Park, CA: Sage, pp. 18–39.

Albrecht, T. L., & Goldsmith, D. J. (2003) "Social support, social networks, and health." In T. L. Thompson, A. M. Dorsey, K. I. Miller & R. Parrott (eds.), *Handbook of Health Communication*. Hillsdale, NK: Erlbaum, pp. 263–284.

Bargh, J. A., & McKenna, K. Y. A. (2004) "The Internet and social life." *Annual Review of Psychology, 55*, 573–590.

Bordia, P. (1997) "Face-to-face versus computer-mediated communication: A synthesis of the experimental literature." *Journal of Business Communication, 34*(1), 99–120.

Braithwaite, D. O., Waldron, V. R., & Finn, J. (1999) "Communication of social support in computer-mediated groups for people with disabilities." *Health Communication, 11*(2), 123–151.

Brewer, M. B. (1991) "The social self: On being the same and different at the same time." *Personality and Social Psychology Bulletin, 17*(5), 475–482.

Burleson, B. R., Albrecht, T. L., & Sarason, I. (1994) *Communication of Social Support: Messages, Interactions, Relationships and Community*. Newbury Park, CA: Sage.

Buunk, B. P., & Hoorens, V. (1992) "Social support and stress: The role of social comparison and social exchange processes." *British Journal of Clinical Psychology, 31*(4), 445–457.

Cohen, S., & Syme, S. L. (1985) *Social Support and Health*. Orlando, FL: Academic press, Inc.

Cohen, S., & Wills, T. A. (1985) "Stress, social support, and the buffering hypothesis." *Psychological Bulletin, 98*(2), 310–357.

Colvin, J., Chenoweth, L., Bold, M., & Harding, C. (2004) "Caregivers of older adults: Advantages and disadvantages of Internet-based social support." *Family Relations, 53*(1), 49–57.

Connolly, T., Jessup, L. M., & Valacich, J. S. (1990) "Effects of anonymity and evaluative tone on idea generation in computer-mediated groups." *Management Science, 36*(6), 689–703.

Cummings, J. N., Sproull, L., & Kiesler, S. B. (2002) "Beyond hearing: Where real-world and online support meet." *Group Dynamics-Theory Research and Practice, 6*(1), 78–88.

Davison, K. P., Pennebaker, J. W., & Dickerson, S. S. (2000) "Who talks: The social psychology of illness support groups." *American Psychologist, 55*(2), 205–217.

Deaux, K. (1993) "Reconstructing social identity." *Personality and Social Psychology Bulletin, 19*(1), 4–12.

Erwin, B. A., Turk, C. L., Heimberg, R. G., Fresco, D. M., & Hantula, D. A. (2004) "The Internet: Home to a severe population of individuals with social anxiety disorder?" *Journal of Anxiety Disorders, 18*(5), 629–646.

Festinger, L. A. (1954) "A theory of social comparison processes." *Human Relations, 7,* 117–140.

Finn, J. (1999) "An exploration of helping processes in an online self-help group focusing on issues of disability." *Health & Social Work, 24*(3), 220–231.

Finn, J., & Banach, M. (2000) "Victimization online: The down side of seeking human services for women on the Internet." *Cyberpsychology & Behavior, 3*(2), 243–254.

Finn, J., & Lavitt, M. (1994) "Computer-based self-help groups for sexual abuse survivors." *Social Work With Groups, 24,* 220–240.

Fox, S. (2005) *Health Information Online: Pew Internet and American Life Project.* Pew Internet and American Life Project. Retrieved May 2006 from the World Wide Web: http://www.pewinternet.org

Frable, D. E. S. (1993) "Being and feeling unique: Statistical deviance and psychological marginality." *Journal of Personality, 61*(1), 85–110.

Granovetter, M. (1973) "The strength of weak ties." *American Journal of Sociology, 78,* 1360–1380.

Heany, C. A., & Israel, B. A. (1995) "Social networks and social support." In K. Glanz & F. M. Lewis & B. K. Rimer (eds.), *Health Behavior and Health Education: Theory, Research and Practice,* second edition. San Francisco: Jossey-Bass, pp. 179–205.

Hiltz, S. R., Johnson, K., & Turoff, M. (1986) "Experiments in group decision-making: Communication process and outcome in face-to-face versus computerized conferences." *Human Communication Research, 13,* 225–252.

Hodges, S. D., & Wegner, D. M. (1997) "Automatic and controlled empathy." In W. Ickes (ed.), *Empathic Accuracy.* New York: Guilford, pp. 311–339.

House, J. S., & Kahn, R. L. (1985) "Measures and concepts of social support." In S. Cohen & S. L. Syme (eds.), *Social Support and Health.* Orlando, FL: Academic Press, pp. 83–108.

House, J. S., Landis, K. R., & Umberson, D. (1988) "Social relationships and health." *Science, 241*(4865), 540–545.

Joinson, A. N. (2001) "Self-disclosure in computer-mediated communication: The role of self-awareness and visual anonymity." *European Journal of Social Psychology, 31,* 177–192.

Kiesler, S., Siegel, J., & Mcguire, T. W. (1984) "Social psychological aspects of computer-mediated communication." *American Psychologist, 39,* 1123–1134.

Lea, M., Spears, R., & de Groot, D. (2001) "Knowing me, knowing you: Anonymity effects on social identity processes within groups." *Personality and Social Psychology Bulletin, 27*(5), 526–537.

Leffler, C., & Dembert, M. (1998) "Posttraumatic stress symptoms among U.S. Navy Divers recovering TWA flight 800." *Journal of Nervous and Mental Disorders, 186*, 574–577.

Leimeister, J. M., & Krcmar, H. (2005) "Evaluation of a systematic design for a virtual patient community." *Journal of Computer-Mediated Communication, 10*(4).

Levenson, R. W., & Ruef, A. M. (1992) "Empathy: A physiological substrate." *Journal of Personality and Social Psychology, 63*(2), 234–246.

Madara, E. J. (1997) "The mutual-aid self-help online revolution." *Social Policy, 97*(3), 20–26.

McKenna, K. Y. A., & Bargh, J. A. (1998) "Coming out in the age of the Internet: Identity 'demarginalization' through virtual group participation." *Journal of Personality and Social Psychology, 75*(3), 681–694.

McKenna, K. Y. A., & Bargh, J. A. (2000) "Plan 9 from cyberspace: The implications of the internet for personality and social psychology." *Personality and Social Psychology Review, 4*, 57–75.

Miller, J. K., & Gergen, K. J. (1998) "Life on the line: The therapeutic potentials of computer-mediated conversation." *Journal of Marital & Family Therapy, 24*(2), 189–202.

Nelson, J. A. (1995) "The internet, the virtual community and those with disabilities." *Disability Quarterly, 15*(2), 15–20.

Parks, R. M., & Floyd, K. (1996) "Making friends in cyberspace." *Journal of Communication, 46*(1), 80–97.

Pennebaker, J. W. (1997) "Writing about emotional experiences as a therapeutic process." *Psychological Science, 8*(3), 162–166.

Pennebaker, J. W., & Harber, K. D. (1993) "A social stage model of collective coping: The Loma Prieta earthquake and the Persian gulf War." *Journal of Social Issues, 49*(4), 125–145.

Pennebaker, J. W., Mayne, T. J., & Francis, M. E. (1997) "Linguistic predictors of adaptive bereavement." *Journal of Personality and Social Psychology, 72*(4), 863–871.

Postmes, T., Spears, R., & Lea, M. (1998) "Breaching or building social boundaries? SIDE-effect of computer-mediated communication." *Communication Research, 25*(6), 689–715.

Postmes, T., Spears, R., Sakhel, K., & de Groot, D. (2001) "Social influence in computer-mediated communication: The effects of anonymity on group behavior." *Personality and Social Psychology Bulletin, 27*, 1243–1254.

Preece, J. J., & Ghozati, K. (2001) "Experiencing empathy online." In R. E. Rice & J. E. Katz (eds.), *The Internet and Health Communication*. Thousand Oaks, CA: Sage, pp. 237–260.

Reeves, P. M. (2000) "Coping in cyberspace: The impact of Internet use on the ability of HIV-positive individuals to deal with their illness." *Journal of Health Communication, 5*, 47–59.

Reicher, S., Spears, R., & Postmes, T. (1995) "A social identity model of deindividuation phenomena." In W. Stroebe & M. Hewstone (eds.), *European Review of Social Psychology* Vol. 6. Chichester, England: Wiley, pp. 161–198.

Rheingold, H. (1993) *The Virtual Community: Homesteading on the Electronic Frontier*. Reading, MA: Addison-Wesley.

Rice, R. E. (2006) "Influences, usage, and outcomes of Internet health information searching: Multivariate results from the Pew surveys." *International Journal of Medical Informatics, 75*(1), 8–28.

Rice, R. E., & Gattiker, U. E. (2001) "new media and organizational structuring." In F. M. Jablin & L. L. Putnam (eds.), *The New Handbook of Organizational Communication*. Thousand Oaks, CA: Sage, pp. 544–581.

Rice, R. E., & Katz, J. E. (2001). *The Internet and Health Communication: Experiences and Expectations*. Thousand Oaks, CA: Sage.

Sarnoff, I., & Zimbardo, P. (1961) "Anxiety, fear, and social affiliation." *Journal of Abnormal and Social Psychology, 62*, 356–363.

Sassenberg, K., & Postmes, T. (2002) "Cognitive and strategic processes in small groups: Effects of anonymity of the self and anonymity of the group on social influence." *British Journal of Social Psychology, 41*, 463–480.

Spears, R., & Lea, M. (1992) "Social influence and the influence of the 'social' in computer-mediated communication." In M. Lea (ed.), *Contexts of Computer-Mediated Communication*. Hemel Hempstead: Harvester Wheatsheaf, pp. 30–65.

Sproull, L., & Kiesler, S. (1986) "Reducing social context cues: Electronic mail in organizational communication." *Management Science, 32*(11), 1492–1512.

Sproull, L., & Kiesler, S. (1991) *Connections: New Ways of Working in the Networked Organization*. Cambridge, MA: The MIT Press.

Swickert, R. J., Hittner, J. B., Harris, J. L., & Herring, J. A. (2002) "Relationships among Internet use, personality, and social support." *Computers in Human Behavior, 18*(4), 437–451.

Tanis, M., & Postmes, T. (2003) "Social cues and impression formation in CMC." *Journal of Communication, 53*(4), 676–693.

Tanis, M., & Postmes, T. (2005) A social identity approach to trust: Interpersonal perception, group membership and trusting behaviour." *European Journal of Social Psychology, 35,* 413–424.

Taylor, S. E., Falke, R. L., Shoptaw, S. J., & Lichtman, R. R. (1986) "Social support, support groups, and the cancer patient." *Journal of Consulting and Clinical Psychology, 54*(5), 608–615.

Thoits, P. A. (1995) "Stress, coping, and social support: Where are we? What next?" *Journal of Health and Social Behavior, 35,* 53–79.

Uchino, B. N., Cacioppo, J. T., & Kiecolt-Glaser, J. K. (1996) "The relationship between social support and psychological processes: A review with emphasis on underlying mechanisms and implications for health." *Psychological Bulletin, 119*(3), 488–531.

Wallace, P. (1999). *The Psychology of the Internet.* Cambridge: Cambridge University Press.

Walther, J. B. (1992) "Interpersonal effects in computer-mediated interaction: A relational perspective." *Communication Research, 19*(1), 52–90.

Walther, J. B. (1996) "Computer-mediated communication: Impersonal, interpersonal, and hyperpersonal interaction." *Communication Research, 23*(1), 3–43.

Walther, J. B., & Boyd, S. (2002) "Attraction to computer-mediated social support." In C. A. Lin & D. J. Atkin (eds.), *Communication Technology and Society: Audience Adoption and Use.* Cresskill, NJ: Hampton Press, pp. 153–188.

Weinberg, N., Schmale, J., Uken, J., & Wessel, K. (1995) "Computer-mediated support groups." *Social Work With Groups, 17,* 43–54.

Wellman, B. (1997) "An electronic group is virtually a social network." In S. Kiesler (ed.), *Culture of the Internet.* Mahwah, NJ: Lawrence Erlbaum, pp. 179–205.

Wills, T. A. (1985) "Supportive functions of interpersonal relationships." In S. Cohen & S. L. Syme (eds.), *Social Support and Health.* New York: Academic, pp. 61–82.

Wright, K. B. (2000a) "Computer-mediated social support, older adults, and coping." *Journal of Communication, 50*(3), 100–118.

Wright, K. B. (2000b) "Perceptions of on-line support providers: An examination of perceived homophily, source credibility, communication and social support within online support groups." *Communication Quarterly, 48,* 44–59.

Wright, K. B. (2002) "Social support within an on-line cancer community: An assessment of emotional support, perceptions of advantages and disadvantages, and motives for using the community from a communication perspective." *Journal of Applied Communication Research, 30*(3), 195–209.

Wright, K. B., & Bell, S. B. (2003) "Health-related support groups on the Internet: Linking empirical findings to social support and computer-mediated communication theory." *Journal of Health Psychology, 8*(1), 39–54.

Social Support Real-World Lab

Name: _____

Date: _____

For this real-world lab, you will spend some time technology free!

Commit to a four-hour block of time during your normal waking hours and turn off *all* your devices. During this time, have two or more face-to-face conversations. These could be with friends, coworkers, or even strangers at the grocery store or coffee shop. Try to really focus on what they are saying to you. Take note of any urges to check your phone or abruptly end the conversation.

Journal throughout and after the block of time to record how the lack of technology affected your day. Attach your typed and printed journal entry to this worksheet or upload it to the online course management system.

After completing your journal entry, answer these reflection questions:

1. How did the technology-free time change your day?

_____

_____

_____

_____

_____

2. Did you offer/were you offered any support during your technology-free time? If yes, describe it. If no, were there missed opportunities for giving or receiving support?

_____

_____

_____

_____

_____

3. How, if at all, do you think technology use has affected our ability to give and receive high-quality support?

_____

_____

_____

_____

4. How, if at all, did your communication change during the technology-free time? How did it feel to not have certain modes of communication available to you?

_____

_____

_____

_____

_____

5. After this experience, how would you describe your relationship with technology?

_____

_____

_____

_____

6. List some pros and cons of technology dependence or frequent use.

_____

_____

_____

_____

CHAPTER 11

Relationship Dissolution
Hurt, Anger, and Forgiveness

Introduction to the Chapter

Have you ever had a close friend or romantic partner break a promise, say hurtful things they couldn't take back, or cheat on you? This chapter defines and describes common relational transgressions that may lead to conflict, ending a relationship, or even forgiveness. Relational transgressions include infidelity (e.g., cheating), hurtful events, and rule violations (e.g., events, actions, and behaviors that break a relationship norm or expectation).

Selection from "Responses to Relational Transgressions: Hurt, Anger, and Sometimes Forgiveness"

By Sandra Metts and William R. Cupach

....

There is perhaps no phenomenon more theoretically interesting but personally devastating than the inexplicable chasm between the words, "I love you," and "How could you?" Few people caught up in the early excitement of a new relationship can envision the person they love committing an act that discounts them, devalues them, or violates the assumptions of trust and good faith they assumed to be enduring qualities of the relationship. Yet the possibility of a relational transgression ranging from unsettling, to hurtful, and even debilitating is a very real possibility. Even the most trusted and valued friend may commit an act of disregard or violate an assumption of privacy that will challenge the continuation of that friendship. Remarkably, although some relationships dissolve as a result of the transgression, many relationships endure and even improve following the transgression. The question of why and how this is accomplished has recently taken the interest of scholars from a variety of disciplines. One factor that seems to emerge from this research is the critical role of forgiveness. Even when a relationship does not endure following a transgression, forgiveness of the transgressor allows the victim to treat the transgressor with positive regard and move forward with greater comfort in subsequent relationships.

Scholarship on the topics of relational transgressions and forgiveness is multidisciplinary and expanding at a remarkable rate (e.g., Emmers-Sommer, 2003; Fitness, 2001; Jones & Burdette, 1994; Jones, Kugler, & Adams, 1995; McCullough et al., 1998; Roloff & Cloven, 1994; Worthington, 1998). The scope and diversity of this body of work motivates this chapter. Our goal is twofold. First, we synthesize both the transgressions literature and the forgiveness literature, noting conceptual and operational issues relevant to each. Second, we integrate research findings from these two areas to focus attention on the factors that are salient in the transgression to forgiveness process. The first step toward this goal is to provide an overview of the domain of untoward relationship behaviors commonly known as transgressions.

Relational Transgressions: Conceptual and Operational Definitions

Most laypeople have a working knowledge of interpersonal transgressions and can describe a transgression they experienced at work, in their friendships, families, and romantic relationships. However, scholars vary in the terminology they use to describe the range of "untoward" behaviors that might be subsumed under the general rubric of relational transgression. These differences in terminology are important because they direct researchers toward somewhat different domains of inquiry. In addition, the notion of transgression that guides a research agenda influences aspects of the methods used for investigation. For example, a researcher's conceptual definition of transgression influences the types of hypothetical scenarios used or the types of instructions given to respondents when describing their own experiences. It also guides the manipulation and measurement of forgiveness and other variables of interest such as the level of severity of the event, the nature of interaction between offenders and offended, and the degree of distress, hurt, or anger that is imagined or experienced.

In general, the approaches evident within the scholarly literature tend to reflect three conceptual distinctions characterized by the aspect of the transgression event that is emphasized. The first approach focuses on the aspect of certain behaviors as a violation of relational norms and rules. The second focuses on the interpretive consequences of certain behaviors, particularly the degree to which they hurt the victim or imply disregard for the victim and for the presumed value of the relationship. The third approach focuses more specifically on behaviors that constitute infidelity (a common prototype of relational transgression) and the potential threat to paternity or loss of relational resources. We offer illustrations for each approach under the headings of rule violations, hurtful events, and infidelity.

Before doing so, however, we acknowledge the permeable boundaries across these distinctions. For example, the term *betrayal* is often used as a synonym when referring to relational transgressions. In some cases, however, betrayal is defined as one form of rule violation that is particularly traumatic or threatening to a relationship, and in other cases as destructive conflict or as a reference to infidelity. For example, Couch, Jones, and Moore (1999) defined betrayal as a "serious violation of the norms and expectations of a close personal relationship" (p. 452) with infidelity and deception ranked as the two most prototypical cases. Hoyt, McCullough, Fincham, Maio, and Davila (2005) defined betrayal as a particular type of conflict that involves "feelings of injury and resentment, and attributions of blame, on the part of one or both parties" and referred to "precipitating causes of these feelings and attendant cognitions as *interpersonal transgressions*" (p. 376). This caveat aside, we offer the following three approaches to transgressions as one way to organize a large body of literature.

Rule Violations

The most inclusive rendering of relational transgressions focuses on events, actions, and behaviors that violate an implicit or explicit relationship norm or rule (Boon & Sulsky, 1997; Metts, 1994; Roloff, Soule, & Carey, 2001). Explicit rules tend to be relationship specific, such as those prompted by the bad habit or dispositions of a friend or partner (e.g., tendency toward excessive drinking), or those that emerge from ongoing attempts to avoid or manage conflict (e.g., the rule to avoid talking about a former spouse or spending time with a certain person). Implicit norms and rules tend to be those that are accepted as cultural mandates for the proper conduct in relationships (e.g., secrets kept private and sexual exclusivity). Of course, a couple might make adjustments to these more generic rules and decide, for example, that they will not be sexually exclusive, but that they will be emotionally exclusive (Metts, 1994).

The advantage of this approach is its utility for soliciting transgressions from members in a variety of relationships including friends, family, and work relationships as well as romantic relationships. It also avoids highly connotative words such as betrayal. As Finkel, Rusbult, Kumashiro, and Hannon (2002) pointed out, when soliciting transgression descriptions they avoid asking respondents to describe instances of betrayal because it "may connote exclusively sexual norm violations or may arouse anxiety or desire to present the self or the relationship in a socially desirable manner" (p. 963).

Research asking respondents to describe a transgression or a rule violation indicates that a number of actions and events are deemed transgressions by research participants. For example, in a series of studies asking college students to describe an instance when a romantic partner or friend committed a transgression (Metts, Morse, & Lamb, 2001; Metts, Pensinger, & Cupach, 2001) nine categories of transgressions emerged consistently:

- Inappropriate interaction: Instances in which a partner performs badly (rudely, excessively, inappropriately) during an interaction, typically a conflict episode.

- Lack of sensitivity: Instances in which a partner exhibits thoughtless, disrespectful, inconsiderate behavior. Offender demonstrates a lack of concern or emotional responsiveness when expected and appropriate.

- Extrarelational involvement: Sexual or emotional involvement with persons other than the offended party. Offender does not confound involvement with deception.

- Relational threat confounded by deception: Instances in which a partner participates in sexual or emotional involvement with persons other than the offended party and then uses deception to conceal the involvement.

- Disregard for primary relationship: Actions that indicate the transgressor does not privilege the primary relationship; chooses other people or activities over partner or changes plans.

- Abrupt termination: Actions that terminate a relationship with no warning and no explanation.

- Broken promises and rule violations: Occasions during which a partner fails to keep a promise, changes plans with no warning or explanation, or violates a rule that the offended person assumes was binding.

- Deception, secrets, privacy: Instances in which a partner lied, kept important information a secret, failed to keep sensitive information private, or violated privacy boundaries.

- Abuse: Verbal or physical threats.

A similar list of transgressions was identified by Cameron, Ross, and Holmes (2002) in participant descriptions of an event in which they were either the perpetrator or victim of a transgression in a relationship that was "somewhat serious at the time." Content analysis of these descriptions yielded 10 categories of negative behaviors:

- Broken promises.
- Overreaction to the victim's behavior.
- Inconsiderate behavior.
- Violating the victim's desired level of intimacy.
- Neglecting the victim.
- Threat of infidelity.

- Infidelity.

- Verbal aggression toward the victim.

- Unwarranted disagreement.

- Violent behavior toward the victim.

As expected, respondents in the perpetrator role estimated greater change and improvement both in themselves and in their relationships than did respondents in the victim role.

One other study is relevant here, although the impetus for the study was to explore hurtful events rather than relational transgressions. When Feeney (2005) analyzed the descriptions of hurtful events respondents had experienced in their relationships, she discovered a rule-violation framework inherent in these narratives. That is, the feature that distinguished among types of hurtful events was the relational rules that respondents perceived the hurtful person to have violated. These rules included autonomy, similarity display, supportiveness, openness, loyalty or fidelity, shared time, equity, romance, and failure to trust the participant.

In sum, the focus on transgressions as rule violations affords the opportunity to examine a wide range of unexpected, inappropriate, and disruptive behaviors across a variety of relationship types. However, it does locate the definition of a transgression within the rule parameters of the relationship rather than the affective responses of the members. The second general approach focuses more directly on behaviors or events that are perceived by victims to devalue them or the importance of the relationship they share with the person who commits the actions.

Hurtful Events

Transgression studies that ask participants to call to mind behaviors that were hurtful to them or a time when their partner hurt their feelings are very common in the literature (see Vangelisti, chap. 5, this volume). For example, Leary, Springer, Negel, Ansell, and Evans (1998) identified six categories of hurtful events in college students' descriptions: active disassociation (explicit rejection); passive disassociation (being ignored); criticism; betrayal; teasing; and feeling unappreciated, used, or taken for granted. Vangelisti, Young, Carpenter-Theune, and Alexander (2005) identified 14 categories for hurt feelings in college students' descriptions of hurtful behaviors including, for example, rejection, behavioral criticism, betrayal (deception or disloyalty), moral affront, ill-conceived humor, relational depreciation, indifference, and personal attack (pp. 450–451).

Some scholars contend that these hurtful events constitute transgressions when targets perceive themselves as victimized and vulnerable (Vangelisti, 2006;

Vangelisti & Crumley, 1998; Young, 2004). Other scholars suggest that the nature of that hurt is embedded in the perceived devaluation of a relationship considered important to the offended person (Leary & Springer, 2001). Leary et al. (1998) analyzed hurtful episodes experienced by college students. Their findings indicated that all but two of them were caused by perceived relational devaluation and that ratings of emotional pain correlated highly with the degree to which they felt rejected. Feeney (2005) confirmed Leary et al.'s categories of hurtful events and the emotions they evoked.

Several variations within the general parameters of hurtful behaviors and events are evident in the literature. For example, a study focused on hurtful messages by Young (2004) indicates that a recipient's appraisal of the intended expression of concern, comfort, and care that might have motivated a hurtful message is influenced to some degree by the quality of the relationship, but more consistently by the degree of message intensity (i.e., harsh or abrasive language used to encode the message).

A systematic set of investigations by Kowalski (1997, 2000, 2001) examines a family of hurtful actions referred to as *aversive behaviors.* Her investigations detail the motivations for, the nature of, and relational consequences arising from such bad behavior as betrayal, lying, teasing, complaining, arrogance, breaches of propriety, and dependency. She argued that such behaviors are not only perceived as indicative of relational devaluation but as intentionally malicious. In a recent investigation of the impact that one's role as victim or perpetrator might play in assessment of the aversive behaviors, Kowalski, Walker, Wilkinson, Queen, and Sharpe (2003) randomly assigned participants to one of seven aversive behavior situations (betrayal, lying, breaches of propriety, teasing, complaining, arrogance, and dependency) and asked them to write two narratives, one when they had been the perpetrator and one when they had been the victim. As expected, ratings of perceived aversiveness, relational damage, and guilt were higher when participants described their experiences as victims compared to perpetrators, and especially so for betrayal, lying, teasing, and arrogance.

Finally, a subset of aversive behaviors not limited to close relationships is known as *provocations.* Fine and Olson (1997) used a checklist of 29 provocations ranging from bad circumstances or luck (e.g., on the first day of your vacation you wake up feeling ill) to disappointments (e.g., you do not receive an expected pay raise), to various types of aversive behaviors in a relationship (e.g., being stood up for a date, you discover that someone you felt close to has lied to you, your boyfriend or girlfriend tells you that he or she "needs more space" in the relationship and that he or she thinks you should both start dating other people, you overhear a friend criticizing you). Each item was rated on the degree of hurt and anger the participant believed he or she would experience. As expected, hurt and anger were positively correlated and anger and life satisfaction were negatively correlated. Interestingly, although women had higher scores for hurt feelings than did men, only men showed a correlation (negative) between hurt and life satisfaction and assertiveness, and only men exhibited a correlation (positive) between hurt and ratings of relationship intimacy.

Infidelity

Perhaps the prototypical example of what most ordinary people would consider a relational transgression or act of betrayal is relational infidelity, both emotional and sexual. Because Tafoya and Spitzberg (chap. 8, this volume) cover the infidelity research in detail, we selectively review only those investigations relevant to relational transgressions and forgiveness.

What distinguishes infidelity from more generic forms of relational transgressions or betrayal is the unique problem that infidelity imposes on the relationship. Although broken promises, rude, disconfirming, deceptive, or devaluing behaviors evoke hurt, fear, and anger and threaten the stability of the relationship, they do not introduce a rival or competitor directly into the relationship. In addition, each type of infidelity evokes somewhat different responses. As Hall and Fincham (2006) noted, sexual infidelity is more likely to result in "hostile or vengeful, shocked, nauseated or repulsed, humiliated, sexually aroused, or homicidal or suicidal feelings" (p. 157) compared to emotional infidelity. Emotional infidelity is likely to evoke feelings of being "undesirable or insecure, depressed, helpless or abandoned, blameworthy" (p. 157). When both types of infidelity are present, couples are more likely to break up than when only one type of involvement is present.

The unique features of relational infidelity have led evolutionary theorists to propose gender differences in reactions to infidelity depending on the particular form it takes; that is, sexual, emotional, or a combination of sexual and emotional involvement. For example, Shackelford, Buss, and Bennett (2002) drew from an evolutionary perspective in arguing that sexual involvement of a partner threatens men because it raises issues of paternity; emotional involvement of a partner threatens women because they face the loss of their partner's commitment and investments, which makes his infidelity reproductively costly. Shackelford et al. presented respondents with three hypothetical situations (your partner developing deep emotional attachment for another person, your partner enjoying passionate sexual intercourse with that other person, or both) and using forced-choice options asked them to indicate which would be more upsetting, more difficult to forgive, and more likely to lead to breaking up with a partner. Results indicated that men found it more difficult to forgive a partner's sexual infidelity than a partner's emotional infidelity, and were more likely to break up in response to sexual than emotional infidelity. Conversely, women found it more difficult to forgive emotional involvement and were more likely to break up in response to emotional than sexual infidelity. This same pattern of distress emerged from a sample that included older respondents (M = 67 years) as well as college students, although older women were less likely to find emotional infidelity distressing relative to younger women (Shackelford et al., 2004).

Although these findings appear to be straightforward and easily explained from an evolutionary perspective, other research suggests that differences in male and female responses to infidelity are more complicated. For example, those scholars who frame sex differences within social learning theory reason that gender role scripts, more than biological imperatives, explain the differential reactions to infidelity (Hendrick & Hendrick, 1995). The feminine gender script encourages women to feel responsible for the affective quality of the relationship and to embed sexual involvement within committed relationships, whereas the masculine gender script encourages men to value sexual prowess and devalue emotional reflection (i.e., signs of emotional weakness). Thus, if women and men do not uniformly adopt these gender role scripts, their sex-based responses to infidelity will be mediated by individual differences in personality. Cann, Mangum, and Wells (2001) offered support for this argument. Although the men in their sample reported sexual infidelity more distressing and the women in their sample reported emotional infidelity more distressing, individual differences in sexual attitudes such as instrumentality and communion (Hendrick & Hendrick, 1987) and romantic beliefs (Sprecher & Metts, 1989) predicted responses to infidelity independent of gender.

Regardless of the theoretical position used to frame an investigation of infidelity, three concerns are important when interpreting sex differences. First, the methods used to assess distress may influence the gender patterns that emerge. Harris (2002) studied actual as opposed to hypothetical situations of emotional and sexual infidelity. She found that both men and women reported focusing more on the emotional aspects of their partner's infidelity relative to the sexual aspects. She later directly compared responses to actual experiences with forced-choice and continuous rating scales of distress (Harris, 2003). When evaluating actual experience, men and women did not differ in levels of distress for sexual and emotional infidelity. However, when forced to choose which hypothetical scenario was more distressful, women rated emotional infidelity as more distressing than sexual infidelity. Finally, when evaluating hypothetical scenarios on continuous rating scales, men and women both rated sexual infidelity as more upsetting than emotional infidelity, and women rated both more upsetting compared to men.

Second, sexual infidelity and emotional infidelity are not unidimensional constructs. In addition to sexual intercourse, sexual infidelity might entail heavy petting, passionate kissing, sexual fantasies, and sexual attraction (Yarab, Sensibaugh, & Rice Allgeier, 1998). It might involve a one-night stand or an extended relationship; it might involve a prostitute or a same-sex partner (Blow & Hartnett, 2005). In addition to strong feelings of love and intimacy, emotional infidelity might also involve nonsexual fantasies about falling in love, romantic attraction, desire to spend time with another just having lunch or dinner, or going to a movie or other events with someone other than one's partner. It might involve a coworker or an Internet partner; it might involve face-to-face interactions or be conducted long distance by telephone (Blow & Hartnett, 2005). As Whitty (2003, chap. 4, this volume) found, even online ("virtual") sexual activity is rated as more unfaithful than pornography because, despite the similarity in behavior, it implies a threat to the relationship.

Finally, the person who is the object of sexual or emotional attraction influences a partner's appraisal of the situation. Yarab and Rice Allgeier (1998) found sexual fantasies about a partner's friend are perceived to be more threatening than fantasies about a stranger or a movie star. Cann and Baucom (2004) found that when infidelity involves a former romantic partner as opposed to a new rival, it is perceived to be more distressing, especially for women. Although both men and women selected situations of sexual infidelity as more distressing than situations of emotional involvement, men only selected the former partner situation when the infidelity was sexual; they made no distinction when the infidelity was emotional. For women, a former partner was selected as the most distressing option in both situations. Ratings of forgiveness indicated that both men and women found emotional and sexual infidelity more difficult to forgive when it involved a former partner.

Conceptualizing Forgiveness

When an individual experiences a serious and hurtful relational transgression, he or she is likely to feel an initial flood of negative emotions, including anger, disappointment, hurt, fear, resentment, and shame. Indeed, when Feeney (2005) asked participants to recall instances in which a partner said or did something that hurt their feelings and describe how they felt at the time, they produced 57 different emotion terms that clustered into four broad categories: sadness, hurt, anger, and shame. Interestingly, a number of terms were associated with more than one of the broader categories. For example, heartbroken and disappointed were associated with both sadness and hurt, betrayed and deceived were associated with both hurt and anger, and humiliated and rejected were associated with both hurt and shame.

Clearly the initial flood of emotions following a transgression is unpleasant and complex. These emotions are also, however, functional at the time. As motivational states, emotions facilitate emotional as well as physical survival. Fear emerges in anticipation of threat (real or imagined) and following a serious transgression we adopt a readiness orientation to protect ourselves from additional pain (Izard & Ackerman, 2000), sadness follows the realization of loss and leads us to contemplation and reflection (Barr-Zisowitz, 2000), and disgust repels us so that we move away from the object of contamination or moral degradation (Rozin, Haidt, & McCauley, 2000). Even anger can serve a protective function. As Pargament and Rye (1998) pointed out, anger "can be a source of energy and power that counteracts feelings of paralysis and loss of control that often accompany mistreatment" (p. 62).

Thus, emotional responses to relational transgressions are to be expected. They become problematic, however, when they endure beyond their utility as an initial coping mechanism. They eventually become psychologically debilitating and even detrimental to one's physical health (Baumeister, Exline, & Sommer, 1998; Berry & Worthington, 2001; Lawler et al., 2003; Thoresen, Harris, & Luskin, 2000). For this reason, many scholars envision forgiveness as a secondary but more productive means of coping with a transgression and the person who committed it.

More specifically, forgiving does not mean pardoning, condoning, excusing, forgetting, and denying (Enright & Coyle, 1998). Such mental gymnastics, in fact, preclude forgiveness by failing to deal with the transgression and the pain it caused. Rather, the essential element in the accomplishment of forgiveness is a transformation of the initial negative emotions elicited by a transgression to more positive motivations toward the offending person, even if he or she has no right to such compassion. For example, Boon and Sulsky (1997) stated that forgiveness is a "decision to forgo retribution and claims for restitution. It requires that the person who has been harmed, put aside feelings of anger and desires to exact reprisal" (p. 20). McCullough, Worthington, and Rachal (1997) defined forgiveness as a

> set of motivational changes whereby one becomes (a) decreasingly motivated to retaliate against an offending relationship partner, (b) decreasingly motivated to maintain estrangement from the offender, and (c) increasingly motivated

by conciliation and goodwill for the offender, despite the offender's hurtful actions. (p. 323)

Recently, personal relationship scholars have begun to characterize forgiveness as a relationship-constructive transformation similar to the more general notion of accommodation (McCullough et al., 1998). From this perspective, the transformational state is not simply an emotional letting go but a manifestation of the tendency for highly invested, satisfied, and committed couples to inhibit negative or retaliatory responses and engage in constructive behaviors even when their partners have behaved badly (Finkel et al., 2002; Menzies-Toman & Lydon, 2005; Rusbult, Verette, Whitney, Slovik, & Lipkus, 1991). At the core of this transformation is the emergent preference to protect the viability and well-being of the relationship rather than to protect one's own self-interest (i.e., the willingness to sacrifice; Van Lange et al., 1997). As a result, appraisals of a partner's untoward behavior are benign and communicative responses are constructive (i.e., voice and loyalty) rather than destructive (i.e., exit and neglect). Moreover, benign appraisals and the forgiveness they foster are more specifically a function of emotional commitment than of structural commitment (Roloff et al., 2001). Although the premises of the investment model and the transformational nature of forgiveness are a reasonable interface, Fincham, Beach, and Davila (2004) cautioned that when destructive behavior of one's partner is ignored, condoned, or excused, the fundamental conditions for forgiveness (e.g., perceiving the wrongfulness of the actions and partner's intentionality) are not met and thus forgiveness is not relevant.

In sum, there is general agreement among scholars that forgiveness involves the victim's recognition of an offender's responsibility in committing a transgression, the awareness at some level that retaliatory actions would be justified, but ultimately the willingness to transform negative emotions, particularly anger and resentment, into positive and prosocial motivational tendencies toward the perpetrator. However, two issues have emerged in the forgiveness literature that merit comment.

First, as indicated in McCullough et al.'s (1997) definition, forgiveness is often linked to the desire to achieve or willingness to work toward reconciliation. The question of whether forgiveness can be accomplished apart from reconciliation is a point of discussion in the forgiveness literature. Baumeister et al. (1998) argued that *total forgiveness* includes both an intrapsychic dimension (i.e., an emotional attitude based on cognitive appraisals and interpretations) and an interpersonal action between people that returns them to conditions existing before the transgression. To simply change one's internal state is *silent forgiveness* and to simply have interpersonal action leading to reconciliation is *hollow forgiveness*.

However, other scholars argue that intrapsychic forgiveness and interpersonal reconciliation should be treated as independent concepts (e.g., Fincham, 2000; Worthington, 1998). At the heart of the independence position is the argument that linking the achievement of intrapsychic forgiveness with interpersonally negotiated reconciliation distorts the complexity of both processes (Enright, Freedman, & Rique, 1998; Enright & Zell, 1989). For example, the injured party may relinquish negative emotions such as hate, anger, or resentment and even feel positive regard toward the offender, but refuse to renew the relationship because trust cannot be restored (Freedman & Enright, 1996). Alternatively, an offended person may rejoin a partner who committed a transgression but withhold forgiveness, choosing to reunite due to other factors such as children, financial obligations, loneliness, or the relative comfort of familiarity. Empirical research provides some support for the position that forgiveness and reconciliation are separable processes, at least in terms of factors that predict them. For example, Walker and Gorsuch (2004) found in a series of path model analyses that the processes leading to emotional forgiveness and to reconciliation were clearly different.

The concerns characterizing these positions on forgiveness are not easily resolved. As Scobie and Scobie (1998) concluded, the differences would appear to have more to do with "a researcher's attitude toward forgiveness, i.e., which model they use, rather than forgiveness per se" (p. 376). Although Scobie and Scobie's point is well taken, recent investigations of ordinary laypersons' views of forgiveness suggest that the issues emerging in the scholarly discourse may, in fact, be inherent in the very notion of what it means to forgive. For example, when asked to define forgiveness, many college undergraduates and community adults defined it as "letting go of negative feelings and grudges" (college sample, 33%; community sample, 39%). However, others defined it as "going back to or continuing the relationship" (college sample, 24%; community sample, 16%; Younger, Piferi, Jobe, & Lawler, 2004). In a set of studies designed to identify a forgiveness prototype, Kearns and Fincham (2004) found considerable variability in features participants listed for the term *forgiveness*. Although only 4% of the participants mentioned saying, "I forgive you," accepting the offender's apology was frequently mentioned. Some respondents mentioned the possible cost of forgiveness (being hurt again), and others mentioned reconciling and continuing in the relationship.

Perhaps most indicative of the complexity of forgiveness are the personal narratives of those who have experienced a relational transgression. Boekhout, Hendrick, and Hendrick (1999) analyzed the narratives of college students who had experienced relationship infidelity in a dating relationship. In most cases the consequences were quite negative and many of the relationships were terminated. For those who eventually reconciled, however, the authors made the interesting observation about the complexity of that process. For example, a forgiveness description provided by a transgressor, "He was very upset. We were immature when it happened, so he eventually realized that after the anger turned to sadness and finally forgiveness," indicates recognition of the victim's struggle to forgive and reconcile the relationship. Moreover, as Boekhout et al. noted, even reconciled relationships may have been "scarred by the infidelity," and illustrate with the following: "I feel bad, my stomach is always in knots, and it causes much unknown tension between us" (p. 118).

We believe there is merit in both positions on the forgiveness–reconciliation issue. We recognize that forgiveness is indeed an intrapsychic, highly personal, emotional transformation and believe that it can occur independently of relational reconciliation. However, we also believe that even when interactions between the offender and offended person do not result in reconciliation, they play an important role in facilitating (or inhibiting) the emotional process of forgiveness. Indeed, Younger et al. (2004) found that 27% of their college respondents said that "offender lack of remorse/apology" was the primary reason to not forgive. Thus, the transgressor's attempts to seek forgiveness or explain his or her actions may not restore the relationship to its previous levels of commitment and satisfaction, but it may help the victim understand the offender's action and separate the offender from the offensive act. This process facilitates transformation of vengeful emotions into more positive emotions, if for no other reason than it serves to activate some degree of empathy for the offender (Macaskill, Maltby, & Day, 2002).

A second issue apparent in the forgiveness research is whether the transformation of negative emotions into more positive orientations toward the offender necessarily entails the complete elimination of all negative affect associated with the offense. Witvleit, Ludwig, and Vander Laan (2001) argued that "forgiveness still allows for holding the offender responsible for the transgression, and does not involve denying, ignoring, minimizing, tolerating, condoning, excusing or forgetting the offense" (p. 118). In a similar vein, Wade and Worthington (2003) proposed that forgiveness and unforgiveness are not reciprocally related and that "reduced unforgiveness does not imply forgiveness" (p. 344). Using a sample of college students attending a psychoeducational training program designed to promote forgiveness among persons who had been unable to forgive, Wade and Worthington compared the pattern of predictors for forgiveness and unforgiveness. Despite several similarities in these patterns, the differences were sufficient for the authors to conclude that forgiveness and un-forgiveness are two distinguishable responses to interpersonal transgressions. Konstam, Holmes, and Levine (2003) reached a similar conclusion after finding that the correlates of forgiveness and unforgiveness (e.g., emotion-focused coping, empathy, and selfism) were distinctly different.

Although these issues reflect, in part, influences from scholars' disciplinary traditions and clinical practices, they are also aspects arising from the inherent complexity of the forgiveness construct. As might be expected, given the diversity in conceptual definitions of forgiveness, variations in measurement are also evident in the literature.

References

Afifi, W. A., Falato, W. L., & Weiner, J. L. (2001). Identity concerns following a severe relational transgression: The role of discovery method for the relational outcomes of infidelity. *Journal of Social and Personal Relationships, 18,* 291–308.

Aron, A., Aron, E. N., & Smollan, D. (1992). Inclusion of other in the self scale and the structure of interpersonal closeness. *Journal of Personality and Social Psychology, 63,* 596–612.

Ashton, M. C., Paunonen, S. V., Helmes, E., & Jackson, D. N. (1998). Kin altruism, reciprocal altruism, and the Big Five personality factors. *Evolution and Human Behavior, 19,* 243–255.

Barr-Zisowitz, C. (2000). "Sadness"—Is there such a thing? In M. Lewis & J. M. Haviland-Jones (Eds.), *Handbook of emotions* (2nd ed., pp. 607–622). New York: Guilford.

Batson, C. D. (1991). *The altruism question.* Hillsdale, NJ: Lawrence Erlbaum Associates.

Baumeister, R. F., Exline, J. J., & Sommer, K. L. (1998). The victim role, grudge theory, and two dimensions of forgiveness. In E. L. Worthington (Ed.), *Dimensions of forgiveness: Psychological research and theological perspectives* (pp. 79–104). Philadelphia: Templeton Foundation Press.

Berry, J. W., & Worthington, E. L., Jr. (2001). Forgivingness, relationship quality, stress while imagining relationship events, and physical and mental health. *Journal of Counseling Psychology, 48,* 447–455.

Berry, J. W., Worthington, E. L., Jr., O'Connor, L. E., Parrott, L., III, & Wade, N. G. (2005). Forgiveness, vengeful rumination, and affective traits. *Journal of Personality, 73,* 183–229.

Berry, J. W., Worthington, E. L., Jr., Parrott, L., III, O'Connor, L. E., & Wade, N. G. (2001). Dispositional forgivingness: Development and construct validity of the Transgression Narrative Test of Forgiveness (TNTF). *Personality and Social Psychology Bulletin, 27,* 1277–1290.

Blow, A. J., & Harnett, K. (2005). Infidelity in committed relationships II: A substantive review. *Journal of Marital and Family Therapy, 31,* 217–233.

Boekhout, B. A., Hendrick, S. S., & Hendrick, C. (1999). Relationship infidelity: A loss perspective. *Journal of Personal and Interpersonal Loss, 4,* 97–123.

Bonach, K., & Sales, E. (2002). Forgiveness as a mediator between post divorce cognitive processes and coparenting quality. *Journal of Divorce and Remarriage, 38,* 17–38.

Boon, S. D., & Sulsky, L. M. (1997). Attributions of blame and forgiveness in romantic relationships: A policy capturing study. *Journal of Social Behavior and Personality, 12,* 19–44.

Cameron, J. J., Ross, M., & Holmes, J. G. (2002). Loving the one you hurt: Positive effects of recounting a transgression against an intimate partner. *Journal of Experimental Social Psychology, 38,* 307–314.

Cann, A., & Baucom, T. R. (2004). Former partners and new rivals as threats to a relationship: Infidelity type, gender, and commitment as factors related to distress and forgiveness. *Personal Relationships, 11,* 305–318.

Cann, A., Mangum, J. L., & Wells, M. (2001). Distress in response to relationship infidelity: The roles of gender and attitudes about relationships. *Journal of Sex Research, 38,* 185–190.

Caprara, G. V. (1986). Indicators of aggression: The dissipation–rumination scale. *Personality and Individual Differences, 7,* 763–769.

Couch, L. L., Jones, W. H., & Moore, D. S. (1999). Buffering the effects of betrayal: The role of apology, forgiveness, and commitment. In J. M. Adams & W. H. Jones (Eds.), *Handbook of interpersonal commitment and relationship stability* (pp. 451–469). New York: Kluwer Academic/Plenum.

Darby, B. W., & Schlenker, B. R. (1982). Children's reactions to apologies. *Journal of Personality and Social Psychology, 43,* 742–753.

Emmers-Sommer, T. M. (2003). When partners falter: Repair after a transgression. In D. J. Canary & M. Dainton (Eds.), *Maintaining relationships through communication: Relational, contextual, and cultural variations* (pp. 185–205). Mahwah, NJ: Lawrence Erlbaum Associates.

Emmons, R. A. (2000). Personality and forgiveness. In M. E. McCullough, K. I. Pargament, & C. E. Thoresen (Eds.), *Forgiveness: Theory, research, and practice* (pp. 156–175). New York: Guilford.

Enright, R. D. (2005). *Enright Forgiveness Inventory and manual.* Redwood City, CA: Mind Garden.

Enright, R. D., & Coyle, C. T. (1998). Researching the process model of forgiveness within psychological interventions. In E. L. Worthington, Jr. (Ed.), *Dimensions of forgive-*

ness: Psychological research and theological perspectives (pp. 139–162). Philadelphia: Templeton Foundation Press.

Enright, R. D., Freedman, S., & Rique, J. (1998). The psychology of interpersonal forgiveness. In R. D. Enright & J. North (Eds.), *Exploring forgiveness* (pp. 46–62). Madison: University of Wisconsin Press.

Enright, R. D., & Zell, R. (1989). Problems encountered when we forgive one another. *Journal of Psychology and Christianity, 8,* 52–60.

Exline, J. J., Baumeister, R. F., Bushman, B. J., Campbell, W. K., & Finkel, E. J. (2004). Too proud to let go: Narcissistic entitlement as a barrier to forgiveness. *Journal of Personality and Social Psychology, 87,* 894–912.

Feeney, J. A. (2005). Hurt feelings in couple relationships: Exploring the role of attachment and perceptions of personal injury. *Personal Relationships, 12,* 253–271.

Fincham, F. D. (2000). The kiss of the porcupines: From attributing responsibility to forgiving. *Personal Relationships, 7,* 1–23.

Fincham, F. D., Beach, S. R. H., & Davila, J. (2004). Forgiveness and conflict resolution in marriage. *Journal of Family Psychology, 18,* 72–81.

Fincham, F. D., Jackson, H., & Beach, S. R. H. (2005). Transgression severity and forgiveness: Different moderators for objective and subjective severity. *Journal of Social and Clinical Psychology, 24,* 860–875.

Fincham, F. D., Paleari, F. G., & Regalia, C. (2002). Forgiveness in marriage: The role of relationship quality, attributions, and empathy. *Personal Relationships, 9,* 27–37.

Fine, M. A., & Olson, K. A. (1997). Anger and hurt in response to provocation: Relationship to psychological adjustment. *Journal of Social Behavior and Personality, 12,* 325–344.

Finkel, E. J., Rusbult, C. E., Kumashiro, M., & Hannon, P. A. (2002). Dealing with betrayal in close relationships: Does commitment promote forgiveness? *Journal of Personality and Social Psychology, 82,* 956–974.

Fitness, J. (2001). Betrayal, rejection, revenge, and forgiveness: An interpersonal script approach. In M. R. Leary (Ed.), *Interpersonal rejection* (pp. 73–104). New York: Oxford University Press.

Fraser, B. (1981). On apologizing. In F. Coulmas (Ed.), *Conversational routine: Explorations in standardized communication situations and prepatterned speech* (pp. 259–271). New York: Mouton.

Freedman, S. R., & Enright, R. D. (1996). Forgiveness as an intervention with incest survivors. *Journal of Consulting and Clinical Psychology, 64,* 983–992.

Goffman, E. (1971). *Relations in public.* New York: Basic Books.

Gordon, K. C., & Baucom, D. H. (1998). Understanding betrayals in marriage: A synthesized model of forgiveness. *Family Process, 37,* 425–450.

Gordon, K. C., & Baucom, D. H. (2003). Forgiveness and marriage: Preliminary support for measure based on a model of recovery from a marital betrayal. *American Journal of Family Therapy, 31,* 179–199.

Hall, J. H., & Fincham, F. D. (2006). Relationship dissolution following infidelity. In M. A. Fine & J. H. Harvey (Eds.), *Handbook of divorce and relationship dissolution* (pp. 153–168). Mahwah, NJ: Lawrence Erlbaum Associates.

Hargrave, T. D., & Sells, J. N. (1997). The development of a forgiveness scale. *Journal of Marital and Family Therapy, 23,* 41–63.

Harris, C. R. (2002). Sexual and romantic jealousy in heterosexual and homosexual adults. *Psychological Science, 13,* 7–12.

Harris, C. R. (2003). Factors associated with jealousy over real and imagined infidelity: An examination of the social-cognitive and evolutionary psychology perspectives. *Psychology of Women Quarterly, 27,* 319–329.

Hendrick, S. S., & Hendrick, C. (1987). Multidimensionality of sexual attitudes. *Journal of Sex Research, 23,* 502–526.

Hendrick, S. S., & Hendrick, C. (1995). Gender differences and similarities in sex and love. *Personal Relationships, 2,* 55–65.

Hoyt, W. T., McCullough, M. E., Fincham, F. D., Maio, G., & Davila, J. (2005). Responses to interpersonal transgressions in families: Forgivingness, forgivability, and relationship-specific effects. *Journal of Personality and Social Psychology, 89,* 375–394.

Izard, C. E., & Ackerman, B. P. (2000). Motivational, organizational, and regulatory functions of discrete emotions. In M. Lewis & J. M. Haviland-Jones (Eds.), *Handbook of emotions* (2nd ed., pp. 253–264). New York: Guilford.

John, O. P. (1990). The "Big Five" factor taxonomy: Dimensions of personality in the natural language and in questionnaires. In L. A. Pervin (Ed.), *Handbook of personality: Theory and research* (pp. 66–100). New York: Guilford.

Jones, W. H., & Burdette, M. P. (1994). Betrayal in relationships. In A. L. Weber & J. H. Harvey (Eds.), *Perspectives on close relationships* (pp. 243–262). Boston: Allyn & Bacon.

Jones, W. H., Kugler, K., & Adams, P. (1995). You always hurt the one you love: Guilt and transgressions against relationship partners. In J. P. Tangney & K. W. Fischer (Eds.), *Self-conscious emotions: The psychology of shame, guilt, embarrassment, and pride* (pp. 301–321). New York: Guilford.

Jones, W. H., Moore, D. S., Schratter, A., & Negel, L. A. (2001). Interpersonal transgressions and betrayals. In R. Kowalski (Ed.), *Behaving badly: Aversive behavior in interpersonal relationships* (pp. 233–255). Washington, DC: American Psychological Association.

Kachadourian, L. G., Fincham, F., & Davila, J. (2004). The tendency to forgive in dating and married couples: The role of attachment and relationship satisfaction. *Personal Relationships, 11,* 373–0.

Karremans, J. C., Van Lange, P. A. M., & Holland, R. W. (2005). Forgiveness and its associations with prosocial thinking, feeling, and doing beyond the relationship with the
offender. *Personality and Social Psychology Bulletin, 31,* 1315–1326.

Kearns, J. N., & Fincham, F. D. (2004). A prototype analysis of forgiveness. *Personality and
Social Psychology Bulletin, 30,* 838–855.

Kelley, D. L. (1998). The communication of forgiveness. *Communication Studies, 49,*
1–17.

Kelley, D. L., & Waldron, V. R. (2005). An investigation of forgiveness-seeking communication and relational outcomes. *Communication Quarterly, 53,* 339–358.

Knapp, M. L., Stafford, L., & Daly, J. (1986). Regrettable messages: Things people wish
they hadn't said. *Journal of Communication, 36,* 40–58.

Konstam, V., Holmes, W., & Levine, B. (2003). Empathy, selfism, and coping as elements
of the psychology of forgiveness: A preliminary study. *Counseling and Values, 47,*
172–183.

Kowalski, R. M. (1997). The underbelly of social interaction: Aversive interpersonal
behaviors. In R. M. Kowalski (Ed.), *Aversive interpersonal behaviors* (pp. 1–9). New
York: Plenum.

Kowalski, R. M. (2000). "I was only kidding!": Victims' and perpetrators' perceptions of
teasing. *Personality and Social Psychology Bulletin, 26,* 231–241.

Kowalski, R. M. (2001). Aversive interpersonal behaviors: On being annoying, thoughtless,
and mean. In R. M. Kowalski (Ed.), *Behaving badly: Aversive behaviors in interpersonal
relationships* (pp. 3–26). Washington, DC: American Psychological Association.

Kowalski, R. M., Walker, S., Wilkinson, R., Queen, A., & Sharpe, B. (2003). Lying, cheating,
complaining, and other aversive interpersonal behaviors: A narrative examination of the
darker side of relationships. *Journal of Social and Personal Relationships, 20,* 471–490.

Lawler, K. A., Younger, J. W., Piferi, R. L., Billington, E., Jobe, R., Edmondson, K., et al.
(2003). A change of heart: Cardiovascular correlates of forgiveness in response to
interpersonal conflict. *Journal of Behavioral Medicine, 26,* 373–393.

Leary, M. R., & Springer, C. (2001). Hurt feelings: The neglected emotion. In R. M. Kowalski
(Ed.), *Behaving badly: Aversive behaviors in interpersonal relationships* (pp. 151–176).
Washington, DC: American Psychological Association.

Leary, M. R., Springer, C., Negel, L., Ansell, E., & Evans, K. (1998). The causes, phenomenology, and consequences of hurt feelings. *Journal of Personality and Social Psychology,
74,* 1225–1237.

Macaskill, A., Maltby, J., & Day, L. (2002). Forgiveness of self and others and emotional
empathy. *Journal of Social Psychology, 142,* 663–665.

Mauger, P. A., Perry, J. W., Freeman, T., Grove, D. C., McBride, A. G., & McKinney, K. E. (1992). The measurement of forgiveness: Preliminary research. *Journal of Psychology and Christianity, 11,* 170–180.

McCullough, M. E., Bellah, C. G., Kilpatrick, S. D., & Johnson, J. L. (2001). Vengefulness: Relationships with forgiveness, rumination, well-being, and the Big Five. *Personality and Social Psychology Bulletin, 27,* 601–610.

McCullough, M. E., Fincham, F. D., & Tsang, J. (2003). Forgiveness, forbearance, and time: The temporal unfolding of transgression-related interpersonal motivations. *Journal of Personality and Social Psychology, 84,* 540–557.

McCullough, M. E., & Hoyt, W. T. (2002). Transgression-related motivational dispositions: Personality substrates of forgiveness and their links to the Big Five. *Personality and Social Psychology Bulletin, 28,* 1556–1573.

McCullough, M. E., Hoyt, W. T., & Rachal, K. C. (2000). What we know (and need to know) about assessing forgiveness constructs. In M. E. McCullough, K. I. Pargament, & C. E. Thoresen (Eds.), *Forgiveness: Theory, research, and practice* (pp. 65–88). New York: Guilford.

McCullough, M. E., Rachal, K. C., Sandage, S. J., Worthington, E. L., Jr., Brown, S. W., & Hight, T. L. (1998). Interpersonal forgiving in close relationships: II. Theoretical elaboration and measurement. *Journal of Personality and Social Psychology, 75,* 1586–1603.

McCullough, M. E., Worthingon, E. L., Jr., & Rachal, K. C. (1997). Interpersonal forgiving in close relationships. *Journal of Personality and Social Psychology, 73,* 321–336.

McLaughlin, M. L., Cody, M. J., & O'Hair, H. D. (1983). The management of failure events: Some contextual determinants of accounting behavior. *Human Communication Research, 9,* 208–224.

Menzies-Toman, D. A., & Lydon, J. E. (2005). Commitment-motivated benign appraisals of partner transgressions: Do they facilitate accommodation? *Journal of Social and Personal Relationships, 22,* 111–128.

Metts, S. (1994). Relational transgressions. In W. R. Cupach & B. H. Spitzberg (Eds.), *The dark side of interpersonal communication* (pp. 217–239). Hillsdale, NJ: Lawrence Erlbaum Associates, Inc.

Metts, S., Morse, C., & Lamb, E. (2001, November). *The influence of relational history on the management and outcomes of relational transgressions.* Paper presented at the convention of the National Communication Association, Atlanta, GA.

Metts, S., Pensinger, A., & Cupach, W. R. (2001, April). *How could you? Relational transgressions, redressive actions, and forgiveness.* Paper presented at the convention of the Central States Communication Association, Cincinnati, OH.

Mullet, E., Houdbine, A., Laumonier, S., & Girard, M. (1998). "Forgiveness": Factor structure in a sample of young, middle-aged, and elderly adults. *European Psychologist, 3,* 289–297.

Ohbuchi, K.-I., Kameda, M., & Agarie, N. (1989). Apology as aggression control: Its role in mediating appraisal of and response to harm. *Journal of Personality and Social Psychology, 56,* 219–227.

Pargament, K. I., & Rye, M. S. (1998). Forgiveness as a method of religious coping. In E. L. Worthington, Jr. (Ed.), *Dimensions of forgiveness: Psychological research and theological perspectives* (pp. 59–78). Philadelphia: Templeton Foundation Press.

Roberts, R. C. (1995). Forgivingness. *American Philosophical Quarterly, 32,* 289–306.

Roloff, M. E., & Cloven, D. H. (1994). When partners transgress: Maintaining violated relationships. In D. J. Canary & L. Stafford (Eds.), *Communication and relational maintenance* (pp. 23–43). San Diego, CA: Academic.

Roloff, M. E., Soule, K. P., & Carey, C. M. (2001). Reasons for remaining in a relationship and responses to relational transgressions. *Journal of Social and Personal Relationships, 18,* 362–385.

Rozin, P., Haidt, J., & McCauley, C. R. (2000). Disgust. In M. Lewis & J. M. Haviland-Jones (Eds.), *Handbook of emotions* (2nd ed., pp. 607–622). New York: Guilford.

Rusbult, C. E., Verette, J., Whitney, G. A., Slovik, L. F., & Lipkus, I. (1991). Accommodation processes in close relationships: Theory and preliminary empirical evidence. *Journal of Personality and Social Psychology, 60,* 53–78.

Schlenker, B. R., & Darby, B. W. (1981). The use of apologies in social predicaments. *Social Psychology Quarterly, 44,* 271–278.

Scobie, E. D., & Scobie, G. E. W. (1998). Damaging events: The perceived need for forgiveness. *Journal for the Theory of Social Behaviour, 28,* 373–403.

Shackelford, T. K., Buss, D. M., & Bennett, K. (2002). Forgiveness or breakup: Sex differences in response to a partner's infidelity. *Cognition and Emotion, 16,* 299–307.

Sprecher, S., & Metts, S. (1989). Development of the "Romantic Beliefs Scale" and examination of the effects of gender and gender-role orientation. *Journal of Social and Personal Relationships, 6,* 385–409.

Takaku, S. (2001). The effects of apology and perspective taking on interpersonal forgiveness: A dissonance-attribution model of interpersonal forgiveness. *Journal of Social Psychology, 141,* 494–509.

Tavuchis, N. (1991). *Mea culpa: A sociology of apology and reconciliation.* Stanford, CA: Stanford University Press.

Thompson, L. Y., Snyder, C. R., Hoffman, L., Michael, S. T., Rasmussen, H. N., Billings, L. S., et al. (2005). Dispositional forgiveness of self, others, and situations. *Journal of Personality, 73,* 313–359.

Thoresen, C. E., Harris, A. H. S., & Luskin, F. (2000). Forgiveness and health: An unanswered question. In M. E. McCullough, K. I. Pargament, & C. E. Thoresen (Eds.), *Forgiveness: Theory, research, and practice* (pp. 254–280). New York: Guilford.

Tomlinson, E. C., Dineen, B. R., & Lewicki, R. J. (2004). The road to reconciliation: Antecedents of victim willingness to reconcile following a broken promise. *Journal of Management, 30,* 165–187.

Toussaint, L., & Webb, J. R. (2005). Gender differences in the relationship between empathy and forgiveness. *Journal of Social Psychology, 145,* 673–685.

Vangelisti, A. L. (2006). Hurtful interactions and the dissolution of intimacy. In M. A. Fine & J. H. Harvey (Eds.), *Handbook of divorce and relationship dissolution* (pp. 133–152). Mahwah, NJ: Lawrence Erlbaum Associates.

Vangelisti, A. L., & Crumley, L. P. (1998). Reactions to messages that hurt: The influence of relational contexts. *Communication Monographs, 65,* 173–196.

Vangelisti, A. L., Young, S. L., Carpenter-Theune, K. E., & Alexander, A. L. (2005). Why does it hurt?: The perceived causes of hurt feelings. *Communication Research, 32,* 443–477.

Van Lange, P. A. M., Rusbult, C. E., Drigotas, S. M., Arriaga, X. B., Witcher, B. S., & Cox, C. L. (1997). Willingness to sacrifice in close relationships. *Journal of Personality and Social Psychology, 72,* 1373–1395.

Wade, N. G., & Worthington, E. L. (2003). Overcoming interpersonal offenses: Is forgiveness the only way to deal with unforgiveness? *Journal of Counseling and Development, 81,* 343–353.

Walker, D. F., & Gorsuch, R. L. (2004). Dimensions underlying sixteen models of forgiveness and reconciliation. *Journal of Psychology and Theology, 32,* 12–25.

Weiner, B., Graham, S., Peter, O., & Zmuidinas, M. (1991). Public confession and forgiveness. *Journal of Personality, 59,* 281–312.

Whitty, M. T. (2003). Pushing the wrong buttons: Men's and women's attitudes toward online and offline infidelity. *CyberPsychology and Behavior, 6,* 569–579.

Witvleit, C., Ludwig, T. E., & Vander Laan, K. (2001). Granting forgiveness or harboring grudges: Implications for emotion, physiology, and health. *Psychological Science, 11,* 117–123.

Wolf-Smith, J. H., & LaRossa, R. (1992). After he hits her. *Family Relations, 41,* 324–329.

Worthington, E. L., Jr. (1998). The pyramid model of forgiveness: Some interdisciplinary speculations about unforgiveness and the promotion of forgiveness. In E. L. Worthington, Jr. (Ed.), *Dimensions of forgiveness: Psychological research and theological perspectives* (pp. 107–138). Philadelphia: Templeton Foundation Press.

Yarab, P. W., & Rice Allgeier, E. (1998). Don't even think about it: The role of sexual fantasies as perceived unfaithfulness in heterosexual dating relationships. *Journal of Sex Education and Therapy, 23,* 246–254.

Yarab, P. W., Sensibaugh, C. C., & Rice Allgeier, E. (1998). More than just sex: Gender differences in incidence of self-defined unfaithful behavior in heterosexual dating relationships. *Journal of Psychology and Human Sexuality, 10,* 45–57.

Young, S. L. (2004). Factors that influence recipients' appraisals of hurtful communication. *Journal of Social and Personal Relationships, 21,* 291–303.

Younger, J. W., Piferi, R. L., Jobe, R. L., & Lawler, K. A. (2004). Dimensions of forgiveness: The views of laypersons. *Journal of Social and Personal Relationships, 21,* 837–855.

Zechmeister, J. S., & Romero, C. (2002). Victim and offender accounts of interpersonal conflict: Autobiographical narratives of forgiveness and unforgiveness. *Journal of Personality and Social Psychology, 82,* 675–686.

Relationship Dissolution Real-World Lab

Name: _____

Date: _____

For this real-world lab, you will analyze the ending of a relationship. You can choose to analyze a breakup of your own or one you are familiar with from TV or a movie. For example, you may choose to discuss a relationship with a significant other or Ross and Rachel from *Friends*.

Knapp describes five stages of coming apart:[1]

1. Differentiating. This stage is a normal part of healthy relationships and is marked by the couple spending less time together and doing things independently. This stage is part of maintenance.

2. Circumscribing. In this stage, partners start to talk to one another less and relationship deterioration becomes more serious. Major violations of trust (e.g., cheating) often result in moving to this stage.

3. Stagnating. In this stage, people feel they have little left to say or that they already know exactly how a fight will play out, so they don't even bother having the fight.

4. Avoiding. Physical avoidance happens in this stage, including staying late at work or spending time with friends to avoid seeing one another or moving into separate bedrooms for couples who live together.

5. Terminating. In this stage, the relationship is over. The people disassociate from each other's social networks (e.g., tell their friends they are no longer a couple). This happens just before "the end."

Answer the following questions:

1. Briefly describe the nature of the relationship you are analyzing and then discuss how it dissolved using the five stages defined.

_____

_____

_____

_____

_____

_____

---

1   Mark L. Knapp, *Social Intercourse: From Greeting to Goodbye.* (Boston: Allyn & Bacon, 1978).

_____

_____

_____

_____

2. Did the breakup follow Knapp's five stages in order or did it go out of order or skip any stages?

_____

_____

_____

_____

3. Now, tell the breakup story from another perspective. There are two sides to every story. If analyzing your own breakup, try to see the situation from your ex's point of view. How would they tell the story of your breakup? How is their version different from yours? If analyzing a fictional breakup, how do the characters' two versions of the same breakup differ?

_____

_____

_____

_____

4. How, if at all, was technology involved in the breakup?

_____

_____

_____

_____

5. What relational transgressions occurred in the relationship? Were those the cause of the breakup? Why or why not?

_____

_____

_____

_____

_____

6. How did hurt, anger, and forgiveness (or lack thereof) play a role in the ending of the relationship?

_____

_____

_____

_____

_____

7. If you analyzed your own breakup, is there anything you would change about how things ended now that you know more about hurt, anger, and forgiveness? If you analyzed a fictional relationship, what would you suggest the characters change or do differently in the future?

_____

_____

_____

_____

_____

CHAPTER 12

Organizational Culture and Workplace Communication

Introduction to the Chapter

Just like any group of people that is created and maintained by communication, all organizations have a culture. Some have stronger and/or healthier cultures than others. Organizational cultures have the power to influence people's performance and satisfaction in their jobs. This chapter explores the concept of organizational culture including communication climates within cultures. Different types of organizational cultures discussed include authoritarian and participative cultures. Management styles that focus on communication are also discussed including theory X and theory Y.

Selection from "Organizational Structure, Culture, and Climate"

By Rita Linjuan Men and Shannon A. Bowen

Organizational Culture

Organizational culture can be thought of as an organization's "personality." The organizational enterprise is comprised of numerous functions, subfunctions, and units. Those factors combined with its environment, policies, and human aspects, including communication and the meaning that is created by it, combine together in a *suis generis* sense to create organizational culture—organizational culture exists holistically, as a whole that is greater than the sum of its parts, as part symbolism and part performance (Eisenberg and Riley 2001). As such, an organizational culture is comprised of symbolism, psychological meanings and processes, representations, symbolism, and power (Smircic and Calas 1987).[1]

Organizational culture is nebulous, yet can be reliably described, felt, and measured (Eisenberg and Riley 2001). Further, organizational culture has a clear impact on performance, effectiveness, employee satisfaction, hiring, and retention. A purposeful and strong organizational culture can even offer a competitive advantage in the marketplace. Although organizational culture is made up of a complex interplay of factors, it can be theorized to exist as two opposite poles: authoritarian culture and participative culture. The reality of an organization would include some mix of factors that place it on the continuum along the spectrum between these two approaches, but they offer an extremely useful conceptualization of organizational culture.

Authoritarian Organizational Culture

Authoritarian organizational culture, as the name implies, is based on authority. This type of organizational culture is based on command and control systems of

---

[1]   For an excellent discussion on the cultural organization, see Morgan (2006), *Images of organization*, chapter 4, pp. 115–48.

hierarchy and formalized structure, as well as standard operating procedures and codified policy. The authority of stakeholders is linked in an escalating chain of command and reporting lines (Goodpaster 2007). Authoritarian systems use an organized chain of command and some degree of reliance on bureaucracy and formalization (Jablin 1987). For example, if an employee's expense report must be approved by a supervisor, and submitted with both signatures to accounting, a formal approval process is in place creating a standardized workflow.

A number of strengths and weaknesses should be noted regarding authoritarian organizational cultures. They are excellent at organizing a large-scale enterprise and offering a standard, recognizable product or service. For example, the enormous fast-food chain McDonald's uses authoritarian culture to organize one of the world's largest new employee training programs in which routines and standard operating procedures are taught. The food is relatively standardized and recognizable at any McDonald's location throughout the world. Employees are organized with a standard and predictable economy of scale, with efficiency in mind. Labor is considered a relatively inexpensive and renewable resource, so that a frequent turnover rate does not hamper efficiency or product quality. Communications are routine and focused on role specificity, in order to help organize this large-scale enterprise. On-boarding is also standardized and a relatively high turnover rate of employees is expected (Jablin 2001).

Authoritarian organizational cultures are predictable and stable, but resistant to change and are slow to evolve. The status quo is valued because it reinforces authority systems. These cultures value stability rather than input and open communication, which is not encouraged or sought from most employees. Employees may feel undervalued or disconnected from the organization in an authoritarian culture, unless specific efforts are made through internal relations to communicate with them frequently and well. Further, input from employees is neither sought nor desired by management at higher levels of hierarchy. Employees are not viewed as a resource for ideas or innovation, so any upward communication is often stifled (Grunig 1992). Feedback on performance is often routine and may only be issued in negative cases because routinely acceptable performance is assumed (Jablin 2001). In an authoritarian culture, communication is often one-way or top–down based on specifics of job-related issues. Two-way symmetrical discussion is rare (Grunig 1992).

Because of the formal lines of hierarchy in authoritarian cultures, internal relations can be challenging. A good practice is to build lines of upward communication for employees, as well as to use the formal downward lines of communication that are in place. Communication can take place horizontally, across peer ranks, as well as in upward and downward fashion. Although two-way symmetrical communication is rare, generating stakeholder feedback and input into organizational processes may actually increase efficiency by gaining expertise from those on the front lines.

Authoritarian cultures should have stakeholder feedback loops built in to their communication programs, because when communication and input are not routinely sought, many problems can be suppressed or overlooked until they become crises. Anonymous channels for employees to communicate about the organization are essential. Because of the rigid hierarchy in place, employees may be afraid of retribution or simply "rocking the boat" and may be wary of doing so. Anonymous means of reporting problems or even asking questions generally encourage a higher degree of employee interaction with the organization, more commitment, and offer an early warning system for identification of potential issues or crises.

Although an authoritarian organizational culture may not be an ideal communication environment because it may lack collaboration and not offer opportunities for stakeholder input, it excels at organizing a large-scale undertaking and offering consistency of product or service. Efficiency and consistency can be valuable competitive advantages in the marketplace. As long as internal relations are attended effectively, an authoritarian organizational culture can offer a satisfactory work environment.

Participative Organizational Culture

A participative organizational culture, as the name implies, encourages participation across organizational levels by stakeholders. This type of organizational culture is able to encourage input, innovation, and collaboration. In a participative organizational culture, stakeholder input and participation in management and decision-making are commonly sought and encouraged (Goodpaster 2007). Rather than focusing on economies of scale and large-scale organization, a participative organizational culture focuses on innovation, input, collaboration, and team performance (Grunig 1992). Good ideas can come from any level within the organization, and thus seeks to be inclusive in seeking input and managerial decision-making. Whereas authoritarian cultures can be seen as top–down communication, participative cultures can be seen as bottom–up communication (Grunig 1992).

It is common to find a participative organizational culture in industries with highly skilled or highly educated workers, and in small- to medium-size enterprises. For example, a consultancy focused on finance and accounting may have a highly educated workforce in which hierarchies between reporting lines are minimized in a team-based structure that seeks input from all members. Some team members may be CPAs, while others may be tax attorneys, yet all have valuable input to contribute to the team.

Participative organizational cultures offer the main competitive advantages of innovation and flexibility. These types of organizational cultures generally foster stakeholder creative thinking and offer a fertile environment for problem-solving and building community (Eisenberg and Riley 2001). Information sharing and two-way symmetrical discussion can improve decision-making by offering inclusion for stakeholders at all levels of the organization. Participative organizational cultures have low turnover rates because they tend to instill commitment to organizational goals.

One should be mindful of the strengths and weaknesses of participative organizational cultures. Because of the high level and frequency of communication in a participative organizational culture, role ambiguity and confusion about responsibilities, or overlapping responsibilities, may be the norm. Some degree of inefficiency is introduced by this heavy reliance on communication and lack of role specificity. Further, participative organizational cultures function best when all are dedicated to the success of the enterprise and use their own initiative to enhance team performance and improve results. Stakeholders who lack motivation or personal initiative may become entirely disengaged from the participative process.

Participative organizational cultures are not as adept at organizing complex or routine enterprises as authoritarian cultures. However, these cultures offer speed and flexibility of problem-solving that make them responsive, agile, and highly competitive environments, such as the technology industry. In environments where innovation is a key component of success, you are likely to find varying degrees of participatory organizational cultures.

In a participative organizational culture, communication is both one-way and two-way. Symmetrical or dialog-based communication is used for more complex problem-solving and to generate stakeholder input. One-way communication is used as an organizational tool and may be more specific to job responsibilities. An interesting and valuable outcome of generating two-way symmetrical communication is that it enhances employee commitment to the organization. For example, asking stakeholders at all levels for ideas input and feedback about revising the organization's mission statement can lead to a greater "buy-in" or commitment to that mission from employees at all levels.

Participative cultures also need to have stakeholder feedback loops built in to their communication programs. Some employees, for instance, may feel that anonymous communication about the organization is safer for them, even in a participative environment. Generating input in such a manner is sometimes called creating *organic communication*, or organic leadership, that naturally grows from all varied levels of an organization. It is essentially two-way symmetrical communication seeking collaborative problem-solving and idea generation throughout the organization. Organizations with a participative culture generally tend to retain employees and have a lower turnover rate, requiring less reinvestment in recruiting, hiring, and training than authoritarian organizations. High employee retention also offers the competitive advantage of retaining more experienced employees who have more institutional knowledge of the organization itself (Goodpaster 2007). Internal relations within a participative organizational culture often tend to flow quickly, be less formalized, and be tailored to the workflow or needs of specific units within the organization.

Conclusions About Culture

In terms of internal relations, it is probably easier to motivate employees in a participative culture than those in an authoritarian one (Eisenberg and Riley 2001). However, the purposes of internal relations themselves may differ. Participative cultures tend to hold internal relations efforts that are focused on team building and innovation, whereas authoritarian cultures focus on individual contribution and efficiency. The scale of the enterprise, as well as its structure, can help to explain these different foci. Knowing which culture an organization predominately holds can help the internal relations program tailor communications that effectively meet stakeholder needs, while also helping an organization solve problems and avert crises.

Both participative and authoritarian organizational cultures have pros and cons. Envisioning them as two ends of an axis or two poles of a continuum allows the internal relations manager to understand the predominant culture and the complexities of differing priorities within specific organizations. Although most organizations fall somewhere toward the middle of the continuum, a predominant organizational culture can usually be identified and then can be used to address communication deficits, inspire performance, and motivate employees according to their needs in that culture.

Communication Climate Within Organizational Culture

A smaller, more specific concern is *communication climate*. Communication climate includes both organizational factors and external influences on communication outcomes (Falcione, Sussman, and Herden 1987). In other words, communication climate is organizational culture's impact on the communication process, combined with other individual variables such as psychological processes (Weick 1987).

Communication climate is smaller than organizational culture because it can exist between as few as two people. However, communication audits can clearly identify the level of open versus closed communication climate in organizational units.[2]

Communication climate can vary between groups within the organization, and is a subjective construct that is regularly created through interaction within the organization. Communication climate can generally be thought of as open or closed, warm and supportive, or cool and detached. Researchers argue that *leadership style* is the most important factor in communication climate, but also note that it depends on a communication network, structure of the organization, autonomy, psychological factors, diversity, and reward or incentive systems (Northouse 2007). In other words, how free and forthcoming is communication? Is communication easily flowing, free, and open, or restrained by protocols, constraints, and procedures?

Fostering a communication climate that is more open and encourages symmetrical dialog is typically the job of internal relations (Grunig 1992). Dispelling fear of speaking out, valuing employee input, and lessening the likelihood of reprisals or negative reinforcement all can instill a more open communication climate. An open communication climate should be fostered within organizations because it can help identify issues, problems, inefficiencies, or areas in need of revision. Doing so can help the organization ultimately become more effective, inclusive, and supportive of stakeholder input. An open communication climate normally supports employee satisfaction, retention, productivity, and can enhance employee engagement.

Management Style

The final dimension of an organization is *management style*. As introduced in Chapter 1 (p. 8), there are two basic dimensions of management style: Theory X and Theory Y management, as developed by McGregor (1960) who studied the human elements of enterprise. Knowing these two approaches to management style can help to refine one's own approach to management and help to conceptualize how management is conducted in the organization—as well as refining how it *should* be conducted. Many studies have been conducted on means to conceptualize management, as well as hybrid forms of these two approaches. Some modern approaches to management style are parts of proprietary programs that study dimensions of managerial behavior, team membership, personal attributes, and

---

2   A communication audit is a major organizational undertaking that surveys all stakeholders, to include senior management, conducts numerous stakeholder focus groups and in-depth interviews across the enterprise, and includes active journaling, whereby selected stakeholders keep daily journals of their communications.

work style. However, the parsimonious approach offered through the Theory X or Theory Y management style offers a robust, yet accessible explanation of how managers approach the process of organizing, leading, controlling, and evaluating.

Theory X

The Theory X management style holds that internal stakeholders—employees—must be firmly controlled by management. Managers who operate under a Theory X paradigm assume that workers need to be controlled because they do not want to work, or not enjoy working, or both and must be forced to do so.

The Theory X management style is similar to an authoritarian organizational culture and they often go hand-in-hand. Rigid systems of authority and reporting chains are in place to help control employee behavior. Innovation, dissent, offering opinion, and individual autonomy are often not encouraged by the Theory X approach to management. Systems of codified authority and centralized power are in place. This approach sometimes puts management against labor and sees monetary motivation or penalty systems as the primary means of controlling employee behavior.

Employees who work for a Theory X manager normally experience relatively low levels of personal autonomy and decreased job satisfaction than workers who are more engaged by their management. Theory X management often results in high turnover and increased costs associated with that turnover, such as recruitment and training expenditures. Even in large-scale, complex organizations that use a highly stratified vertical organizational structure along with authoritarian culture, the Theory X management style is not necessarily productive or helpful. Other means of controlling stakeholder behavior are in place in the organizational structure and through hierarchical authority, so the Theory X management style becomes rather redundant and even can hamper the effectiveness of the organization.

Theory Y

The Theory Y management style holds that employees will accomplish more and better work when empowered to do so by the management. Managers who adopt a Theory Y style offer greater levels of decision-making freedom to their employees, encourage them to offer feedback and opinions, and incentivize problem-solving behavior. Theory Y style managers believe that employees are gratified by doing good work and strive to do so for recognition and commitment to a team or cause, in addition to material gains or avoiding penalties. Similar to two-way symmetrical communication (Grunig 1992), the Theory Y management style values dialog and open lines of input.

The Theory Y approach holds that motivated employees are more productive and successful than those who are unmotivated or disengaged. Even employees who prefer to work autonomously can still be motivated to accomplish the collective goals of an organization or contribute to a team effort by encouraging their input. Communication is used as both a means to empower employees and to understand their needs in the Theory Y management. Theory Y managers engage in team building and motivating others to strive for team goals. By encouraging input, they allow employees to buy into the mission of the organization and create a personal sense of belonging and gain when goals are accomplished.

The drawback to the Theory Y management style is that not everyone knows how to do it. Inexperienced managers—easily threatened by a loss of control or do not understand how to engage their employees—tend to fail at creating an engaged workforce because they naturally resort to more authoritarian Theory X management. Building symmetrical systems of feedback for employees, asking for input and ideas, recognizing good work, shared problem-solving, and creating team-oriented goals based on shared vision can overcome these problems and create a Theory Y management style. Although a common myth holds that the best managers are charismatic leaders, best practices in internal relations and research in the field both show that *authentic* managers are the best. Authentic managers seeking to create genuine communication and honest effort to motivate their employees are the most effective. Theory Y style based on authenticity can also be argued to create more ethically responsible management (Seeger 1997), more committed stakeholders (Sims 1994), and more conscientious organizations overall (Goodpaster 2007).

Theory Y style managers tend to be comfortable sharing control, listening to the ideas of others, and confident in their abilities to handle day-to-day challenges of managing. They also tend to have a high degree of vocational competence, on the individual, group, and organizational level (Jablin and Sais 2001). Sharing control does not threaten managers who use a Theory Y style, and they often ask for the input of others before making decisions. Often times, successful Theory Y managers display a sense of resilience, flexibility, a sense of humor, and humility.

Conclusions

Although this book seeks balance in describing the organizational variables and dimensions based on differences such as industry, competition, socioeconomic environment, and situation, it does not seek balance in this case. Both research and practice show that the Theory Y management style is clearly superior to the Theory X management style. Theory Y management excels in creating positive

Communication	Structure	Culture	Management style
One-way predominates	Vertical/centralized	Authoritarian	Theory X
Two-way predominates	Horizontal/decentralized	Participative	Theory Y

Figure 12.1 Summary of communication by dimensions of an organization

organizational outcomes and stakeholder experiences, such as higher rates of job satisfaction (Azanza, Moriano, and Molero 2013). Internal relations should be used to foster a Theory Y style of management among individual managers and throughout organizations to engage stakeholders, create satisfaction, input, dialog, and retention, and foster organizational excellence.

Because of the complexity of studying organizational communication, the concepts represented here are simplifications of much more complex real-world constructs. However, they offer a readily accessible way to understand the organizational variables that can influence internal communication. Figure 12.1 summarizes the organizational dimensions discussed earlier, grouped along the lines of predominantly one-way communication (providing information) to predominantly two-way communication (persuasive communication or symmetrical dialog). Knowing the predominant communication style, structure, culture, and management style of an organization can help internal relations be optimized to fulfill the needs of employees and internal publics.

Organizational Dimensions

The flow of communication, as well as organizational structure, culture, and management style all influence the type of internal communications employed by an organization. Sometimes, two-way communication is undertaken to persuade, but at its best it is undertaken to create understanding through dialog (Grunig 1992). In that manner, symmetrical systems of internal communication contribute to overall organizational excellence through problem-solving and integrative or collaborative decision-making.

Focusing on two-way communication in which symmetrical systems of generating input and feedback are in place, the Theory Y management style can be used to create a positive communication climate within organizations relatively independently of structure and culture. In that manner, different sizes and types of industries are able to maximize the benefit of internal relations and create more engaged employees, resulting in retention and efficacy.

Summary

This chapter discussed the context of organizations in terms of their socioeconomic environment and the responsibilities of management under different forms of governance, from totalitarian control to free-market competition. Organizational structure was discussed to illustrate how communication would differ, from vertical and centralized organizational structures to horizontal and decentralized organizational structures. Stratified hierarchy and reporting chains were discussed as affecting the degree of formalization of communication along the lines of standard operating procedures. Decentralized organizational structure offers a number of advantages for communication flow and efficacy, as well is higher degrees of employee autonomy and participation. A brief review of organizational culture offered two polarized approaches: authoritarian culture, which is highly controlled and based on hierarchy, and participative culture that involves input across all levels of an organization for integrative decision-making.

Two differing styles of management were discussed. Theory X management is a highly controlled and authoritarian management style that is based on dictates from management, and reward and punishment for employees. The Theory Y management style is an approach using shared control in which managers seek input and use team-building strategies to motivate employees based on commitment to the success of the enterprise. Theory Y management has been found to be superior to the Theory X management style.

It should be noted that organizational structure is resistant to change, but positive communication climates can be instilled in vertical and horizontal structures. Both participative organizational culture and Theory Y management style were said to hold parallels with two-way symmetrical communication involving dialog that is used to create organizational excellence. An internal communication approach based on the Theory Y style management should drive internal relations. Feedback for internal stakeholders and channels of input using internal relations systems should be undertaken to help foster dialog, input, and shared or collaborative decision-making.

References

Azanza, G., J.A. Moriano, and F. Molero. 2013. "Authentic Leadership and Organizational Culture as Drivers of Employees Job Satisfaction." *Journal of Work and Organizational Psychology* 29, no. 2, pp. 45–50.

Eisenberg, E.M. and P. Riley. 2001. "Organizational Culture." In *The New Handbook of Organizational Communication: Advances in Theory, Research, and Method*, eds. F.M. Jablin, and L.L. Putnam, 291–322. Thousand Oaks: Sage.

Falcione, R.L., L. Sussman, and R.P. Herden. 1987. "Communication Climate in Organizations." In *Handbook of Organizational Communication: An Interdisciplinary Perspective*, eds. F.M. Jablin, L.L. Putnam, K.H. Roberts, L.M. Porter, 195–227. Newbury Park: Sage.

Goodpaster, K.E. 2007. *Conscience and Corporate Culture*. UK: Blackwell.

Grunig, J.E. 1992. "Symmetrical Systems of Internal Communication." In *Excellence in Public Relations and Communication Management*, ed. J.E. Grunig, 531–75. Hillsdale, NJ: Lawrence Erlbaum Associates.

Grunig, L.A. 1992. "Activism: How it Limits the Effectiveness of Organizations and How Excellent Public Relations Departments Respond." In *Excellence in Public Relations and Communication Management*, ed. J.E. Grunig, 503–30. Hillsdale, NJ: Lawrence Erlbaum Associates.

Jablin, F.M. 1987. "Formal Organizational Structure." In *Handbook of Organizational Communication: An Interdisciplinary Perspective*, eds. F.M. Jablin, L.L. Putnam, K.H. Roberts, L.M. Porter, 389–419. Newbury Park: Sage.

Jablin, F.M. 2001. "Organizational Intrigue, Assimilation, and Disengagement/Exit." In *The New Handbook of Organizational Communication: Advances in Theory, Research, and Methods*, eds. F.M. Jablin and L.L. Putnam, 732–818. Thousand Oaks: Sage.

Jablin, F.M., and P.M. Sais. 2001. "Communication Competence." In *The New Handbook of Organizational Communication: Advances in Theory, Research, and Methods*, eds. F.M. Jablin and L.L. Putnam, 819–64. Thousand Oaks: Sage.

Morgan, G. 2006. *Images of Organization*. Beverly Hills, CA: Sage.

McGregor, D. 1960. *The Human Side of Enterprise*. New York: McGraw-Hill.

Northouse, P.G. 2007. *Leadership: Theory and Practice*, 4th ed. Thousand Oaks, CA: Sage.

Seeger, M.W. 1997. *Ethics and Organizational Communication*. Cresskill, NJ: Hampton.

Sims, R.R. 1994. *Ethics and Organizational Decision Making: A Call for Renewal*. Westport, CT: Quorum.

Smircich, L., and M.B. Calas. 1987. "Organizational Culture: A Critical Assessment." In *Handbook of Organizational Communication: An Interdisciplinary Perspective*, eds. F.M. Jablin, L.L. Putnam, K.H. Roberts, and L.M. Porter, 228–63. Newbury Park: Sage.

Weick, K.E. 1987. "Theorizing About Organizational Communication." In *Handbook of Organizational Communication: An Interdisciplinary Perspective*, eds. F.M. Jablin and L.L. Putnam and K.H. Roberts and L.W. Porter, 97–122. Newbury Park, CA: Sage.

Organizational Culture
Real-World Lab

Name: _____

Date: _____

For this real-world lab, you will reflect on your experiences of university culture. This chapter defines organizational culture, in part, as an organization's "personality." Answer the following questions about your university's culture.

1. How would you define the culture of your university or college?

_____

_____

_____

_____

2. To help you define the culture, answer the following:

   • What are the values and shared beliefs of your university?

   _____

   _____

   _____

   _____

   • What are the important stories or myths told at your university?

   _____

   _____

   _____

   _____

- What are important rituals or traditions at your university?

_____

_____

_____

_____

3. Many students are familiar with the university culture before they even set foot on campus. This type of learning is called anticipatory socialization. Some students learn about the culture from older siblings or parents who attended the same university, from the media, or from campus tours as high school students. How did you learn about the culture of your university before you started as a first-year student? Think about stories you were told and expectations you had about what it would be like to be a student at your university.

_____

_____

_____

_____

4. After a few months on campus, you likely adjusted your understanding of the university culture. How did you learn about the culture when you first arrived on campus? What surprised you or changed your mind from what you thought you knew about the culture before you came?

_____

_____

_____

_____

5. How does your university's culture affect the way you communicate with your fellow classmates? What about with your professors?

_____

_____

_____

_____

CHAPTER 13

Family Relationships

Introduction to the Chapter

Families are unique in that they are often not chosen, the relationships are long lasting, and the members develop a long-standing shared history with one another. This chapter takes a close look at family as interpersonal relationships. This chapter lays out different types of families, different ways to define family, and how the family form has changed over time. As you read, take note of which definition of family makes the most sense to you and matches with your idea of who is included in your family and who is not.

Selection from "Defining Family Variations"

By Gene H. Starbuck and Karen Saucier Lundy

Prelude

Throughout our lives, many of our deepest sorrows, our most profound joys, and our most mundane moments are associated with family relationships we have had or hope to have someday. We experience these as intensely personal, unique, individual events. We seldom stop to think about the influence our society has on these family experiences.

Yet, the makeup of our family, who we include as family members, and what shape we expect our families to take are all subject to significant social influence. Out of the extensive menu imaginable for constructing families, our society supports only a few possibilities. As individuals, we select from this limited menu only a few possibilities for ourselves. This chapter is about the broader universe of cultural choices that might be possible.

Would all these options be feasible in American society today?

The study of marriage and the family is complicated by the fact that we each have a somewhat different image of what a family is. When asked about their families, one person might think of his mother, father, sister, and two brothers. Another might have her own husband and children in mind. Someone else might immediately think of a grandmother, mother, and brother. In some cultures, a man might think of his 4 wives, 26 children, and 65 grandchildren.

Despite different ethnic backgrounds, the four children in this photograph are siblings. Dad has the 1–1/2 year old on his shoulders, mom is in the foreground with the two 5–year olds behind her, and an aunt has the 2–1/2–year-old boy on her shoulders.

This book is primarily about families in the United States today, but it puts those families in historical and cultural context. To do this requires definitions that apply to all types of families, from the earliest groups of people who survived solely by hunting and gathering their food to today's complex postindustrial societies.

This chapter will explore various types of definitions of family, using symbolic human groups as illustrations. In the process, several terms that refer to diverse family forms will be introduced, and a variety of analytic tools for studying families will be presented.

> **Thinking Ahead** Write a definition of the family. Make sure that your definition includes all those groups of persons you think of as being a family, while ruling out all groups that you think do not constitute a family.

Basic Considerations

Social scientists have developed a set of symbols for describing different kinds of family relationships. These symbols (see Figure 13.1) can help define types of families and provide models of groups that might or might not be called families. To get the most out of this section of the text, students can refer to their own definition of family as they consider each symbolic group of people.

What Is a Family?

Figure 13.2 represents a man and woman we will call John and Jennifer. They are married to each other and have a son and daughter we will call Kyle and Kayla. By anyone's definition, this group is a family. In fact, it is an important enough type that it has a specific name: the **nuclear family.** As the word *nuclear* implies, this is the nucleus, or central unit of the family. It is not, however, the smallest kind of family unit.

In Figure 13.3 John and Jennifer are married to each other but have no children. This group, too, has a specific term because of its importance to the family. The husband-wife pair is called the *conjugal unit.* A family containing this unit would be called a *conjugal family.* The term derives from the Latin word that means "to join," as does the word *conjunction.* Thus, *conjugal* implies the bringing together of previously unrelated units.

Figure 13.4(a) represents a more complicated, three-generation, group. Jennifer is labeled Ego in the diagram, indicating that she is the reference point for defining relationships. She and her husband John are parents of Kyle and Kayla, and her brother and parents are also represented in the diagram. This entire unit is an example of an **extended family;** it extends, or goes beyond, a nuclear family. While extended families typically include three generations, they can include a variety of other arrangements (for example, see Figure 13.4b).

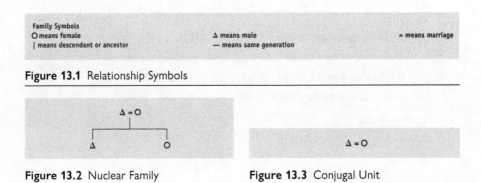

Family Symbols
O means female
| means descendant or ancestor
Δ means male
— means same generation
≈ means marriage

Figure 13.1 Relationship Symbols

Figure 13.2 Nuclear Family

Figure 13.3 Conjugal Unit

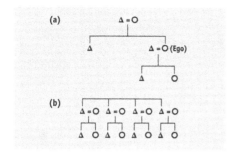

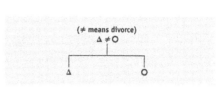

Figure 13.4 Relationship Symbols

Figure 13.5 Divorce

Jennifer in Figure 13.4(a) is actually part of several family units. In addition to the extended family, she and John constitute a conjugal unit. She is also a member of two nuclear family units: one involves her parents and brother, the other includes her husband and children.

To avoid confusion, the two nuclear units to which Ego belongs are sometimes given separate names. The family that includes her parents and siblings is the one in which she is "oriented" into the world. For that reason it is called her **family of orientation.** The other family is the one into which she married and had children. This is called her **family of procreation.**

Now, unfortunately, John and Jennifer get a divorce, as depicted in Figure 13.5. From Kyle and Kayla's perspective, John and Jennifer each maintain their family-related terms; they remain mother and father. The relationship terms in the former conjugal unit of John and Jennifer, however, now become ex-husband and ex-wife. This unit as a whole might no longer be called a family, although the children/father unit could be, as could the children/mother unit. In either case the children would be part of a single-parent family, even though they still have two parents.

Figure 13.6 depicts Jennifer's remarriage to Jackson. Particularly if the children live with their mother and her new husband, they would be members of a **stepfamily.** This unit is also called a *blended family* or a *reconstituted family.*

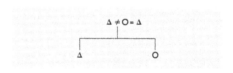

Figure 13.6 Remarriage

Figure 13.7 provides a somewhat different case. Although it cannot be determined from the diagram, we can assume for purposes of illustration that Jennifer and her children are

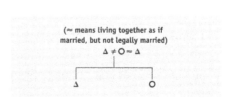

Figure 13.7 Mother's cohabiting boyfriend

living in the same household. In this case the mother formed an intimate cohabiting relationship with Jackson, but there was no legally recognized wedding ceremony. Jackson has not entered into a formal relationship with Jennifer and her children. Because no marriage is present, some people might not call this entire group a family.

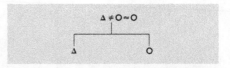

Figure 13.8 Mother's cohabiting girlfriend

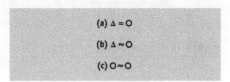

Figure 13.9 Couple families?

Even more controversy is likely about the group represented in Figure 13.8, where Judy moves into the household. It is identical to that in Figure 13.7 except that the new adult in the household is female rather than male. While intimacy and long-term commitment exist between Jennifer and Judy, the same-sex couple is less likely to be thought of as being part of a family than would Jennifer and Jackson. Some same-sex couples, of course, have children without either having been previously married. Such couples and their children provide yet another question about defining families.

To illustrate further, consider the childless couples in Figure 13.9. The relationship between John and Jennifer in Figure 13.9(a) has previously been defined as a conjugal unit, but this might not be true for the case of Jennifer and Jackson (13.9b). The only obvious difference would be that in the first instance the marriage has been officially registered with the state. Jennifer and Judy in case (c) might have the same feelings for each other as those in case (a) or (b), but, in most jurisdictions, they are not allowed to enter into legally defined marriages. Americans are divided about whether this could still be called a family.

Today's families are diverse, but such has always been the case. Single-parent families have always existed, although in the past such families more commonly resulted from parental death than from divorce or out-of-wedlock birth. There have always been couples without children, either because no child has yet been born or because those born have died or left the home. Also, many individuals spend at least part of their lives belonging to both a family of orientation and a family of procreation, and some spend part of their lives living alone.

One way to compare the way individuals live at any given time is to divide them into **households.** Although the majority of households in the United States contain families, the percentage of people living in families is declining. Table 13.1 reveals the percentage of households of various types. The percentage of households

Table 13.1 Household Composition in the United States, 1970–2010, in Percent of Total Households

Type	1970	1980	1990	2000†	2010†
Married Couples with Children*	40.3	30.9	26.3	23.9	20.1
Married Couples without Children*	30.3	29.9	29.8	29.8	31.5
Other Families with Children*	5.0	7.5	8.3	8.2	7.9
Other Families without Children*	5.6	5.4	6.5	7.5	8.3
Men Living Alone	5.6	8.6	9.7	10.8	11.7
Women Living Alone	11.5	14.0	14.9	14.6	15.1
Other Nonfamily Households	1.7	3.6	4.6	5.2	5.4

†Projections calculated from U.S. Bureau of Census, *Statistical Abstract of the United States: 1998,* Table 70.

*Own children, under age 18

Sources: U.S. Bureau of Census, *Statistical Abstract of the United States: 1994* and *Statistical Abstract of the United States: 1996,* Table 68.

containing married couples, both with children (nuclear families) and without children (conjugal units) continues to decrease. In 1970, 40.3% of households consisted of married couples with children. By 2010, that figure is expected to drop to half of the 1970 rate.

Criteria for Judgments

Agreeing on a definition of the family is difficult for several reasons. The purpose of constructing the definition is one factor. In everyday conversation we can usually figure out what definition is implied by the context of the conversation. For legal purposes, however, a more precise definition is required so that legal distinctions between family groups and other types of groups are more clear. These definitions affect inheritance rights, hospital visitation rights, the right to live together in certain parts of town, the right to be included in a "family health plan," and a number of other legal issues. Quite often, the values held by the persons doing the defining will affect the definition and the legal consequences for family and nonfamily groups.

Values

Values are more or less shared by members of a particular society. Especially in today's complicated and diverse societies, however, significant disagreement about values exists. The last few years have witnessed considerable discussion in the United States about what the values ought to be with respect to the family. The phrase "family values" itself has become controversial because it seems to be used primarily by those who support more traditional ideas about what families ought to be.

Religious traditions include values related to families. Support for the traditional image of the family is often based on an interpretation of the Judeo-Christian ethic, as defined by a literal reading of the Bible. This perspective places a high value on the type of nuclear family unit in which the father is the provider, protector, and spiritual leader, while the mother works in the home as a caregiver and nurturer to the children. Nontraditionalists, on the other hand, sometimes refer to values such as fairness, equality, and individualism. To these people, the nuclear family is only one kind of family that is, perhaps, no better than alternative types.

Norms

Norms are another important element in defining a family. While values are general ideas about what is good, right, or proper, norms are more specific guidelines about behavior and are enforced by rewards or punishments of varying degrees of seriousness. **Formal norms** are written down and enforced by some socially regulated mechanism. In the United States the formal norms are called laws and are enforced by police officers and courts. The most serious violations, such as murder, can sometimes be punishable by death. Less serious crimes can be punished by a prison sentence or fine. Formal family norms regulate violent behaviors among family members and the responsibility of parents to support their minor children.

Informal norms, on the other hand, are not enforced by agencies like the police, but uncounted numbers of these unwritten rules guide behavior nonetheless. Violation of informal norms might bring a dirty look, gossip, a rude comment, or other informal sanction. For example, we all know that the norm is to get in the back of the line at the grocery store. Cutting in line will not bring the police, but it is likely to bring stares and grumbling from others in the line. Informal norms affect the way family members interact in public. Parents might scream at their children at home, but they try to resist doing so in the grocery store. In most American groups, children are expected to call their parents "Mom" and "Dad," or perhaps "Mother" and "Father." They do not typically call their biological parents by the parent's first name.

One informal norm is that, when a young couple gets married, they should have children. This is referred to as **pronatalism.** No "fertility police" will lock up couples without children, but they face many informal pressures. Friends and relatives might ask them when they are going to have children, or even whose "fault" it is that they do not. Generally, persons who follow the norms are not asked to explain their behavior, but those who deviate from expectations are. In this case, couples who never have children are called upon to explain themselves. In today's society, people who have "too many" children—probably more than three—are sometimes called upon for an explanation.

As both the values and norms change, images of families change. In a diverse society like the United States, not everyone holds the same values and norms. Different ethnic groups, social classes, religious groups, occupational groups, and other categories of people have somewhat different values and norms.

Roles and Scripts

Individuals play parts in the family in ways similar to the parts played by actors on the stage. In the theater, a **role** is a part played by an actor. The **script** prescribes how various roles are expected to interact. Actors are told what to say, what costumes are appropriate, when to enter and exit the stage, and what emotions to portray.

Role playing is not limited to actors on the stage. In everyday life, too, persons play roles. During the course of any day, John and Jennifer are likely to play several roles. They might, at different times, behave in ways appropriate to being a student, a son or daughter, a worker, a friend, and a husband or wife.

Real-life roles are not as detailed as those found in a movie script. In real-life roles there is usually considerable room for individual variations. At most universities, the student role has only a loosely defined set of expectations regarding the proper costume to wear, but acceptable options have limits. Imagine the reaction to a student who wears a bikini or tuxedo to class. Sanctions, in the form of gestures, expressions, and comments, are brought to bear on persons who depart too widely from the expectations of their group.

In a family group, the name that two related individuals call each other provides a tremendous amount of information about how they should treat each other. When Jennifer meets an old friend and wants to introduce the man to whom she is married, she can use the family term *husband* as a way of defining the kind of relationship the two of them have: "Margaret, this is my husband, John." Several other terms define family or kinship relationships, including *niece, nephew, cousin, father, mother, brother, sister, grandfather, grandmother, aunt,* and *uncle.*

Some of the groups of persons depicted in the diagrams above have family terms available to describe the role relationship; others do not. Consider again the possibilities that are listed in Figure 13.9. John and Jennifer ($\Delta = O$) have the recognizable family terms of husband and wife. Jackson and Jennifer ($\Delta \approx O$)

might have the emotional and sexual ties of husband and wife, but they lack a widely accepted name for the social relationship and role. How does the woman in this relationship introduce the man? She might simply say "Margaret, this is my *friend,*" but that term does not quite fully capture the nature of the relationship. Nor, quite, do *significant other, boyfriend,* or *lover.* The term *partner* is increasingly popular; it can apply to same-sex or opposite-sex couples, married or cohabiting. *Partner* is a bit ambiguous, however, since it can also be applied to a business relationship. The U.S. Census Bureau suggested the term *POSSLQ* (pronounced "posselque"), an acronym for "person of the opposite sex sharing living quarters." One implication is that, although cohabitation ("Mother, this is my cohabitant") is becoming increasingly acceptable, the cohabiting union might not be considered a family because the kinship terms have not yet been established. This is even truer for the other possibilities in Figure 13.9: Jennifer and Judy ($\Delta \approx \Delta$) or John and Jackson ($O \approx O$).

If a child calls an adult "mother" or "father," there is a fairly clear understanding of the responsibilities and prohibitions the adult has with regard to the child. Some of those role expectations have become formal norms, written into the law. The parent has the legal responsibility to feed, clothe, and provide medical care; failure to do so can result in punishments for child neglect. These formal expectations are supplemented with such informal ones as providing affection and positive regard. Informal norms change constantly; a new one seems to be developing that mothers and fathers should not smoke in their homes where children might be exposed to second-hand smoke.

A stepparent, too, has role responsibilities toward the stepchild, but they are not as clearly defined as that for a parent (more on this in chapter 15). The matter is less clear in the POSSLQ relationship between

Father Knows Best was typical of television shows of the 1950s, with an intact nuclear family and a stay-at-home mom.

Jennifer and Jackson as represented in Figure 13.7. The role relationship is ambiguous between Jennifer and Jackson, but it is even less clear between Jackson and the children. He might behave as if he is a father, but Kyle and Kayla already have someone in that role. The relationship is more like that of stepfather to stepchild, but since no legal marriage exists with Jennifer, it is not formally a step relationship.

By the 1990s, television shows such as *Fresh Prince of Bel-Air* depicted a wide variety of family and living arrangements.

Types of Definitions

We know that a family is a group of individuals who interact in a close, personal way, but emphasis on different elements of these groups can result in different types of definitions. Some definitions focus on what the family does (a **functional definition**) and others on what components a family must have (a **structural definition**). Both types can refer to the interaction among family members.

Functional Definitions

A **microfunctional** definition focuses on how the family serves its individual members. Steinmetz's example (see Highlight 13.1.a) refers to mutual sharing of various kinds. By this definition, the John and Jackson couple depicted in Figure 13.9(d) could be a family. All of the illustrations, in fact, could be families because of the functions each group serves for the individuals involved.

Microfunctional definitions can include a wide variety of forms under the "family" umbrella. For example, sorority "sisters" live together and share some values, goals, commitment, and resources. They even have a house "mother." Similarly, an urban juvenile gang shares values and commitment while providing a sense of belonging to interacting members. These two groups, however, are not what most people have in mind when they use the term *family*.

A **macrofunctional** definition (see Highlight 13.1.b) deals with the functions the family serves for society as a whole. Rather than focus on how the family serves individuals, a macrofunctional definition treats the family as a social **institution** that contributes to society by performing such functions as reproduction, socialization of children, and economic cooperation. The homosexual couples represented in Figure 13.9 might not be considered families using a macrofunctional definition because such couples do not, by themselves, serve the social function of reproduction. They do, however, cooperate economically and sometimes participate in socialization of the young.

Structural Definitions

While functional definitions have their uses, they are not very precise in determining whether a particular group is a family. The Census Bureau, faced with the responsibility of counting the actual number of families in the United States, needs a definition that clearly distinguishes what a family is. The Census Bureau definition (see Highlight 13.1) refers to the parts of a family and how they are held together, rather than what the parts do. It is much easier to decide whether a particular group is a family with this definition than with others. By this definition neither juvenile gangs nor college fraternities would qualify as families.

By the Census Bureau definition, a family must share a common residence; that is, they must form a household. Extended families would not count as a family unless they all lived in the same domicile. The Census Bureau definition also recognizes **kin groups.** Kin can be uncles, aunts, grandparents, and others, but they do not need to live in the same housing unit. This definition would not include the couples represented either by Figure 13.9.b (POSSLQs) or by Figure 13.9.c or d (homosexual couples) because they are not related by blood, marriage, or adoption.

Sometimes persons with no "real" kinship ties end up with kin-like roles. The children might call an elderly neighbor who takes care of young children "Grandma Martha," even though she has no blood relationship to them. These are referred to as fictional or **fictive kin.** In some cases the fact that the kinship is fictional is all but forgotten; in other cases, such as that of godparents, the relationship has its own set of rules and is kept separate from the "real" kin relationships (Vandekerckhove, 1981; Kutsche, 1983). Fictive kin might be counted as family members by a functional definition but not by a structural one.

Because they require kinship relationships, structural definitions are more limiting than functional ones. It is quite possible that the male in Figure 13.6 (a mother's POSSLQ) is the "functional equivalent" of a husband and father, making that unit a family by a functional definition but not by a structural one. The mother/child unit would be a family by either definition. A divorced woman, her two children, and her cohabiting boyfriend might functionally be a family. To the Census Bureau, however, such a household would be categorized as a family with an unrelated individual. The same would be true if it involved the mother and her live-in girlfriend.

Highlight 13.1 *Definitions of Family*

(a) Microfunctional definition:

A unit of intimate, transacting, and interdependent persons who share some values, goals, resources, and responsibility for decisions, as well as a commitment to one another over time (Steinmetz et al., 1990:12).

(b) Macrofunctional definition:

The intimate group in which reproduction, socialization of the young, economic cooperation, and social status placement occurs.

Definition stressing dysfunctions of the family for some participants:

"The major institution for perpetuating patriarchy and women's oppression" (Tuttle, 1986:100).

(c) A structural definition of family:

Two or more individuals who share a housing unit and are related by blood, marriage, or adoption (U.S. Census Bureau, 1983).

(d) Definitions with a combination of elements:

"A group of persons united by ties of marriage, blood, or adoption; constituting a single household; interacting and communicating with each other in their respective social roles (husband and wife, mother and father, sons and daughter, brother and sister); and creating and maintaining a common culture" (Burgess & Locke, 1953).

"A set of persons related to each other by blood, marriage, or adoptions and whose basic societal function is replacement" (Winch, 1971).

"The basic social institution. One or more men living with one or more women in a socially-sanctioned and more or less enduring sex relationship, with socially recognized rights and obligations, together with their offspring" (Fairchild, 1970).

"A social group in society typically consisting of a man and woman and their offspring. 1. Two or more people who share goals and values, have long-term commitments to one another, and reside usually in the same dwelling place. 2. All the members of a household under one roof. 3. A group of persons sharing common ancestry" (American Heritage Dictionary).

"Particular societal arrangement whereby persons related by ancestry, marriage, or adoption live together, form an economic unit, and raise children" (Zinn & Eitzen, 1993:460).

Defining Marriage

Some structural approaches identify **marriage** as an essential element of the family; others do not. We have been reserving the symbol = only for those relationships that fit the legal definition of marriage and have used ≈ for relationships that are marriage-like but are not legal marriages. This would follow the legalistic definition of marriage, which requires formal recognition of the relationship.

Other definitions are more commonly used in anthropology and sociology. Societies without a written language have no formal records, but they do have forms of relationships that could be considered marriage. In yet other societies, religious rather than political authorities formally record marriages.

The beginning of a marriage is nearly always accompanied by a **rite of passage** called a wedding. When an individual's **status** changes from "single person" to "married person," role expectations change. Once John and Jennifer are married, they see themselves, and are seen by others, to have new rights, privileges, immunities, responsibilities, and duties.

As is true with the term *family,* definitions of marriage are affected by formal and informal norms. Virtually all societies have norms about who can marry whom. An **incest taboo** is universal, although societies differ about which relatives are included. Some societies allow exceptions in certain cases; brother-sister marriage among the rulers in ancient Egypt and Hawaii are examples (Vivelo, 1978).

Other normative expectations are less seriously sanctioned, so they are more openly violated. These include **pronuptialism,** the informal norm that people should get married. Although this norm is not as strong as it was in the past, the vast majority of young adults still follow expectations.

Based on values of chastity, a traditional norm was that young persons should not have sexual intercourse until they were married. Unmarried couples who lived together were considered to be "living in sin," and by this formal norm they could not form the legal basis for a marriage. Laws forbidding premarital sex and adultery began to change in the 1960s but remain on the books in some states. As a practical matter, these laws were not often enforced, but they were a symbolic barrier to nonmarital sexual activity. The sexual component of marriage is also recognized in the provision that a marriage is not technically legal until it is consummated by the first complete act of sexual intercourse.

While societies vary in their norms about nonmarital sex, sexual access is universally a privilege of marriage. The sexual distinction between married and unmarried persons in the last few decades has blurred, but other role expectations remain. Economic cooperation and the merging of assets acquired during the marriage still form part of the legal expectations of marriage.

One difference between the legally wed couple and the functionally wed one is that the legally wed are entitled to certain privileges when the relationship ends either by death or by divorce. The exact laws vary from one jurisdiction to another, but all recognize the married couple as a distinct legal unit. One consequence of this is that the state must be asked for permission, in the form of a divorce petition, to end the legal relationship. Couples who are only functionally wed do not have to do this. Legal spouses also have certain assumed rights to inheritance that cohabitants do not.

Married persons are entitled to certain other legal privileges, such as coverage under family medical plans and other job benefits. Here too, however, the line between those who are legally married and those who are not has blurred. In some cases, legal protection has been granted to those who are functionally but not legally married. Homosexual couples might go through a wedding in their church and are sometimes granted some privileges of legally married couples. In 1989, San Francisco enacted a "domestic partners" law; many other jurisdictions have followed suit. Such laws extended marriage-like rights, dealing with such things as health benefits and bereavement leave, to both homosexual and heterosexual cohabitants.

In 2000, Vermont legalized "civil unions" for same-sex couples. Although a civil union is not exactly the same as marriage, registered couples are entitled to the same rights as married couples in such matters as health benefits and inheritance rights. These unions, unlike marriages, are valid only in Vermont, and other states to which the couple might move are not required to extend the same benefits. In spite of this, as many as two-thirds of couples who took advantage of the new law in the first few weeks were from out of state. Some participants anticipate court battles to extend the benefit of their civil union to their home states (Goldberg, 2000). In 2004, Massachusetts became the first state to legally recognize same-sex marriages, and the issue has been considered in several other states.

Thirteen states (Alabama, Colorado, Georgia, Idaho, Iowa, Kansas, Montana, Ohio, Oklahoma, Pennsylvania, Rhode Island, South Carolina, and Texas) and the District of Columbia recognize what is called a **common-law marriage** (Skoloff, Skoloff, & Wolfe, 1997). Such a relationship has all the rights and responsibilities of a legal marriage, but it lacks the legal registration of a wedding ceremony. In some states the requirement includes a certain length of time that the couple must be together; in others it is a matter of "intent" to live as husband and wife. The intent might be demonstrated in several ways, including the filing of a joint income tax return. The state is still involved, however, because a judge's approval is required before legal status is fully granted, and a legal divorce is required if the common-law marriage breaks up.

Key Terms

Nuclear family: A two-generation group that includes parents and their children.

Conjugal unit: The husband-wife pair.

Extended family: A family composed of the nuclear family plus additional relatives, usually a third generation.

Family of orientation: The family unit that includes one's parents and siblings.

Family of procreation: The family unit that includes one's spouse and, at least potentially, one's children.

Stepfamily: Family unit consisting of a married man and woman, plus children from a previous relationship. A *simple stepfamily* includes children of one parent; a *complex stepfamily* includes children from both adults. Also called a *blended family* or a *reconstituted family*.

Household: A living unit; a group of persons sharing living quarters.

Values: Shared ideas about what is good, right, or proper.

Norm: Widespread expectations governing behavior. *Prescriptive norms* determine what *should* be done; *proscriptive norms* determine what *should not* be done.

Formal norms: Behavioral expectations that are written and enforced by specialized social mechanisms; laws.

Informal norms: Behavioral expectations that lack codified, enforceable sanctions.

Pronatalism: A belief system that encourages childbearing.

Role: Expectations associated with a particular position in the social system.

Script: Expectations governing the interaction of two or more roles.

Functional definition: Definition based on how the family serves the participating individuals (*microfunctional*) or how it serves society (*macrofunctional*).

Structural definition: Definition describing the components and makeup of a family.

Microfunctional definition: Focusing on consequences for individuals.

Macrofunctional: Focusing on consequences for institutions or societies.

Institution: 1. A system of norms, values, statuses, and roles that develop around a basic social goal. 2. A regular and traditional way of meeting a society's needs.

Kin group: Network of persons related by blood, marriage, or adoption.

Fictive kin: Persons treated as if they are related.

Marriage: (1) (legalistic definition) The legal union of a man and woman as husband and wife. (2) A socially sanctioned sexual and economic union between two (or more) members of opposite sexes (occasionally between members of the same sex) (from Howard,

1989:454). (3) A socially approved sexual union of some permanence between two or more individuals (Robertson, 1981:630).

Rite of passage: A public ceremony in recognition of a change in status.

Status: A position in the social system.

Incest taboo: A rule forbidding marriage or sexual activity among closely related persons.

Pronuptialism: A belief system that encourages marriage

Common-law marriage: A union legally recognized as a marriage in spite of not having been solemnized by the state.

References

Burgess, Ernest W., & Harvey J. Lock. [1945] 1953. *The Family: From Institution to Companionship.* New York: American Book.

Fairchild, Henry Pratt. 1970. *Dictionary of Sociology and Related Sciences.* Totowa, NJ: Helix Books.

Goldberg, Carey. 2000. "Same-sex Unions Draw Couples to Vt. from Afar." *The Denver Post* July 23:8A.

Howard, Michael C. 1989. *Contemporary Cultural Anthropology,* 3rd. ed. Glenview, Illinois: Scott, Foresman.

Kutsche, Paul. 1983. "Household and Family in Hispanic Northern New Mexico." *Journal of Comparative Family Studies* 14:151–65.

Skoloff, Gary N., Skoloff, & Wolfe. 1997. "Marriage Laws." P. 728 in Robert Famighetti, ed., *The World Almanac and Book of Facts, 1997.* Mahwah, NJ: World Almanac Books.

Tuttle, Lisa. 1986. *Encyclopedia of Feminism.* New York: Facts on File Publications.

Vandekerckhove, Lieven A. 1981. "The Role of Godparents: On the Integration of a Non-Familial Role in the Structure of the Kinship System." *Journal of Comparative Family Studies* 12:56–59.

Vivelo, Frank R. 1978. *Cultural Anthropology Handbook.* New York: McGraw-Hill.

Winch, Robert F. 1971. *The Modern Family.* New York: Holt.

Zinn, Maxine Baca, & D. Stanley Eitzen. 1993. *Diversity in Families,* 3rd ed. New York: HarperCollins.

Family Communication and Advice
Real-World Lab

Name: _____

Date: _____

For this real-world lab, you will apply what you have learned about family relationships to a certain type of communication: advice. "Good" advice is advice that is "perceived positively by its recipients, facilitates the recipient's ability to cope with the problem, and is likely to be implemented."[1] Think of a relationship problem you have had recently, or a decision you need to make. Briefly describe the problem.

1. Go ask *three* people for advice on the problem/decision.

   These should be different "types" of people: family members, friends, significant others, even strangers! Make sure to ask at **least one family member** so you can use what you learned about family in this chapter to analyze the advice.

   Don't tell them this is part of a project (at least not at first)—just see what kind of advice they give you.

2. Write out the advice you received (feel free to leave out names/details if it is personal) and the sources of the advice (e.g., mom, best friend).

   Advice #1   Source:

   _____

   _____

   _____

   _____

   _____

   _____

1   Erina L. MacGeorge, Bo Feng, Elizabeth R. Thompson. "'Good' and 'Bad' Advice: How to Advise More Effectively," in *Studies in Applied Interpersonal Communication*, ed. Michael T. Motley (Thousand Oaks, CA: Sage, 2008), 146.

Advice #2   Source:

_____

_____

_____

_____

Advice #3   Source:

_____

_____

_____

_____

3. Analyze the advice you received using the following prompts:

    • How did the source of the advice make a difference in the (a) quality and
      (b) style of the advice received? For example, how was the advice from
      family different from the advice from other sources?

      _____

      _____

      _____

      _____

    • What is unique about family relationships that might make their advice
      different from that of other sources?

      _____

      _____

      _____

      _____

    • Was the advice you received "good advice" according to the definition?
      Why?

      _____

      _____

      _____

      _____

- Will you take any of the advice you received? Why or why not? If yes, which piece?

_____

_____

_____

_____

- Rewrite any "weak" pieces of advice you received to be "better" based on what you have learned over the course of the semester so far.

_____

_____

_____

_____

CHAPTER 14

Cultural Differences in Interpersonal Communication

Introduction to the Chapter

Culture shapes people to communicate differently, and communication in turn has the power to shape and transform culture. There are many challenges and benefits of communicating with people from other cultures. This chapter provides a clear description of culture and explores how cultures are created, learned, and sustained by people and communication. Dimensions of culture are discussed, along with the concepts of high- and low-context cultures. Social identity theory, social cognitive theory, and cultivation theory are all presented. The chapter wraps up by asking the question, "Does culture change?"

What Is Culture? How Does Culture Affect Communication?

By Alexis Tan

....

I ntercultural communication is communication in general, with one important distinction: the participants bring with them differing worldviews, values, behavioral norms, and communication styles to the interaction. Let's take a look at culture in more detail and see how culture can affect communication.

In doing the research for this chapter, I came across two quotes originally cited in the book *Management Across Cultures* by Steers, Nardon, and Sanchez-Runde (2013) that tell us something about culture:

> "We do not see things as they are; we see things as we are."
>
> —Talmud Bavli, Ancient Book of Wisdom, Babylonia

> "Water is the last thing a fish notices."
>
> —Lao Tzu

What do these quotes tell us about culture? To me, Bavli says that how we see the world (our realities) is influenced by our cultures; Lao Tzu reminds us that we may not be aware of this influence at all.

Defining Culture

If culture is such a powerful force on how we see and make sense of our environment and other people, then how can we not be aware of its influence? Before we can answer this question, let's define what we mean by culture. This won't be an easy task, considering that there are at least 150 definitions, by one estimate (Kroeber & Kluckhohn, 1952), in anthropology, sociology, social psychology, and communication. Here are some examples:

Culture ... is that complex whole which includes knowledge, belief, art, law, morals, custom, and any other capabilities and habits acquired by man as a member of society. (Taylor, 1871, p. 1)

Culture may be defined as the totality of the mental and physical reactions and activities that characterize the behavior of individuals composing a social group collectively and individually in relations to their natural environment, to other groups, to members of the group itself and of each individual to himself. It also includes the products of these activities and their role in the life of the groups. The mere enumerations of these various aspects of life, however, does not constitute culture. It is more, for its elements are not independent, they have a structure. (Boas, 1911, p. 149)

Culture means the whole complex of traditional behavior which has been developed by the human race and is successively learned by each generation. A culture is less precise. It can mean the forms of traditional behavior which are characteristics of a given society, or of a group of societies, or of a certain race, or of a certain area, or of a certain period of time. (Mead, 1937, p. 17)

Culture has been distinguished from the other elements of action by the fact that it is intrinsically transmissible from one action system to another by learning and diffusion. (Parsons & Shills, 1976, p. 172)

Man is a biological being as well as a social individual. Among the responses which he gives to external stimuli, some of the full product of his nature, and others to his condition (culture). (Levi-Strauss, 1949, p. 4)

Culture ... is ways of thinking, the ways of acting, and the material objects that together shape a people's way of life. Culture can be nonmaterial or material. (Macionnis & Gerber (2011, p. 11)

The term culture refers to what is learned ... the things one needs to know in order to meet the standards of others. (Goodenough, 1971, p. 19)

The culture concept denotes an historically transmitted pattern of meanings embodied in symbols, a system of inherited conceptions expressed in symbolic forms by means of which men communicate, perpetuate, and develop their knowledge about and toward life ... (Geertz, 1966, p. 89)

The collective programming of the mind that distinguishes the members of one human group from another. (Hofstede, Hofstede, & Minkov, 2010, p. 3)

An integrated system of learned behavior patterns which are characteristic of the members of a society and which are not the result of biological inheritance. (Hoebel, 1976, p. 2)

The collection of beliefs, values, behaviors, customs, and attitudes that distinguish the people of one society from another. (Kluckhohn, 1949, p. 1)

As you can see, there is no lack of definitions for culture. From these definitions, let's identify the characteristics that stand out and about which there is agreement.

1. Culture is a characteristic of people who identify with a group. This identification may be based on shared geographical boundaries (such as a country); a shared demographic category, such as race or ethnicity, religion, or socio-economic level; or simply shared interests and goals, such as a corporation or student club (organizational culture).

2. Since culture is dependent on group membership and identification, the individual must be aware of the group's existence and acknowledge his or her membership in the group.

3. Culture includes agreement within the group about how to make sense of or assign meanings to its environment, which behaviors in response to the environment are acceptable, what is important in life, and how to feel about other people and objects in the environment. These components are the *dimensions* of culture: beliefs and worldviews (to make sense), action norms (acceptable behaviors), values (what is important in life), and attitudes (how

to feel). Culture is manifested in these nonmaterial human tendencies, but also represented in material artifacts such as art, language, architecture, laws, rituals, literature, and so on. Our concern in this book is nonmaterial culture.

4. Culture therefore guides an individual's response to and interpretation of the environment. Its influence is distinct from our natural human tendencies, which are hardwired into our genes, such as, according to some scholars, the tendency to be prejudiced or to favor in-groups over out-groups.

5. Culture is a pattern of shared dimensions, each related to and reinforcing the other. For example, beliefs are related to attitudes, attitudes to behavior.

6. Culture is shared by group members using signals, verbal and nonverbal.

7. Culture is transmitted over time from one generation to the next through a process of socialization (discussed later in this chapter).

8. Culture can change, as a response to changes in the environment, such as economic growth (Inglehart, 1997), encroachment by other cultures (Inglehart, 1997), proliferation of foreign media (Tunstall, 1977; Scotton & Hatchten, 2008), and migration (Inglehart, 1997).

Incorporating these commonalities, here is my simplified definition that applies to intercultural communication:

> Culture is a pattern of shared beliefs, values, attitudes, behavioral norms, and worldviews shared by members of a group and transmitted over time from one generation to the next. Although generally resistant to change, culture is malleable, as a response to environmental changes. The major form of transmission is communication.

My definition of culture, as well as the other definitions I cited, share a common problem: How do we know that a worldview is shared? One hundred percent agreement? (highly unlikely). By a majority? What about those who don't agree, the outliers?

Scholars have taken different approaches to solving the problem. Some, like Hofstede (1984) and Hofstede et. al. (2010) use statistics (i.e., means, standard deviations, factor analysis, and correlations, which I discuss later in this chapter) to analyze results of surveys, looking for commonalities within a group, in his case, countries, and then comparing groups. Kluckhohn (1951) also used statistics to compare indigenous groups in the United States on several dimensions of culture. Others have used critical analysis of the artifacts of culture to identify themes representing cultural dimensions, such as in law, literature, the mass media, and observations of everyday behaviors and activities. Still others (Wood & Smith, 2004; Schwartz et al., 2001) have analyzed culture both at the individual and group levels, looking for individual differences in how cultural dimensions are internalized and demonstrated. In this latter approach, outliers, members of a group who deviate from cultural norms, are given special attention by analyzing possible reasons for their deviations. In intercultural communications and other interactions, there is a risk in automatically ascribing to a person a group culture simply because of membership, which is a form of stereotyping. (Perhaps we are interacting with an outlier.) While these generalizations are a useful guide, and in fact they are often accurate in describing a majority, the prudent approach is to use culture as a guide while being cognizant of possible individual differences or deviations. Strategies for accomplishing this are discussed in Chapter 7, "Know Others."

Dimensions of Culture

Culture is defined by its dimensions—worldviews, beliefs, values, attitudes, and behavioral norms. In this section, I discuss those dimensions that have the most impact on intercultural communication.

Hofstede's National Cultural Dimensions

According to Hofstede (1984) and Hofstede et al. (2010), culture has six dimensions that can differentiate between countries. Here are three of them:

- *Power distance* is the "extent to which the less powerful person accepts inequality in power and considers it as normal" (Hofstede, 2001, p. 139). In a high power distance culture, society is highly stratified into institutionalized hierarchies based on wealth and political authority. People with high power consider people with low power to be different from them; they consider the unequal distribution of power and authority to be "a fact of life," and believe that everybody has a rightful place in society determined by how much power he or she has. In high power distance societies, there is greater centralization of political power, less participation by people with low power, positions of authority are held by people with power, and more importance is placed on status and rank.

- In low power distance cultures, people believe that inequality is undesirable and should be minimized, all people should have access to power, and people in power should be held accountable to the publics they serve. In low power distance cultures, laws, norms, and everyday behaviors minimize power distance.

- According to Hofstede (2001), Malaysia, Guatemala, Panama, and the Philippines are high power distance cultures, whereas Austria, Israel, Denmark, and New Zealand are low power distance cultures. The United States ranks 38 out of 53 countries (53 being the country with the lowest power distance). These rankings were based on a survey of IBM employees in over 50 countries in the late 1960s and early 1970s by Hofstede and his colleagues (Hofstede, 2001).

- *Individualism/collectivism* is a cultural dimension that measures the degree to which members of a culture use the group or the individual as a basis for personal identities (Schwartz, 1994). In collectivist cultures, the group is the most important identity source, meaning that people's identities are anchored on group memberships. Therefore, there is greater emphasis on needs and goals of the in-group; on collaboration, shared interests, and harmony; and on preserving the "face," or positive image, of the group. In contrast, in individualist cultures, personal goals take precedence over group goals, independence of the individual rather than reliance on the group is stressed, and an individual's personal identity and self-image are more important than group identity in guiding behaviors and interpersonal relations. Hofstede et al. (2010) identified the United States as the most individualist culture among more than 50 countries in the IBM surveys, followed by Australia, Great Britain, Canada, the Netherlands, and New Zealand. The most collectivist cultures were Guatemala, Ecuador, Panama, and Venezuela.

- *Uncertainty avoidance* refers to the degree that people in a culture are uncomfortable (or comfortable) with situations that are unstructured, unpredictable, unknown, unfamiliar, or unclear, and the extent to which they are willing to cope with and tolerate these situations. In high uncertainty avoidance cultures, members try to avoid uncertainty and ambiguity because these situations are uncomfortable. To prevent high uncertainty situations from occurring, and to cope with them when they do occur, high anxiety avoidance cultures establish formal rules, seek consensus, rely on authority figures, and are less tolerant of deviant ideas and behaviors. Members of low uncertainty avoidance cultures are more comfortable with unfamiliar, new, and unstructured situations. They are more tolerant of unusual and nonconforming behavior, have fewer rules governing social behavior, dislike hierarchies and rigid social structures, and are more willing to take risks. Hofstede et al. (2010) identified Greece, Portugal, Guatemala, and Uruguay as high uncertainty avoidance countries (do not like uncertainty), and Singapore, Jamaica, Denmark, and Sweden as low uncertainty avoidance countries (do not feel uncomfortable with uncertainty). The United States ranked 43 out of 53 countries (the higher the rank, the lower anxiety avoidance).

These cultural dimensions were identified by Hofstede and his colleagues in a series of studies beginning in 1967, the most recent in 2010. I discuss them in more detail, the country rankings, and how the dimensions affect intercultural communication in Chapter 7 ("Know Others.").

Hall's High- and Low-Context Cultures

According to Hall (1981), intercultural communication can be analyzed by considering how much emphasis is placed on the context of information and how much emphasis is placed on the explicit message. The context of communication is the physical environment in which communication takes place, including its setting (e.g., formal board room or informal wine bar); the status and social positions of the participants; and nonverbal signs, such as gestures and facial expressions. In high-context cultures, most of the meanings exchanged among participants depend more on context and less on the explicit verbal message. High-context participants often come from homogeneous cultures in which tradition and past experience have taught them what behaviors are expected in social relationships and how to respond to messages from others. Much of the exchange of explicit verbal messages is ritualistic and formal. The real meaning of the interaction is in its context—roles, nonverbal signs, and other situational cues. Communication is often indirect to promote harmony and to avoid public expressions of discord.

In contrast, members of low-context cultures place more emphasis on the explicit verbal message. "Tell me what you think, and put it in writing" is a common expectation. Low-context people have difficulty reading meanings from the context of communication. They expect that meanings will be expressed in explicit verbal messages. Communication is direct, and people are expected to express themselves.

Some high-context cultures, according to Hall (1981) are Japanese, Chinese, and Korean. Examples of low-context cultures are German, Scandinavian, and North American.

In Chapter 7, "Know Others," I discuss how high- and low-context orientations affect intercultural communication.

Kluckhohn and Strodtbeck's Cultural Dimensions

According to Kluckohn and Strodtbeck (1961), culture is best understood by analyzing how people respond to human problems. The solutions to these problems, which could be caused by environmental stresses like drought and earthquakes or by human conflicts like war, depend on values held by members of a group or community. They define a value as "a conception, explicit or implicit, ... of the desirable which influences the selection from available modes, means and ends of action," a definition they borrowed from Kluckhohn (1951, p. 395). Therefore, values are deeply held beliefs about what is important in life (goals), what are the best means to achieving these goals, and what are the important results (ends). In a group, community, or society (an aggregate of many communities), members will share a few values that guide the selection of solutions to problems and which are manifestations of the group's, community's, or society's culture. Kluckhohn and Strodtbeck (1961) identified five problems confronted by human societies with different possible strategies for finding solutions. The preferred strategies are based on cultural values. Here are the societal problems, posed as questions, and possible strategies for solving them (Hills, 2002):

- *Time*: Should we focus on the past, present, or future?

- *Humans and the natural environment*: Should we master the environment? Live in harmony with it? Submit to it?

- *Relations with other people*: Should we relate to others hierarchically (*lineal*)? As equals (*collateral*)? According to individual merit?

- *Motivation for human behavior*: Is the prime motivation to express one's self, to grow, or to achieve?

- *Human nature*: Are humans naturally good, bad, or a mixture?

The possible answers to these questions indicate a society's values, which, in turn, reflect that society's culture. The preferred solutions help us understand how people in the culture respond to common problems. Here is a summary adapted from Hills (2002, p. 5):

- Time
  - Past: Focus on the time before now—or the past—and on preserving and maintaining traditional teachings and beliefs.
  - Present: Focus on what is now—the present—and on accommodating changes in beliefs and traditions.
  - Future: Focus on the time to come—the future—and on planning ahead and seeking new ways to replace the old.
- Natural environment
  - Mastery: Can and should exercise total control over nature.
  - Harmonious: Can and should exercise partial, but not total, control by living in balance with nature.

- ○ Submissive: Cannot and should not exercise control over nature; subject to the "higher power" of these forces.
- Relating to other people
  - ○ Hierarchical (lineal): Deferring to higher authorities within the group.
  - ○ As equals (collateral): Seeking consensus within the group as equal members.
  - ○ Individualistic: Making decisions independently from others in the group.
- Motive for individual actions
  - ○ To express oneself: Emphasizes activity valued by the individual but not necessarily by others in the group.
  - ○ To grow: Emphasizes growth in abilities that are valued by the individual, but not necessarily by others.
  - ○ To achieve: Emphasizes activity valued by the individual and approved by others.

As you can see, each of these values leads to a particular response that might be used in solving a problem. According to Kluckhohn and Strodtbeck (1961), these values are indicative of a group's culture, and agreement on which values are important can be found within many groups. They began their research to determine how much agreement can be found within cultural groups by interviewing Navahos, Mexican Americans, Texan homesteaders, Mormon villagers, and Zuni pueblo dwellers in the American Southwest. They developed scenarios to describe real-life situations that all five cultural groups would find realistic and relevant. They then asked their participants how they would respond to the situations, and assigned the participants, based on responses, to a value orientation category (e.g., past, present, or future time orientation). They drew value orientation profiles of each group, showing how much agreement there was within the groups, and how similar or different the groups were from each other. These profiles described the cultures of each group based on their value orientations.

Other researchers have used Kluckhohn and Strodtbeck's value orientation model to describe and compare cultures in different contexts and geographical regions. Russo (2000) and Russo, Hills et al. (1984) analyzed the value orientations of the Lumni, an indigenous community in Washington state. Hills (1977) and Hills & Goneyali (1980) studied generational changes in values between young people and their parents as a result of migration. They looked at samples of migrants to New Zealand from Samoa, Fiji, and the Cook Islands. Using Kluckhohn and Strodtbeck's value orientations, they interviewed young people ages 16 to 18 and their parents, using tape-recorded questions in the respondent's native language. Here are some examples of the interview questions (from Hills, 2002, p. 8):

> I will ask you 25 questions. There are three possible answers to each question. Please listen carefully to each question and then each of the three suggested answers to that question. I can play them again if you would like to listen to them again. We do not want your name. There are no right or wrong answers to these questions—we want to know how you feel about them. Take as much time as you need to answer them.
>
> Here is the first one.
>
> When our group sends a delegate to a meeting I think it's best—
>
> *Relational*
>
> 1. To let everyone discuss it until everyone agrees on the person.
>
> > Collateral
>
> 2. To let the important leaders decide. They have more experience than us.
>
> > Lineal
>
> 3. For a vote to be taken and the one with the most votes goes, even if some people disagree.
>
> > Individualistic
>
> Now please tell me the answer which comes closest to the way you feel.
>
> Now tell me the answer which is your second choice.

Thanks. Here's the next one.

When I get sick I believe:

Humanity and Nature

1. Doctors will be able to find a way to cure it.

    Mastery

2. I should live properly so I don't get sick.

    Harmony

3. I cannot do much about it and just have to accept it.

    Subjugation

Here's the third ...

When I send money for use overseas, I think it should be
spent to:

Time

1. Make a better life for the future.

    Future

2. Make a better life now.

    Present

3. Keep the old ways and customs alive.

    Past

Using this interview protocol, Hills (1977) and Hills and Goneyali (1980) showed changes in value orientations between young immigrants and their parents, which he attributed to migration. Young people showed more agreement with the predominant values of the new environment (New Zealand) than did their parents.

Kluckhohn and Strodtbeck (1961) provide us with a useful tool for differentiating between cultures. However, we should be aware of two possible weaknesses in their theory. First, the definitions of values are heavily influenced by the researchers' perceptions of how cultures might differ from each other. The starting point is their theory, which they then test in different cultures. An alternative strategy is to first ask people to describe their cultures and then build a theory based on the responses. Thus, theory is developed from the ground up, respondents to researcher, rather than from the top, researcher to respondents. Second, the theory does not adequately provide for the possibility that respondents may use different values as a basis for solving a problem, depending on context. These values are not necessarily mutually exclusive. For example, on the relational value orientation, I may be individualistic at work but lineal in my family.

Nonetheless, Kluckhohn and Strodtbeck's values orientation theory has provided researchers with a useful tool for differentiating between cultures. These weaknesses are not unique to their theory, but are weaknesses of most of the other cultural dimension theories as well. The common problem is how do we generalize from individual data or information obtained from the individual through interviews and questionnaires to the entire group, and how do we account for individual differences within the group? Researchers continue to grapple with this problem with varying degrees of success.

Trompenaars and Hampden-Turner's Seven Dimensions of Culture

According to Trompenaars and Hampden-Turner (1997), culture has seven dimensions, which they identified from surveys of 40,000 teenagers in 40 countries. These dimensions are as follows:

1. *Universalism (rules) versus particularism (relationships)*: People with a universalism point of view place a high value on laws, rules, and obligations; rules come before relationships. People who are particularistic place relationships above rules; their actions are determined by the situation and who is involved, rather than by rules and laws.

2. *Individualism (the individual) versus communitarianism (the group)*: Individualistic people value personal freedom and achievement, and believe that the individual should make his or her own decisions. People who value communitarianism believe that the group is more important than the individual, the group provides help and safety in exchange for loyalty, and the group always comes before the individual.

3. *Specific versus diffuse relationships at work*: People with a specific perspective believe that personal relationships are separate from work and that people can work together without having a good relationship. People with a diffuse relationship believe that good relationships are important at work and are necessary for success at work.

4. *Neutral versus emotional*: Neutral people control their emotions. They believe more in reason than in emotions. They keep their emotions to themselves. Emotional people express how they feel more openly; their behaviors are influenced by emotions.

5. *Achievement versus ascription*: People who value ascription believe that a person's worth should be based on performance, what a person does. People who subscribe to ascription believe that a person's worth is based on status, power, title, and position.

6. *Sequential time versus synchronous time*: People who value sequential time believe that time is valuable and that events should happen in order, in a linear fashion. They value punctuality, planning, and sticking to a schedule. To people who value synchronous time, the past, present and future are interchangeable and related. Therefore, time is not linear, but circular. It's more important to complete many tasks and projects rather than sticking to a schedule to finish one task.

7. *Internal direction (internal locus of control) versus outer direction (external locus of control)*: People who are internally directed believe that they can control their environment to achieve goals. People who are externally directed believe that their environment controls them; therefore, they must work within the constraints of what is around them, including other people.

The dimensions of culture defined above give the end points of a scale, meaning that they are bipolar extremes. A culture could be assigned to any point between these extreme anchors based on responses to a questionnaire by individuals within the culture. Again, we are faced with the problem of generalizing from individuals to the group and accounting for individual differences.

The cultural dimensions I have discussed are a convenient way of describing and categorizing cultures based on their worldviews and values. And, as you can see, there is quite a bit of commonality among these dimensions. In Chapter 7,

"Know Others," I discuss how the cultures of several countries have been placed along several of these dimensions. I also suggest communication strategies that might be appropriate and effective in several cultures based on their placement on the continuum. A word of caution, though: these dimensions are generalizations, so we should take care to first know whether the individual we are interacting with fits into the cultural mode we have assigned to him or her. There is no substitute, as we shall see in Chapter 7, to treating people as individuals first before we consider their culture.

How Do We Learn Culture?

So far, we have looked at several dimensions on which culture can be described. These dimensions do not exhaust all the possible manifestations of culture, but they are the ones that are most relevant to intercultural communication. Remember that culture is learned and transmitted from one generation to the next. Further, culture is patterned, meaning that the dimensions are all related to and consistent with each other and they, taken together, provide a general guide for making sense of and acting within a person's environment in the context of membership in a group. How then is such a complex pattern of accepted norms for action and believing learned within a group?

A number of theories from anthropology, sociology, education, and social psychology explain how culture is learned. In this section, I focus on those theories that assign an important role to communication.

Motivation to Learn a Culture: Social Identity Theory

Why should a person be motivated to learn a culture? Tajfel and Turner's (1986) social identity theory gives us a clue. First, group membership provides us with a source of identity, a sense of who we are. Research has shown that, indeed, our sense of who we are is determined by groups we strongly identify with—for example, student organizations, work organizations, ethnic and racial groups, religious groups, countries, or nationalities. Not all of these groups will be salient or will influence our actions, perceptions, and beliefs at all times; group influence on the individual is situational rather than general. For example, organizational culture may influence my behavior at work (e.g., I work 12-hour days because everybody else seems to do so) while national or country culture (e.g., "American") may influence my behavior when travelling abroad. In intercultural communication, much of the emphasis has been on national cultures. We ask, how does culture at this level affect communication interactions? We are also interested in how co-cultures, defined as smaller group cultures within a nation, such as the cultures of racial and ethnic groups, interact with each other. The basic premises of social identity theory hold regardless of the level of analysis from small to large groups for two reasons. First, group membership is a source of self-identity. Second, the stronger the individual's identification with the group, the greater the motivation to learn its culture.

Another motivation for learning a group's culture is self-preservation, meaning that the individual needs the group to survive and thrive in the natural and social environment. The group provides the resources needed by the individual to function effectively in interactions with other groups and with nature. At the national level, consider social security, laws, disaster relief, health insurance, and the military. These resources are available to us because we identify as "Americans" and are members of this national group.

The Process of Learning Culture: Enculturation and Socialization

Learning a culture continues over time from childhood to adulthood. Although most of the research emphasis has been on children and adolescents, attention has also been given to how immigrants, sojourners (temporary visitors to a country), and adults in new environments learn cultures.

Two general and related theories explain the process of learning culture. *Enculturation* is defined by Kottak (2011) as:

> the process where the culture that is currently established teaches an individual the accepted norms and values of the culture or society where the individual lives. The individual can become an accepted member and fulfill the needed functions and roles of the group. Most importantly the individual knows and establishes a context of boundaries and accepted behavior that dictates what is acceptable and not acceptable within the framework of that society. It teaches the individual their role within society as well as what is accepted behavior within that society and lifestyle.

Socialization is a similar concept, defined as:

1. A lifelong process of learning the norms, customs and ideologies of a society that are needed for participation, functioning, and continued membership (Macionis, 2010);

2. A learning process influenced by agents such as the family (Macionis & Gerber, 2011); peers (other members of the group who are important to the learner, sometimes referred to as "significant others") (Macionis & Gerber, 2011); teachers and schools (Macionis & Gerber, 2011); and the media, new and traditional (McQuail, 2005).

These definitions help us understand what is learned and who the teachers might be, but gives little information on how culture is learned. The next two theories tell us about the learning process.

Social Cognitive Theory

Most theories of how behaviors, beliefs, values, and other dimensions of culture are learned include two processes: learning by direct experience and by purposive teaching. Traditional learning theories, for example, explain that learning occurs by actually performing the behavior and then experiencing its consequences. Learning is facilitated by reinforcement, or the extent to which the behavior is rewarded or punished. People will learn culture by acting out its components and then repeating the actions if they are rewarded. They learn these behaviors from information and instruction given to them by parents, peers, and teachers. For example, how does a child learn that in American culture he or she is supposed to act independently and not depend too much on a group? The child may be instructed to do so by parents or teachers; then he or she does a class assignment independently of a group; parents or teachers show approval; and consequently, this behavior, acting independently, becomes part of the child's pattern of responses to the environment.

Unlike traditional learning theories, *social cognitive theory* (SCT) explains how behaviors are learned from observation. The opportunity to learn and practice or enact behaviors from direct instruction is present in most cultures, particularly in classrooms and the home. However, there is also a great deal of opportunity to learn indirectly from observation without direct instruction—for example, children observing their parents' interaction with people in the mall; actions of their favorite characters in television and the movies, and the consequences of these actions; and the behavior of classmates in the playground. Developed by Albert Bandura

(1986, 2002), SCT explains how we learn by observation. This theory is particularly relevant to intercultural communication because many of the behaviors we can learn, such as those included in cultural dimensions, are presented in new and traditional media, including television and the movies.

According to SCT (Bandura 1985, 2002), learning by observation occurs in sequential steps:

1. The learner, such as a child being socialized into a culture, is motivated to acquire knowledge about a behavior. Motivation will depend on the child's sense of self-efficacy, the ability to learn and repeat the observed behavior, and on perceived rewards from performing the behavior, such as parental approval: the higher the sense of self-efficacy, the greater the motivation; also, the greater the expectation that the behavior will be rewarded, the greater the motivation to learn it.

2. The behavior to be learned is presented in a medium that reaches the learner. Children watch television. They play video games on their electronic devices. Behaviors and values demonstrated or implied in these media can be observed by children and potentially learned.

3. The learner pays attention to the behavior presented in a medium. Attention is facilitated by repetition; portrayals of characters that the observer identifies with because they have similar characteristics ("They are just like me"); portrayals of situations that the learner identifies with because of experience (e.g., "I have been there") or relevance (e.g., "This applies to me"); distinctiveness (portrayals that stand out); simple (easy to understand and follow); and positive emotional arousal ("This makes me feel good," "This is funny," "The good people won").

4. The learner remembers the behavior learned, stores it using symbolic codes (language and visually), and rehearses it mentally. Retention is facilitated by simplicity of the act and its prevalence or repetition in the environment.

5. When the occasion arises, the remembered behavior is enacted or produced, such as a child preferring to work alone rather than in a group. Enactment will be consistent and repeated when the behavior is rewarded, as when a child is praised by parents and teachers.

SCT, as you can see, is a powerful model for explaining how *deliberate* learning occurs by observation. The learner actively processes information from observed events and reenactment occurs consciously and with purpose. Because much of a culture's values and behavioral norms are indeed reenacted by socialized members repeatedly in everyday life and in the media, the opportunity for deliberate observational learning is not only present, but inviting to the novice learner. But what about unconscious learning?

Cultivation Theory

Not all learning is deliberate and conscious. We also learn cultural beliefs and behaviors unconsciously. That is, we are learning them but we do not actively exert effort to learn them. And we are not consciously aware of having learned these behaviors until we enact them. Bias and prejudice, which are discussed in Chapter 4, are examples of cultural behaviors that many of us learn unconsciously.

So how do we learn culture unconsciously? *Cultivation theory* (CT) provides an explanation of unconscious learning from the mass media. Developed by George Gerbner and Larry Gross more than 30 years ago, CT continues to be an influential theory about how we learn from television (e.g., Morgan & Shanahan, 2010). The basic premise of CT is that heavy viewers of television learn to believe the social realities portrayed in television. And most of us, especially children, are heavy viewers. This learning is cumulative, happens over time after repeated exposure, and is unconscious and not deliberate. We learn from constant exposure; we do not deliberately seek out behaviors and norms that will help us adapt and function in a culture.

Gerbner and his colleagues propose the following propositions about television's effects on culture:

1. Television is "the source of the most broadly shared images and messages in history. Television cultivates from infancy the very predispositions that used to be acquired from other primary sources. The repetitive pattern of television's mass produced messages and images forms the mainstream of a common symbolic environment" (Gerbner, Gross & Signorielli, 1986). Further, Gerbner et al. (1986) propose that "the substance of consciousness cultivated by television is not so much specific attitudes and opinions as more basic assumptions about the facts of life and standards of judgment on which conclusions are based."

   In other words, television has supplanted parents, peers, and the school as the primary agents of cultural socialization because of its ubiquity (especially today, with availability in a variety of platforms); the effects of television are not on specific attitudes, but on a person's worldview (dimensions of culture in our previous discussion); and these effects are cumulative and happen over time.

2. Television presents a reality that supports existing institutions, power structures, and cultural norms. Television's reality does not always (one might say rarely) coincide with realities in our natural environment. For example, more violence is portrayed in television than actually happens in the real world. Although Gerbner's cultural indicators project, which maps out television realities through content analysis, does not address most of the cultural dimensions I discussed earlier, several themes related to culture have been identified. These include gender roles; racial and ethnic representation and status; fear of crime; police presence and effectiveness; mistrust of people; and, the television reality that has attracted the most attention from researchers, violence in the real world.

3. Heavy viewers of television have accepted television realities as their own and natural realities. For example, research has found that heavy viewers in comparison to light viewers:

   a. Are more afraid of being victims of crime;

   b. Believe that there are more police officers in the real world and that police are more effective in solving crimes than they are in the real world;

   c. Have a greater mistrust of people.

There is, therefore, evidence that television "cultivates" in heavy viewers some indicators of a culture and that this cultivation can be found across co-cultures, such as racial groups within a society, thereby resulting in a common outlook, at least on some cultural indicators, a process Gerbner calls "mainstreaming." Further research can confirm our expectation that television might be able to similarly influence viewer adaptations of other cultural dimensions discussed earlier in this chapter.

Does Culture Change?

The short answer is "yes." Learned patterns of behavior and beliefs can be unlearned and replaced with new ones when human needs change or when external pressures support change (Rochon, 1998). Although resistant to change, considering that its many dimensions are imbedded in group members over a long period of time, culture can change in response to the following forces (Rochon, 1998):

1. *Discovery and invention.* Discovery is "addition to knowledge" and invention is "new application of knowledge" (Linton, 1955). To lead to cultural change, an invention or discovery would first have to be understood and accepted and then used regularly. Acceptance comes after the invention or discovery is shown to be beneficial to the individual and society. Examples

in the United States are technological inventions such as the automobile, new energy sources, and new digital technologies, all of which have affected how Americans view the world and related behaviors.

2. *Internal changes within a society, such as changes in political and economic structures.* Much has been written in the media about changes in some values and related behaviors, particularly among young people, in some Middle Eastern countries and China because of changes in political and economic conditions. Whether and to what extent the cultural dimensions discussed earlier in this chapter have changed in these countries is a matter for empirical research.

3. *Influence from foreign countries.* Powerful countries and cultures such as the United States have the potential to change cultures in less powerful countries. This process is called *acculturation*, the replacement of native cultures with foreign cultures. This process can take many forms: conquest through war; economic domination; and, most relevant to intercultural communication, influence through the media. Many scholars have expanded on the original notion that "the media are American" (Tunstall, 1977; Scotton and Hatchen, 2008), showing that American media, particularly movies and television, have indeed influenced young people around the world to adopt the American cultural realities portrayed (accurately or not), from the more superficial manifestations in dress, music, and food to values emphasizing consumption and hedonism.

4. *Influence of a new culture.* To be accepted, an immigrant is expected to adapt the values and behavioral norms of the new culture. When this change occurs, the process is called *transculturation.* The extent to which total transculturation is functional for the immigrant and the new culture continues to be subject of debate, especially as migration increases around the world, significantly changing the demographics in host societies, including the United States. One view says that complete transculturation is necessary to preserve the culture of the host country. Another view says that the diversity in cultures brought by immigrants adds to the richness of the host culture. Others say that diverse values, worldviews, and behavioral norms indeed add to the host culture and should be accepted and respected, but that certain fundamental values, such as those identified in the host country's constitution, should be upheld. (In the United States these values include freedom and equality.)

References

Bandura, A. (1985). *Social foundations of thought and action*. Englewood Cliffs, NJ: Prentice Hall.

Bandura, A. (2002). Social cognitive theory in cultural context. *Applied Psychology, 51*(2), 269–290.

Boas, F. (1911). *The mind of primitive man*. New York, NY: Macmillan Publishing.

Geertz, C. (1966). Religion as a cultural system. In M. Banton (Ed.), *Anthropological approaches to the study of religion*. New York, NY: Routledge.

Gerbner, G., Gross, L., Morgan, M., & Signorielli, N. (1986). Living with television: The dynamics of the cultivation process. In J. Bryant and D. Zillman (Eds.), *Perspectives on media effects* (pp. 17–40). Hillsdale, NJ: Lawrence Erlbaum Associates.

Goodenough, W. (1971). *Culture, language, and society*. Reading, MA: Addison-Wesley.

Hall, E. (1981). *Beyond culture*. New York, NY: Anchor Books.

Hills, M. D. (2002). Kluckhohn and Strodtbeck's values orientation theory. *Online Readings in Psychology and Culture, 4*(4). Retrieved from http://dx.doi.org/10.9707/2307-0919.1040.

Hills, M.D. (1977). *Values in the South Pacific*. Paper presented at the Annual Conference of the New Zealand Psychological Society, Auckland, New Zealand.

Hills, M. D., & Goneyali, E. (1980). *Values in Fijan families* (Monograph). Hamilton, New Zealand: University of Waikato, Dept. of Psychology.

Hoebel, E. A. (1976). *Cultural and social anthropology*. New York, NY: McGraw-Hill.

Inglehart, R. (1997). *Modernization and postmodernization: Cultural, economic, and political change in 43 societies*. Princeton, NJ: Princeton University Press.

Hofstede, G. (1984). *Culture's consequences: International differences in work-related values*. Beverly Hills, CA: Sage.

Hofstede, G. (2001). *Culture's consequences: Comparing, values, behaviors, institutions, and organizations across nations*. Beverly Hills, CA: Sage.

Hofstede, G., Hofstede, G. J., & Minkov, M. (2010). *Cultures and organizations: Software of the mind*. New York, NY: McGraw-Hill.

Kluckhohn, C. K. (1949). *Mirror for man: The relation of anthropology to modern life*. Berkeley, CA: Whittlesey House.

Kluckhohn, C. K. (1951). Values and value orientations in the theory of action. In T. Parsons and E. A. Shils (Eds.), *Toward a general theory of action*. Cambridge, MA: Harvard University Press.

Kluckhohn, F. R., & Strodtbeck, F. L. (1961). *Variations in value orientations*. Evanston, IL: Row, Peterson.

Kottak, C. P. (2011). *Window on humanity: A concise introduction to Anthropology*. New York: McGraw-Hill.

Kroeber, A. L., & Kluckhohn, C. K. (1952). *Culture: A critical review of concepts and definitions.* Cambridge, MA: Peabody Museum.

Levi-Strauss, C. (1949). *Myth and meaning.* New York, NY: Schocken Books.

Linton, R. (1955). *The tree of culture.* New York, NY: Alfred Knopf.

Macionis, J. (2010). *Sociology.* New York, NY: Pearson Education.

Macionis, J., & Gerber, L. (2011) *Sociology.* New York, NY: Pearson Education.

McQuail, D. (2005). *McQuail's mass communication theory.* Beverly Hills, CA: Sage.

Mead, M. (1937). *Cooperation and competition among primitive peoples.* New York, NY: McGraw-Hill.

Morgan, M., & Shanahan, J. (2010). The state of cultivation research. *Journal of Broadcasting & Electronic Media, 54*(2), 337–355.

Parsons, T., & Shils, A. (Eds.). (1976). *Toward a general theory of action.* Cambridge, MA: Harvard University Press.

Rochon, T. (1998). *Culture moves: Ideas, activism, and changing values.* Princeton, NJ: Princeton University Press.

Russo, K. W. (Ed.). (2000). *Finding the middle ground: Insights and applications of the value orientations method.* Yarmouth, ME: Intercultural Press.

Russo, K., Hills, M.D. et al. (1984). *Value orientations in the Lumni Indian community and their commercial associates.* Report to the Lumni Indian Council. Bellingham, WA.

Schwartz, S. (Ed.). (1994). *Beyond individualism/collectivism: New cultural dimension of values.* Thousand Oaks, CA: Sage.

Schwartz, S., Melech, G., Lehmann, A., Burgess, S., Harris, M., & Owens, V. (2001). Extending the cross-validity of the theory of basic human values with a different method of measurement. *Journal of Cross-Cultural Psychology, 32*(5), 519–542.

Scotton, J., & Hachten, W. (2008). *New media for a new China.* New York, NY: Wiley.

Steers, R., Nardon, L., & Sanchez-Runde, C. (2013). *Management across cultures: Developing global competencies.* Cambridge: Cambridge University Press.

Tajfel H., & Turner, J.C. (1986). The social identity theory of intergroup behavior. In S. Worchel & W.G. Austin (Eds.). *Psychology of intergroup relations* (pp. 7–24). Chicago, IL: Nelson-Hall.

Taylor, E. (1871). *Primitive culture.* London: John Murray.

Trompenaars, F., & Hampden-Turner, C. (1997). *Riding the waves of culture: Understanding diversity in global business.* (3rd ed.). New York, NY: McGraw-Hill.

Tunstall, J. (1977). *The media are American.* New York, NY: Columbia University Press.

Wood, A., & Smith, M. (2004). *Technology, identity, & culture.* New York, NY: Psychology Press.

Random Acts of Kindness
Real-World Lab

Name: _____

Date: _____

This activity was adapted from Tolman.[1]

A random act of kindness (RAK) is a generous gesture that is completed for a stranger or acquaintance (not a friend or family member) with the expectation of receiving nothing in return. Do not take money for completing the RAK and do not do anything that threatens your safety or makes you or the other person feel uncomfortable. **Be sure to choose a person who is from another culture or has "different" social identity from you in some way (e.g., race, ability, sex).** A RAK might be shoveling a neighbor's driveway or scraping ice off a person's car, buying a person's coffee (inside the store, so you can observe), helping find a missing neighborhood cat, giving another customer a coupon at a store, or helping a person in need load their groceries, and so on. You can find more examples at www.randomactsofkindness.org and www.payitforwardmovement.org.

1. Complete one RAK. Make sure you can observe the reaction of others so you can report back about your observations.

2. Describe your RAK. Give some background information and include how you felt before, during, and after the interaction. Describe whether the RAK was truly random or planned out ahead of time.

_____

_____

_____

_____

_____

_____

_____

_____

---

1   Elizabeth Tolman, "Creating Opportunities for Interaction and Critical Reflection in the Interpersonal Communication Course: Completing Random Acts of Kindness," *Communication Teacher* 23 no. 3 (2009), 132.

3. Describe the communication that occurred surrounding your RAK. Include at least two concepts from class in your analysis of the communication and reactions (yours, the target person, and bystanders) to your RAK.

_____

_____

_____

_____

_____

_____

_____

_____

4. How, if at all, did culture or difference play a role in your RAK and/or the target person's reaction?

_____

_____

_____

_____

_____

_____

_____

CONCLUSION

Throughout this textbook, you have learned how and why communication works, including how your brain makes sense of communication and shapes the way you see the world. You know the importance of listening closely and actively. You have learned how to build and maintain interpersonal relationships online and off. You know how to persuade others to help you reach your goals. You have learned how relational transgressions can dissolve relationships and how forgiveness can help mend them. You have also learned what makes certain types of relationships unique such as family, coworker, long-distance, and cross-cultural relationships.

In addition to all that you have read, you have practiced what you have learned in the real world through activities that have encouraged you to get out into your communities and reflect on your communication with others. You have taken note of how your communication changes when there are no technology distractions and how people react and respond to the messages you put out into the world.

Take these lessons with you into the rest of your life to engage in meaningful and effective communication, connect with others, and enjoy your relationships.

INDEX

Printed in the USA
CPSIA information can be obtained
at www.ICGtesting.com
LVHW060427220823
755870LV00004B/30